REGULATORY POLICY
AND PRACTICES

REGULATORY POLICY AND PRACTICES

Regulating Better and Regulating Less

Fred Thompson
and L. R. Jones

PRAEGER SPECIAL STUDIES • PRAEGER SCIENTIFIC

Library of Congress Cataloging in Publication Data

Thompson, Frederick.
  Regulatory policy and practices.

  Includes index.
  1. Industry and state—United States.
I. Jones, L. R.   II. Title.
HD3616.U47T47   1982   338.973   82-13131
ISBN 0-03-062178-X

Published in 1982 by Praeger Publishers
CBS Educational and Professional Publishing
A Division of CBS Inc.
521 Fifth Avenue, New York, New York 10175 U.S.A.

3456789   052   98765432
Printed in the United States of America

PREFACE

This book, like most, is a product of research conducted over a long period of time. During this period the authors have benefited from the advice, assistance, counsel, and sympathy lent by a number of colleagues, and we would like to acknowledge these efforts. We would first like to thank Professor William T. Stanbury of the University of British Columbia and former director of the Regulation Reference of the Economic Council of Canada for his support, stimulation, and assistance. Bill coauthored Chapters 2 and 3 of this volume, and his ideas influenced the book throughout. Part of the research for this book was supported by the Economic Council of Canada and for this we thank Professor Stanbury and R. A. Jenness, Bill's successor as director of the Regulation Reference of the ECC. We also thank members of the Regulation Reference staff, especially Margot Priest and Paul Gorecki, for lending their assistance to our research, and to William M. Zumeta of UCLA for coauthorship of Chapter 4 of this volume. We also wish to thank the director and staff of the California Office of Administrative Law for their cooperation. In addition, we express our gratitude to colleagues who made helpful comments on manuscript drafts and encouraged our work, including John Byrd, University of Oregon; G. Bruce Doern, Carleton University; Charles V. Maichel, Center for Regulatory Evaluation; William Niskanen, Council of Economic Advisors; Barry Siegal, University of Oregon; Paul Slovic, Decision Research; and Aaron Wildavsky, University of California, Berkeley. We appreciate their advice, although we did not always follow it and, of course, do not share with them or others any responsibility for the views expressed in this book. We are also grateful to all the regulatory reform researchers from whom we have learned in completing this book.

Also to be thanked for their valuable work in manuscript preparation are Kelly Bombardier, Nancy McKaughan, and Marilynne Musso.

Finally, we would like to dedicate this book to our children Mackendree and Kyrié and Alyson and Cameron.

ACKNOWLEDGMENTS

This book includes materials drawn from the following articles published previously:

Fred Thompson and Larry R. Jones, "Fighting Regulation: The Regulatory Review," California Management Review 23, no. 2 (Winter 1981):5-19.

Fred Thompson and L. R. Jones, "Reforming Regulatory Decision Making: The Regulatory Budget," Sloan Management Review 22, no. 2 (Winter 1980):53-61.

L. R. Jones and Fred Thompson, "Improving the Evaluation of Regulation," The Bureaucrat 10 (Fall 1981):25-31.

W. T. Stanbury, Fred Thompson, and William Zumeta, "Regulatory Reform: American Experience and Canadian Prospects," Journal of Contemporary Business 10, no. 4 (Winter 1981):81-96.

Fred Thompson et al., "On the Definition of Economic Regulation," pp. 1-16; "The Scope and Coverage of Regulation in Canada and the United States: Implications for the Demand for Reform," pp. 17-67; "Regulatory Reform and Deregulation in the United States," pp. 193-238; "More and Better Analysis? The Case of Health, Safety and Environmental Regulation," pp. 239-67 in Government Regulation: Growth, Scope, Process, ed. W. T. Stanbury (Montreal: Institute for Research on Public Policy, 1980).

Fred Thompson, "Closeness Counts in Horseshoes and Dancing . . . and Elections," Public Choice (forthcoming, 1982).

CONTENTS

LIST OF TABLES AND FIGURES

LIST OF ABBREVIATIONS

The list of abbreviations below may simplify the task of the reader in interpreting the acronym-laden jargon that describes regulatory departments, agencies, and other regulatory terms. While we have attempted to identify acronyms clearly before they are used in the text, a single reference point should be of assistance.

ANPRM	Advanced Notice of Proposed Rule Making
APA	Administrative Procedure Act
CAB	Civil Aeronautics Board
CAC	California Administrative Code
CBO	Congressional Budget Office
CEA	Council of Economic Advisors
CEQ	Council on Environmental Quality
CFR	Calendar of Federal Regulations
CWPS	Council on Wage and Price Stability
CPSA	Consumer Product Safety Administration
CSAB	Center for the Study of American Business
CSH	Consumer Safety and Health
DOE	Department of Energy
DOI	Department of the Interior
DOJ	Department of Justice
E&E	Environment and Energy
EIA	Economic Impact Analysis
EIS	Economic Impact Statement
EO	Executive Order (of the President)
EPA	Environmental Protection Agency
EPRG	Economic Policy Review Group
FDA	Food and Drug Administration

FDIC	Federal Deposit Insurance Corporation
FEA	Federal Energy Agency
FMC	Federal Maritime Commission
FR	Federal Register
FTC	Federal Trade Commission
GAO	General Accounting Office
ICC	Interstate Commerce Commission
IIS	Inflation Impact Statement
MARAD	Maritime Administration
MESA	Mine Enforcement Safety Administration
NGPA	Natural Gas Policy Act
NHTSA	National Highway Traffic Safety Administration
NPRM	Notice of Proposed Rulemaking
NRC	Nuclear Regulatory Commission
NTIA	National Telecommunications and Information Administration
OAL	Office of Administrative Law (California)
OIRA	Office of Inflation and Regulatory Affairs
OMB	Office of Management and Budget
OSHA	Occupational Safety and Health Administration
OSP	Office of Statistical Policy (Department of Commerce)
OSTP	Office of Science and Technology Policy
RARG	Regulatory Analysis Review Group
RIA	Regulatory Impact Analysis
RIP	Office of Regulatory and Information Policy (OMB)
SEC	Securities and Exchange Commission
TFRR	Task Force on Regulatory Relief
USCFR	U.S. Code of Federal Regulations
USDA	U.S. Department of Agriculture

1

INTRODUCTION

In the fall of 1974, President Gerald R. Ford summoned representatives of every area within the discipline of economics to attend a summit conference on inflation. On the question of what should be done about inflation there was little or no agreement. Indeed, several of the economists disputed that a problem existed. However, on one point, they all did agree—that government regulation of business was, in some cases, doing more harm than good and that the government should eliminate a number of outdated, inefficient regulatory policies.[1] Actions recommended by the economists included the following:

Prohibit restrictions on the interstate movement of specified types of agricultural products, supply controls for products, state fluid milk price and output controls, and production quotas on individual producers.

Remove all route and commodity restrictions imposed on motor carriers.

Approve automatically all railroad and truck rates within a zone of reasonableness.

Repeal the antitrust exemption of railroad and trucking rate bureaus (the Reed-Bulwinkle Act).

Reduce or eliminate entry barriers into trucking.

Approve automatically all (requests for changes in) air fares, including discount fares.

Eliminate regulations that prevent financial institutions from paying competitive rates for deposits (Regulation Q).

Prohibit resale price maintenance.[2]

Motivated by the somewhat questionable proposition that he could fight inflation by fighting regulation, shortly thereafter President Ford announced to Congress his intention to give the issue of regulatory reform higher priority.[3] Over the next two years, the Ford administration devoted considerable attention to regulatory reform.

The history of dissatisfaction with both the outcomes of regulation and its processes can be traced back to the infancy of the federal government's involvement in the direct regulation of business. The history of reform efforts begins here as well.[4] Previous reform proposals have been concerned primarily with regulatory practice and procedure—with problems of accountability to elected officials,[5] policy coordination and administrative overlap and duplication,[6] increasing the influence of the general public in regulatory decision making,[7] inconsistent and poorly articulated policies,[8] and the burden of delay and excessive paperwork.[9] What is striking about the Ford administration's approach to regulatory reform is that it sought to look past procedural problems to the major issues underlying regulation, to the objectives, purposes, and justifications of government regulation of business, and to the fundamental shortcomings of regulatory decision-making processes. This position is stated with clarity in the report of the Domestic Council Review Group on Regulatory Reform:

> As government has increasingly relied on regulation
> to achieve public policy objectives, some flaws in the
> regulatory process have become glaringly clear. Too
> much public attention, however, has been directed
> toward the more visible regulatory abuses and not
> enough consideration devoted to the underlying prob-
> lems. For example, the formal nature of the rule-
> making process often leads to cumbersome, confused,
> and legalistic regulation. Undue focus on the symptoms
> of delay and complexity, however, tends to divert at-
> tention from the examination of alternatives to regula-
> tion that may offer more effective means to accomplish
> a given purpose. Relieving the caseload backlog in the
> Interstate Commerce Commission would be a beneficial
> management step, helping to reduce some of the costs
> and frustrations with the current process. But exclusive
> concentration on how the ICC can make speedier deci-
> sions begs the question of whether it makes sense at all
> for the Commission to rule on all new applications and
> to set rates.[10]

The attention given regulatory reform by the Ford and Carter administrations, and more recently by the Reagan administration, has had several consequences. First, attitudes have changed toward the use of regulation to achieve public policy objectives. It is now assumed by many that existing regulatory policies and practices are frequently mistaken—that much regulation no longer makes economic sense, or that it is inefficient or ineffective. Second, there have been changes in regulatory decision-making processes, and existing and proposed regulations are being subjected to more rigorous scrutiny. Third, in a few cases substantive policy change has occurred. For example, legalized price fixing of brokers commissions in the securities industry has been abolished. Legislation permitting state fair-trade laws has been repealed. Trucking and rail freight have been deregulated. The Civil Aeronautics Board has decontrolled airline prices and routes (entry) and is scheduled to terminate in 1982. Air freight has been completely deregulated. The Federal Communications Commission has relaxed its opposition to cable television. Congress has provided for the gradual decontrol of the wellhead price of natural gas. Controls on the pricing, production, and allocation of crude oil have also been lifted.

Weighed against the overall scope and domain of government regulation of economic activity, perhaps these changes are not very significant. However, weighed against previous reform efforts, they are remarkable. It is also noteworthy that much of the thrust behind recent reform efforts appears to be motivated by an interest in increasing allocative efficiency.[11] Proponents of reform generally believe that economic analysis can identify mistaken regulatory practices and policies, that further mistakes can be avoided, and that past mistakes can be corrected.[12]

The purposes to be served by this book within this context are as follows:

To define regulation, to indicate what is regulated, and to demonstrate how regulatory policies and practices operate

To indicate what ought and ought not to be regulated and to indicate how regulation should be accomplished where it is appropriate

To prescribe an agenda for reforming regulatory policy, procedures, and strategy

To point out some of the limits of reform, in addition to pure ignorance, and what can be done to overcome these limits.

The organization of chapters reflects these purposes. Chapter 2 provides a comprehensive definition of regulation, sifted from the miasma of confusion on this topic, that is suitable to the authors.

Chapter 3 attempts to document the extent of federal regulation, although rapid changes in regulatory policy make this task difficult and may render some of our efforts out of date. The purpose of Chapter 4 is to clarify the objectives of regulation and to indicate where regulation is likely to be more or less effective than other instruments of public policy. Chapter 5 presents our view, however, biased, of the politics and prospects for regulatory reform. Chapter 6 analyzes a number of procedural reform options available to the federal government and also addresses alternatives for regulatory reform in state government.

A theme that persists throughout the book is that improved analysis of the need for and outcomes of regulation is crucial to satisfactory achievement of reform. Chapter 7 investigates some of the problems involved in the conduct of economic analysis. Employing the example of health and safety regulation, it indicates how economic analysis ought to be approached, if it is attempted at all, and how it might be made more useful. Chapter 8 provides a summary of our conclusions on regulation and reform, identifying some of the key variables that are likely to influence reform efforts.

This book is concerned primarily with the reform of economic rather than purely social regulation, acknowledging that economic regulation often has considerable social consequences. As indicated in Chapter 2, our definition of economic regulation is comprehensive and includes social regulation that has significant economic effect. The reform of purely social regulation, although necessary and laudable, is beyond the scope of this work. The distinction between economic and social regulation, in itself, is not very useful for purposes of analysis or reform. We recognize that the impediments to comprehensive reform of government regulation are numerous and formidable. Moreover, reform efforts will result inevitably in a flurry of political confrontation and no small amount of social discontent. Critics will analyze disagreements over proposed policy changes simplistically as contests between exclusive interests and the general public welfare. And in some cases, the critics will be right. Be that as it may, we have attempted here to demonstrate how we all may benefit when governments regulate better and regulate less.

NOTES

1. "Twenty-one of the twenty-three participants agreed that almost two dozen 'sacred cows' (long standing and politically unassailable laws and regulations) were having a detrimental effect on the economy." See The Challenge of Regulatory Reform, Report to

the President from the Domestic Council Review Group on Regulatory Reform, January 1977, p. 20, referenced to Economists Conerence on Inflation Report 1, September 5, 1974, pp. 11-13.

2. Ibid., p. 63.

3. Ibid., p. 13.

4. Congress established the Interstate Commerce Commission in 1887. The first federal commission on the paperwork burden presented its report the same year. See Commission on Federal Paperwork, Final Summary Report (Washington, D.C.: U.S. Government Printing Office, October 3, 1977).

5. The President's Committee on Administrative Management (Brownlow Committee), Report of the Committee with Studies of Administrative Management in the Federal Government, 1937; Louis J. Hector, "Problems of the CAB and the Independent Regulatory Commissions," Yale Law Journal (May 1960), originally prepared as a memorandum to President Eisenhower, September 10, 1959; Emmette S. Redford, "The President and the Regulatory Commissions," prepared for the President's Committee on Government Organization, November 17, 1960; James M. Landis, Report on Regulatory Agencies to the President-Elect, Committee Print, Subcommittee on Administrative Practice and Procedure, Committee on the Judiciary, U.S. Senate, 1960, pp. 81-87; The President's Advisory Council on Executive Organization (Ash Council), A New Regulatory Framework: Report on Selected Independent Regulatory Agencies, 1971; Subcommittee on Oversight and Investigations Committee on Interstate and Foreign Commerce, U.S. House of Representatives (Moss Committee), Federal Regulation and Regulatory Reform, October 1976, pp. 487-501, 547-49; Committee on Government Operations (later, Governmental Affairs), U.S. Senate (Ribicoff Committee), Study on Federal Regulation, Vol. 1, The Regulatory Appointments Process, January 1977, pp. ix-x, and Vol. 5, Regulatory Organization, December 1977.

6. Ash Council, op. cit.; Moss Committee, op. cit.; Ribicoff Committee, op. cit.

7. Moss Committee, op. cit., pp. 3, 462-65, 469-83, 529-67; Ribicoff Committee, op. cit., Vol. 2, pp. xix, xx, 135, and Vol. 3, passim; Subcommittee on Administrative Practice and Procedure, Committee on the Judiciary, U.S. Senate, Public Participation in Federal Agency Proceedings Hearings, 94th Congress, 2nd Session, January-February 1976; James M. Graham and Victor H. Cramer, Appointments to the Regulatory Agencies: The Federal Communications Commission and the Federal Trade Commission (1949-74), printed at the direction of the Committee on Commerce, U.S. Senate, 94th Congress, 2nd Session, April 1976; Special Subcommittee on Legislative Oversight, Committee on Interstate and Foreign Com-

merce, U.S. House of Representatives, Independent Regulatory
Commissions, H.R. Report 2711, 85th Congress, 2nd Session, 1959.
See also Simon Lazarus, "Halfway Up from Liberalism: Regulation
and Corporate Power," in Corporate Power in America, ed. Ralph
Nader and Mark Green (New York: Grossman, 1975); Simon Lazarus,
The Genteel Populist (New York: Holt, Rinehart and Winston, 1974);
and Simon Lazarus and Joseph Onek, "The Regulators and the
People," Virginia Law Review 57 (1971):1069-1108. See also Marver
Bernstein, Regulating Business by Independent Regulatory Commis-
sion (Princeton, N.J.: Princeton University Press, 1955); Paul
Sabatier, "Social Movements and Regulatory Agencies: Toward a
More Adequate—and Less Pessimistic—Theory of 'Clientele Cap-
ture.'" Policy Sciences 6 (1975):301-42; James Q. Wilson, The
Responsibility and the Business Predicament (Washington, D.C.:
Brookings Institution, 1974), pp. 135-68; Mancur Olson, Jr., The
Logic of Collective Action (Cambridge, Mass.: Harvard University
Press, 1965); Alan Stone, Economic Regulation and the Public In-
terest (Ithaca, N.Y.: Cornell University Press, 1977); and Mark J.
Green, ed., The Monopoly Makers: Ralph Nader's Study Group
Report on Regulation and Competition (New York: Grossman, 1973).

8. Hector, op. cit.; Ash Council, op. cit., pp. 34-37;
Ribicoff Committee, op. cit., Vol. 9, p. viii, and Vol. 2, pp. 66,
94. See also Henry J. Friendly, "A Look at the Federal Administrative Agencies," Columbia Law Review, April 1960; The Need
for Better Definition of Standards (Cambridge, Mass.: Harvard
University Press, 1962); Kenneth C. Davis, Administrative Law of
the Seventies (San Francisco: Bancroft-Whitney, 1975); Theodore
Lowi, The End of Liberalism (New York: Norton, 1969).

9. Attorney General's Committee on Administrative Pro-
cedure, Administrative Procedure in Government Agencies, Senate
Document No. 8, 77th Congress, 1st Session, 1941, Committee on
Administrative Procedure, U.S. Senate; U.S. Commission on
Organization of the Executive Branch of Government (First House
Commission), The Independent Regulatory Agencies: A Report with
Recommendations (Washington, D.C.: U.S. Government Printing
Office, 1949); U.S. Commission on Organization of the Executive
Branch of Government (Second Hoover Commission), Legal Services
and Procedures (Washington, D.C.: U.S. Government Printing
Office, 1955); Landis, op. cit.; Moss Committee, op. cit.; Ribicoff
Committee, op. cit., Vol. 4, Delay in the Regulatory Process;
Commission on Federal Paperwork, Final Summary Report (Wash-
ington, D.C.: U.S. Government Printing Office, 1977); Subcom-
mittee on Administrative Law and Government Relations, Committee
on the Judiciary, U.S. House of Representatives, Congressional
Review of Rulemaking Hearings, 94th Congress, 1st Session,

October-November 1975; Subcommittee on Administrative Practice
and Procedure, Committee on the Judiciary, U.S. Senate, Administrative Procedure Act Amendments of 1976, Hearings, 94th
Congress, 2nd Session, April-May 1976. See also Herbert Kaufman,
Red Tape (Washington, D.C.: Brookings Institution, 1976).
    10. The Challenge of Regulatory Reform, p. 3.
    11. Again we should note that the attention given to allocative
efficiency seems to be a by-product of the concern with inflation.
The link between these two issues may not, however, be readily
apparent to an outside observer. Inefficient regulation is, by definition, a drag on the economy, but its effect is not necessarily cumulative or increasing. While we accept that "stagflation" is exacerbated by supply constraints, to demonstrate that regulation leads to
inflation (a continuous, general increase in prices), it must first be
demonstrated that the drag on the economy resulting from regulation
is both increasing and increasing at an increasing rate. While some
proponents of regulatory reform assert that this is the case (see
James C. Miller III and Bruce Yandle, eds., Benefit-Cost Analysis
& Social Regulation [Washington, D.C.: American Enterprise Institute, 1979], p. 1), they offer little in the way of proof aside from a
list of new agencies and some page counts from the Federal Register
suggesting that regulation has been expanding at an exponential rate.
    12. For examples of different viewpoints on the manner in
which regulatory policies and practices should be modified, see
Paul W. MacAvoy, The Regulated Industries and the Economy (New
York: Norton, 1979); Barry M. Mitnick, The Political Economy of
Regulation: Creating, Designing and Removing Regulatory Forms
(New York: Columbia University Press, 1980); Murray L. Weiden-
baum, The Future of Business Regulation: Private Action and Pub-
lic Demand (New York: AMACON, 1979/1980). See also U.S.
Senate Committee on Government Operations/Governmental Affairs,
Study on Federal Regulation, 6 volumes (Washington, D.C.: U.S.
Senate, January 1977/December 1978).

2

REGULATION DEFINED

As interest in government regulation has increased, definitions of the term have become more numerous. A broad definition of regulation has been offered by the Committee on Government Operation of the U.S. Senate. It states:

> "Regulation," if defined in the broadest possible way, could include virtually everything which the government undertakes, since most of what the Federal Government does provides benefits and imposes restrictions. Thus in the large sense, grant programs, research and development programs, tax code provisions, and the numerous benefits which the government provides for individuals have regulatory aspects.[1]

A more systematic yet still quite broad definition of regulation is offered by Barry Mitnick: "regulation is the intentional restriction of a subject's choice of activity, by an entity not directly party to or involved in that activity."[2] Mitnick's definition holds that "regulation is the public administrative policing of a private [economic] activity with respect to a rule prescribed in the public interest."[3] Warren Buhler, formerly staff director of the U.S. Commission of Federal Paperwork, is only slightly less abstract when he states that regulation "should be defined as any activity of government which directs or substantially influences a specific course of action by persons outside government as a means for achieving government's goals."[4]

The U.S. Domestic Council Review Group on Regulatory Reform also notes that "almost everything government does requires

the prescribing of rules," and then defines federal regulation as
"federal laws or rules imposing government established standards
and significant economic responsibilities on individuals or organizations outside the federal establishment."[5] The U.S. Senate Committee on Government Operations emphasized similar criteria in study-
ing regulatory agencies that have decision-making authority, that
establish standards or guidelines conferring benefits or imposing
restrictions on business conduct, and that operate largely in the
sphere of domestic business activity.[6]

The American Bar Association's Commission on Law and the
Economy, in its report Federal Regulation: Roads to Reform, does
not give a definition of regulation. Rather, it argues that "Almost
all classical examples of regulatory programs can be grouped into
one of five types," and indicates the three major types as "cost-of-
service ratemaking," "allocation in accordance with a public interest standard," and "standard setting." The two minor types are
"historically based price setting" and "historically based allocation."[7]

We believe a more precise definition of regulation is required.
The problem with these other definitions is that they do not distinguish between regulation and other instruments of public policy.
Regulation is only one of a variety of policy instruments governments have at their disposal to influence the behavior of citizens.[8]
In order to identify the characteristics of economic regulation, it
may be useful to look briefly at some policy instruments other than
regulation. These include:

Moral persuasion, exhortation, or negotiation, including
speeches, conferences, reports of task forces or advisory bodies,
and threats of government action.

Direct expenditures, including both capital and current outlays for the provision of public services; grants, subsidies, and
transfer payments to individuals and to firms.

Taxation, that is, direct or indirect taxes, fees or prices for
public services monopolistically supplied, and compulsory con-
tributions to pension plans or insurance schemes. Tariffs are also
included in this category.

Tax expenditures, that is, the use of the tax system, through
exemptions, incentives, preferential treatment, to achieve an economic or social result that could be reached through a direct subsidy or loan program. The cost of tax expenditures is measured in
terms of revenue foregone.[9]

Public ownership, including joint ventures in which government is the controlling partner.

What is it that makes economic regulation different from these other instruments of public policy? It cannot be that economic regulation is the only policy instrument that is used to alter economic behavior. Aside from the broad generalization that any action of government will have some economic effects, it is still true that other policy instruments may be aimed specifically at altering the economic behavior of firms or individuals, for example, a tax incentive for oil exploration or an increase in rate of tax applied to capital gains.[10] To some degree, these policy instruments may be interchangeable, either among themselves or with regulation to achieve a particular objective. By definition, the objective of a tax expenditure could be achieved by some form of direct spending or loan program.[11]

Economic regulation is based on statute, but this also is not a unique characteristic. Most of the policy instruments of government derive their authority from statute. Even techniques of moral suasion or exhortation may depend for their effectiveness on the government's capacity to take other forms of action, that is, to introduce legislation or to enforce existing statutes or subordinate legislation.

It should also be stressed that while much economic regulation is carried out through subordinate legislation called "regulations," this term has no special significance. A regulation is simply a form of subordinate legislation, that is, an issuance by a body or individual to whom the power to legislate has been delegated by the legislature.[12] A regulation may give particular effect to the statutes on which other policy instruments are based. Of course, a regulation may also be subordinate legislation under an economic regulatory statute. This is true frequently because of the necessity for detail in regulatory statutes. Furthermore, it may be interesting to note the relatively high proportion of regulations promulgated under economic regulatory statutes because they share the same characteristics as the statutes themselves and because they are not passed by Congress.

The enabling statutes, and the subordinate legislation of economic regulation, do appear to have one special characteristic that makes them different from the statutes that authorize other policy instruments. Economic regulatory statutes rely solely on rules or commands. They require that certain behavior take place or they prohibit certain behavior. Whereas other policy instruments may rely in a secondary fashion on legal commands, it is the primary form of control used to influence behavior of firms in economic regulation. A system of pure command[13] relies on penalties to enforce the government's will. As noted above, Mitnick emphasizes that regulation is the "public administrative policing of private activity." This does not necessarily imply that the firm or individual toward which the command is directed objects or is unwilling to submit to such commands. Economic regulation may be imposed at the request of and for the chief benefit of the regulated.[14] The penalty aspect of command relates to its form and not necessarily to the political or social context in which it is imposed.[15]

Inherent in the concept of commands or rules enforced by penalties is the narrowing of choice. This point is implicit or explicit in all of the definitions provided in this chapter. As emphasized by Herbert Spencer in 1860: "Regulations have been made in yearly-growing numbers, restraining the citizen in directions where his actions were previously unchecked, and compelling actions where previously he might perform or not as he liked."[16] Although other policy instruments affect alternatives and may reduce the number of alternatives available to a given set of actors, the narrowing of choice is a primary purpose of economic regulation.[17] For example, a tax or subsidy on an activity will change the cost of engaging in that activity and affect its attractiveness relative to other activities. Hypothetically, a command in the form of a prohibition will eliminate the prohibited activity from the set of choices available to the actors.[18]

Economic regulation, taking the form of rules or commands promulgated and enforced by a government, is thus primarily aimed at narrowing certain choices. Because the behavior to be modified is the economic behavior of firms or individuals in the private sector, the choices affected are typically in the following areas:

Price, for example, airline fares, minimum wages, certain agricultural products, telephone rates

Supply, for example, broadcasting licenses, occupational licensing, agricultural production quotas, pipeline certificates "of public convenience and necessity"

Rate of return, for example, public utilities, pipelines

Disclosure of information, for example, securities prospectuses, content labeling

Methods of production, for example, effluent standards, worker health and safety standards

Attributes of a product or services, for example, automobile fuel efficiency standards, safety of children's toys, quality or purity of food products, the "local generation" program requirements in broadcasting

Conditions of service, for example, requirements to act as a common carrier, or not to discriminate in hiring or providing goods and services.

It may be noted that the areas affected by economic regulation include not only the traditional forms of "economic" or "direct" regulation but also what has been called the "new regulation" or "social regulation."[19] Direct regulation is industry-specific and affects price, output, rate of return, and entry or exit. Social regulation typically affects a broad range of industries, although its impact on some may be much greater than it is on others. It includes environmental regulation, consumer production legislation, "fairness" regulation,[20] health and safety regulation, and cultural legislation. Nonetheless, economic behavior is controlled by the preponderance of social regulation. William Lilley and James Miller contrast economic and social regulation as follows:

> While all regulation is essentially "social" in that it affects human welfare, the economic/social distinction emphasized some very significant differences. The old-style economic regulation typically focuses on markets, rates, and the obligation to serve. . . . On the other hand . . . social regulation affects the conditions under which goods and services are produced [and sold] and the physical characteristics of products that are manufactured. . . . The government often becomes involved with very detailed facets of the production process.[21]

Both traditional direct regulation and a great proportion of social regulation, therefore, are included in our definition of economic regulation. Consequently, we believe that economic regulation ought to be defined as the imposition of rules by a government, backed by the use of penalties, that are intended specifically to modify the economic behavior of individuals and firms in the private sector.[22]

The essential characteristics of our definition of regulation should be noted. First, it is concerned with the intentional alteration of economic behavior. Governments impose a very large number of rules designed to alter human behavior. Many are based on moral or ethical precepts. Although the laws dealing with heroin or robbery have an economic impact, their justification and primary objectives are the alteration of behavior that is not seen as economic in nature. Economic regulation is intended to change economic behavior. In general, the choices open to individuals or firms are to be constrained.

Second, as we define it, economic regulation consists of actions by a government aimed at firms and individuals in the private sector. We exclude the vast panoply of rules one segment or level

of government imposes on another. Excluded are the activities by
which one level of government "regulates" another, for example,
federal mandates for affirmative action hiring practices in state or
local government.[23]

A third element of our definition is that, unlike other instruments of government intervention, economic regulation is conducted
through the imposition of rules backed by penalties. Although the
penalties may be economic in character, for example, fines or
loss of a franchise, economic regulation does not rely primarily on
economic incentives to achieve its objectives. For example, taxes
amount to a compulsory levy on assets, income, sales, value added,
and so on. Tax expenditures seek to induce desired behavior by
altering the relative prices/costs of certain activities. Grants and
subsidies operate in much the same way. Direct expenditures on
public services provide income/consumption benefits in kind, often
at zero price. In general, these other instruments of public policy
seek to induce changes in behavior by altering the economic incentives faced by decision makers. In contrast, the statement "there
ought to be a law," as Douglas Hartle points out, "is the demand
for an enforced rule requiring that individuals or corporations or
unions, or whatever, be compelled to stop doing something they are
doing or start doing something they are not doing."[24] The fact that
such a large proportion of legislators are lawyers may account for
their faith in the efficacy of regulatory instruments. Finally, the
idea of regulation as "rules backed by penalties" also stands in contrast to such techniques as exhortation, negotiation, and information dissemination by government aimed at altering economic behavior. There are, of course, grey areas such as when a government urges "voluntary" changes in behavior implicitly backed by the
threat of even more restrictive legislative action. The use of wage
and price guidelines before the imposition of wage and price controls
is an excellent example.

While we believe that our conception provides a satisfactory
definition of economic regulation in a general sense, we wish to
explore the limits and implications of this definition in greater
detail.

LEGAL DOMAIN

A number of conceptual issues arise from the definition of
economic regulation as a particular set of rules or commands promulgated by and backed by the authority of a government. The
rules or commands, like all rules, have a subject dimension and
an object dimension. The subject is typically expressed in terms

of characteristics such as type of product or service, location or market boundaries, or revenue. The object may be expressed as a function, that is, the behavior to be regulated—the setting of price or the maintenance of specified work-place conditions. Taken together, the subject and object constitute a legal domain. Each rule has a legal domain. A statute providing for economic regulation may be composed of several or many rules, the total of which constitutes the legal domain of the statute. The boundaries of the legal domain of a statute are coextensive, therefore, with the authority or vires of the statute. The complete set of rules, we argue, constitutes the legal domain of economic regulation.

In comparing regulatory domains, then, it must be understood that they are made up of many rules, each with a specified subject(s) and objective(s). Unambiguous conclusions may be drawn only when one rule (or several related rules) is equivalent or broader than the other in terms of both subject and object. Furthermore, because the subject, like the object, has many dimensions, it may be difficult to establish firm conclusions about the breadth of the subject without making a detailed investigation. A rule may be more inclusive than another rule on the subject dimension, but less inclusive on the object dimension (or vice versa). One rule may apply to an entire population, but only functionally affect behavior in limited areas. Another rule may apply to a small number of firms but regulate virtually every aspect of their behavior.

These problems are compounded when one tries to sum the domains of individual rules—whether it be to compare statutes, areas of regulation, or the total domain of business regulation in a given country. Transportation again provides an excellent example. In the United States three different levels of government make rules about entry, price, quality of service, safety, and so on. These rules may apply to all modes of transportation or they may apply only to one mode. They may apply broadly or narrowly in terms of cargo, length of trip or destination, and so forth. In other words, there are hundreds of local governments and 50 state governments, each with one or more rule-making body or bodies making different rules that apply to different parts of the transportation industry. Consequently, the investigations and judgments that have to be made to determine comparability of the subject and object dimensions of the domain of transportation regulation present a formidable task.

SCOPE AND COVERAGE

Determination of the dimensions of legal domain of regulation does not complete the definition. Regulation is a political and administrative process carried out by organizations and individuals who impose and enforce rules. In some cases they also create the rules. This means that the actual or de facto regulatory domain may not be identical to the legal or de jure domain. To refer to the actual subjects of regulation, we use the term "coverage." To refer to the objectives of regulation, we use the term "scope." Regulatory organizations may use additional resources to extend the scope and/or coverage of regulation. They may also use additional resources to intensify their efforts at enforcement of regulation with a given scope and coverage.

EFFECT OF REGULATION

As observed, regulation is intended to influence certain kinds of behavior. Hence, when one talks about the "amount of regulation," what is often meant is the degree to which behavior is influenced by it. This is what we mean by the effect of regulation. Moreover, if one wishes to draw normative conclusions about these effects, it is necessary to subtract the social costs of regulation from its social benefits. This is what we mean by net effects, or consequences, of economic regulation. To the extent that the effect of regulation is the elimination of alternatives from the choices of decision makers, net effect may be measured by the difference in value between the alternative that would have been chosen and the best alternative under regulation. Unfortunately, it is very difficult to measure net benefits and nearly impossible to measure them precisely.

There is no necessary relationship between, first, the breadth of the subject and the object or regulation or the scope and the coverage and, second, the magnitude of effect. This is so because some rules imposed upon firms may be trivial. For example, they may mandate behavior that would have occurred in their absence. It should be understood that a few significant rules may have far greater effect than countless trivial ones. Pareto's law or the 80-20 rule probably applies to regulations as to other phenomena. On the other hand, even if the content of the rule is not trivial, the subject's behavior may not be influenced if the rule is not properly enforced. In such a case, regulation would not have an effect. Therefore, information about the scope and coverage of regulation is not sufficient to draw exact conclusions as to the relative effects of regulation. To draw such conclusions, information about the amount of enforcement effort and its effectiveness is also necessary.

We assume that, where other things are equal, the effectiveness of enforcement effort will depend upon the motivation of the regulators, the resources at their disposal, the enforcement technology employed, and, of course, the resultant motivation of those regulated. Motivation may be difficult to determine, with regulators being accused on one hand of being captives of the regulated industry,[25] and on the other hand of being crusading zealots who view the firm or individuals to be regulated as "enemies."[26]

Regulators may choose from an array of enforcement strategies, some of which make their job easier and less costly, and others, more difficult and more costly. The choice of enforcement technology appears often to be governed by the objective of minimizing administrative costs.[27] Therefore, if other things were equal, we could infer that greater resources devoted to regulation implies greater regulatory effectiveness. Together with a greater regulatory domain, this would imply greater regulatory effect.[28] Care must be exercised here because it may be claimed that effectiveness is greatest when compliance is obtained merely by making a regulation backed up by the possibility of enforcement action. However, if there are economic benefits associated with noncompliance, and those subject to regulation treat such benefits as ordinary goods (that is, the morality of noncompliance is ignored), then the usual optimizing calculus applies. In most cases, therefore, more resources or more regulatory effort will be required to increase effectiveness.[29]

In addition, an enforcement strategy that minimizes administrative costs will likely shift costs to the regulated industry. If we look only at the effect associated with enforcement, it appears that where other things (for example, domain) are held equal, the less the regulators' effort, the greater the effect on firms. Much of the effect may be only indirectly related to the ultimate purpose of the regulation in question.

However, in most cases, other things are not equal. As noted, regulators do two things: They make rules and they enforce rules. There is typically a relatively fixed cost to make a given type of rule, although costs may differ with different types of rules. Enforcement effects, in contrast, are probably roughly proportional to effort, at least where enforcement technologies are similar. There are likely to be substantial external economies of scale reflected in regulatory cost functions. How much depends upon the relative importance of rule making and rule enforcement. For example, the occupational health regulation cost function ought to be heavily weighted toward hazard identifications and rule making (that is, establishing threshold levels, dose-response relationships, and so on). In fact, administration of occupational safety and health tends to be heavily weighted toward enforcement. (This point is analyzed further in Chapter 7.) Consequently, it seems likely that the resources devoted to safety and health regulation yield a greater effect and a lesser net effect than they would if they had been directed toward hazard identification and rule making. This approach also means that the net effect is much less likely to be positive.

At least one factor may offset external economies of scale in regulation: complexity. Complexity clearly dominates the regulatory cost function in the case of price controls. The number of prices that a regulator might have to set is an exponential function of the number of product or service attributes subject to regulation. In other words, a linear expansion of domain will result in an exponential increase in the number of prices to be set or controlled. For example, if a regulator had to set surface freight rates for two products and three city pairs, it would be necessary for him to promulgate a maximum of six rates. However, if there were four products and six city pairs, it might be necessary to establish 60 rates. In general, the greater the number of special circumstances, the more costly rule making will be. Therefore, an assessment of complexity must be made in estimating enforcement effort and effect.

CONCLUSION

Economic regulation may be defined as the imposition of rules by a government, backed by the use of penalties, that are intended specifically to modify the economic behavior of individuals and firms in the private sector. This definition distinguishes economic regulation as an instrument of public policy from others such as exhortation, direct expenditure, taxation, tax expenditures, and public ownership. The subject and object dimension of government-imposed rules constitutes the legal domain of the legislative authority. A rule may be more inclusive than another on the subject dimension, but less inclusive on the object dimension, or vice versa. This fact, among others, makes intergovernment comparisons of regulatory domains extremely difficult. Because economic regulations impose or confer both costs and benefits, the net effect or consequences of such regulations must account for both. The net effect of a regulation is highly dependent upon enforcement strategy and the effort devoted to enforcement.

NOTES

1. Committee on Government Operations, U.S. Senate, Study on Federal Regulation, Vol. I, The Regulatory Appointments Process

(Washington, D.C.: U.S. Government Printing Office, January 1977), p. v. Similarly, the U.S. Congressional Budget Office noted: "The broadest definition of federal regulation would include all governmental activities which somehow affect the operations of private industry or the lives of private citizens. Such a definition would result in the identification of most federal activities as regulatory. "The Number of Federal Employees Engaged in Regulatory Activities," staff paper prepared for the Subcommittee on Interstate and Foreign Commerce, U.S. House of Representatives (Washington, D.C.: U.S. Government Printing Office, 1976), as quoted in Barry M. Mitnick, "The Concept of Regulation," Bulletin of Business Research (Ohio State University) 53, no. 5 (1978):1.

    2. Mitnick, op. cit., p. 3.

    3. Ibid. We inserted the word "economic" in the definition as Mitnick notes that "in the literature most usages of the term 'regulation' assume that the private activity regulated is economic in nature."

    4. Warren Buhler, "The Origins and Costs of Regulation," in The Dialogue That Happened: Proceedings of Workshop on the Private Costs of Regulation, ed. G. David Hughes and E. Cameron Williams (Cambridge, Mass.: Marketing Science Institute, 1979), p. 46.

    5. The Challenge of Regulatory Reform, A Report to the President from the Domestic Council Review Group on Regulatory Reform (Washington, D.C.: January 1977), p. 4.

    6. Committee on Government Operation, op. cit., p. vi.

    7. American Bar Association, Commission on Law and Economy, Federal Regulation: Roads to Reform, Exposure Draft (Washington, D.C.: American Bar Association, August 1978), p. 43. The commission notes (p. 60) that regulation may also involve disclosure requirements, but this can easily be seen as a form of standard setting.

    8. See Theodore Lowi, "Four Systems of Policy Politics and Choice," Public Administration Review 32 (May–June 1970):314–25.

    9. Stanley Surrey, Pathways to Tax Reform: The Concept of Tax Expenditures (Cambridge, Mass.: Harvard University Press, 1973).

    10. Ibid.

    11. Ibid.

    12. The particular meaning of "regulation" as subordinate legislation obviously may differ in different contexts. Beyond the issue of subordinate legislation created by a body to whom Congress has delegated authority, there is the problem of subdelegation. The latter refers to the practice of making regulations so as to further delegate rule-making authority to agency or department directors, (for example, the director of the Environmental Protection Agency.

13. For a short discussion of the characteristics of command as a control device, see Robert A. Dahl and Charles E. Lindblom, Politics, Economics, and Welfare (New York: Harper & Row, 1953).

14. See, for example, George J. Stigler, "The Theory of Economic Regulation," Bell Journal of Economics and Management Science 2, no. 1 (1971):3-21; Richard A. Posner, "Theories of Economic Regulation," Bell Journal of Economics and Management Science 5, no. 2 (1974):335-58; Sam Peltzman, "Toward a More General Theory of Regulation," Journal of Law and Economics 19, no. 2 (1976):211-48; James Q. Wilson, "The Politics of Regulation," in Social Responsibility and the Business Predicament, ed. James W. McKee (Washington, D.C.: Brookings Institution, 1974).

15. The choice of regulation with its inherent characteristics of command may have political advantages, however, as the more covert costs of regulation may obviate politically awkward explanations; see Douglas G. Hartle, Public Policy Decision Making and Regulation (Montreal: Institute for Research on Public Policy, 1979), Chap. 4. The penalty characteristic may also provide opportunities for symbolic reassurances to certain interest groups; see Murray Edelman, The Symbolic Uses of Politics (Urbana: University of Illinois Press, 1964).

16. Herbert Spencer, "Parliamentary Reform: The Dangers and the Safeguards," Westminster Review, April 1860, as cited in the Preface to Herbert Spencer, The Man Versus the State (London: Watts, 1940), p. xi.

17. Although regulation seeks to constrain the choice set of those subject to it, in some cases it is imposed to improve the choice set of those who buy from, work for, or invest in the regulated firm. An obvious example is a regulation requiring the disclosure of information such as product content labeling, occupational health hazard identification, or "blue sky" regulations for securities prospectuses.

18. Of course, it is possible to view the penalty, particularly if it takes the form of a moderate fine, as simply a tax on the "prohibited" activity. A firm may prefer to pay the "tax" rather than eliminate the activity from its choice set. See W. T. Stanbury, "Penalties and Remedies Under the Combines Investigation Act, 1889-1976," Osgoode Hall Law Journal 14, no. 3 (December 1976):571-631. Generally, however, society views payment of a tax as a legitimate cost to a firm, while activity that involves frequent payment of fines is usually viewed with less favor. Taxes are a deductible expense in the calculation of net income while fines may not be. In a corporate context, it might even raise questions of breach of the duties and good faith of the offices and directors.

19. For further amplification of the origins and definitions of the "new social regulation," see, for example, Lawrence J. White, Reforming Regulation: Processes and Problems (Englewood Cliffs, N.J.: Prentice-Hall, 1981); James Q. Wilson, ed., The Politics of Regulation (New York: Basic Books, 1980); Lee Fritschler and Bernard Ross, Business Regulation and Governing Decision Processes (Cambridge, Mass.: Winthrop, 1980); see also Chap. 4.

20. We would include legislation that seeks to prevent discrimination in employment and in the sale/purchase of goods and services in the "fairness" category.

21. William Lilley III and James C. Miller III, "The New 'Social Regulation,'" The Public Interest, no. 47 (Spring 1977):53-54.

22. An earlier version of this definition was given in Sylvia Ostry, Regulation Reference: A Preliminary Report to First Ministers (Ottawa: Economic Council of Canada, November 1978), p. 15.

23. A pessimistic view on the ability of government to regulate itself is contained in James Q. Wilson and Patricia Rachal, "Can the Government Regulate Itself?" The Public Interest, no. 46 (Winter 1977):3-14. Their thesis, admirably defended, is that "in general, it is easier for a public agency to change the behavior of a private organization than of another public agency" (p. 4). Wilson and Rachal conclude that "large-scale public enterprise [that is, the shifting of functions from the private to the public sector] and widespread public regulation may be incompatible" (p. 14).

24. Hartle, op. cit., p. 86.

25. See Marver Bernstein, Regulating Business by Independent Commission (Princeton, N.J.: Princeton University Press, 1955). Samuel P. Huntington, "The Marasmus of the ICC," Yale Law Journal 61 (1952):467 et seq. More recently, see Paul Sabatier, "Social Movements and Regulatory Agencies: Toward a More Adequate—and Less Pessimistic—Theory of 'Clientele Capture,'" Policy Sciences 6 (1975):301-42.

26. See, for example, Burt Schorr, "FTC's Mike Pertschuk Tilts Against Congress to Keep Agency Power," Wall Street Journal January 15, 1980, pp. 1, 34; Stan Crock and Burt Schorr, "FTC Stirs Up a Vast Array of Opponents, and Congress Weighs Curb on Its Power," Wall Street Journal, October 18, 1979, p. 48; "Congress Wants to Slow the Regulators," Business Week, November 5, 1979, pp. 164, 168; Steven Rattner, "Regulating the Regulators," New York Times Sunday Magazine, June 17, 1979, pp. 112-13, 122; Tom Alexander, "It's Roundup Time for the Runaway Regulators," Fortune, December 3, 1979, pp. 126-28, 130, 132; Walter Oi, "Safety at Any Price?" Regulation, November-December 1977, pp. 16-23; Walter Guzzardi, Jr., "The Mindless Pursuit

of Safety," Fortune, April 9, 1979, pp. 54-56, 58, 60, 62, 64; and
Tom Alexander, "Time for a Cease-Fire in the Food-Safety Wars,"
Fortune, February 27, 1979, pp. 94-96, 98, 99.

27. The important point here is that the compliance costs incurred by those in the private sector may be many times larger than
the government's administrative costs. This point is emphasized by
Murray Weidenbaum and Robert De Fina, "The Cost of Federal
Regulation," Reprint No. 88 (Washington, D.C.: American Enterprise Institute, 1978). Green and Waitzman challenge their estimate of about $97 billion in costs to comply with U.S. federal regu-
lation administrative costs, in fiscal 1979, of about $ 5 billion. See
Mark Green and Norman Waitzman, Business War on the Law: An
Analysis of the Benefits of Federal Health/Safety Enforcement
(Washington, D.C.: Corporate Accountability Research Group,
1979).

28. If one could assume that other things were equal, that
regulators seek to maximize their effect, and that increasing enforcement intensity increases regulatory effect at a decreasing rate,
it follows that a real increase in regulatory resources would result
in an increase in regulatory scope and coverage; in which case, so
long as the regulators were not constrained by the boundaries of
their legal domain, effect would be proportional to resources.
This, however, is a very special case.

29. Because we are dealing with uncertain events, the analysis
is done in terms of expected values, adjusted for individual risk
propensities. Therefore, if enforcement effort is thought only to
influence the probability of catching and convicting those violating a
regulation, the expected cost (benefits ignored) of violating a regulation can be increased merely by increasing the size of the economic
penalty involved.

3

THE EXTENT OF REGULATION

Employing the definition of regulation developed in Chapter 2, our task now is to gain some greater understanding of the extent and status of regulation. As noted in Chapter 1, within the past few years some progress has been achieved in regulatory reform. Comprehensive reform, including partial deregulation, has occurred in some areas, and a number of procedural reforms also have been made, for example, institution of a federal regulatory calendar, increased ex ante analysis of proposed regulations, and greater use of economic analysis in assessing the costs, benefits, and overall economic impact of regulation. In addition, a number of proposals for additional deregulation are under consideration, and a broad review of federal regulatory performance has been undertaken by the Reagan administration.

The challenge presented to reform efforts is evident given the extent of existing regulation. For example, the 1977 Code of Federal Regulations is approximately 75,000 fine print pages in length.[1] The hazardous products section of the consolidated consumer products safety statutes encompasses 93 pages, motor vehicle statutes cover 81 pages, and food and drug and cosmetics statutes fill 145 pages. Furthermore, the portions of the statutes that explain to regulatory agencies what they may and may not do are lengthy. For example, the food and drug and cosmetics statutes contain eight pages of explicit directions in fine print and six more pages that specify appeal procedures. General statute language explaining regulatory function and jurisdiction in this area covers 20 pages.

Explanations for the lengthiness of federal regulatory statutes may be found in the nature of congressional efforts to control the behavior of regulatory agencies and departments. Congressional control over regulatory outcomes is accomplished from a distance. Congress passes laws that include implementation instructions, but regulatory programs are run by the independent regulatory agencies and the regulatory departments of the executive branch of government under the direction of the cabinet-level appointees of the presidential administration in power. Congress also attempts to influence regulatory agency performance through appropriation in the annual budget process. Consequently, because of its distance from the actual implementation of regulatory statutes, Congress attempts to ensure that regulatory outcomes are consistent with its expectations through the enactment of laws that carefully specify the jurisdictions and functions of the regulators.

An additional reason for the specificity of regulatory statutes appears to result from the fact that U.S. society has become highly litigious; individuals and organizations sue each other frequently in order to test the applicability of the law to their predicaments. This requires Congress and state legislatures to specify the intent and expectation of statutes in great detail in an attempt to prevent the courts from misconstruing the purposes of the law. Furthermore, enabling legislation passed by Congress attempts to comprehend a wide array of contingencies in providing directions to regulators. Congress attempts to provide directions in statute to enable the coordination of regulatory controls within and between agencies and functional areas.

A better measure of regulatory domain is provided by examining the function and jurisdiction of federal regulatory departments and agencies. Table 3.1 provides a summary of regulatory agency function; the classification system shown was developed by Marcia Wallace and Ronald Penoyer and updated by Kenneth Chilton.[2] The conclusion we draw from this survey is a reiteration that the scope of federal regulation is tremendous. In addition, we observe the extensiveness of industry-specific or direct regulation. By direct regulation we mean government control, usually directed at specific industries, of supply (including restrictions on the number of participants in a given industry, that is, entry and specification of conditions of participation, as well as direct restrictions on output) and price (including regulation of return on investment, as well as direct restrictions on prices). Frequently, direct regulation is extended to quality and mix of output and to specification of input mixes and characteristics, that is, investment in plant and equipment, specification of optimal production technology, and so on.

We may also note the extent of federal regulation and its relationship to state-level regulation in three important areas: occupational health, safety, and working conditions, industry-specific or direct regulation, and the regulation of financial activities.

TABLE 3.1

U.S. Regulatory Agencies and Departments by Regulatory Area

Consumer Safety and Health

1. Consumer Product Safety Commission
   To protect the public against unreasonable risks of injury associated with consumer products
2. Department of Agriculture
   i. Agricultural Marketing Service
      To regulate the price and production of various agricultural commodities and the marketing practices of producers
   ii. Agricultural Stabilization and Conservation Service
      To administer specified commodity and related land use programs as part of the overall agricultural farm price support program
   iii. Animal and Plant Health Inspection Service
      To conduct regulatory and control programs to protect and improve animal and plant health
   iv. Federal Grain Inspection Service
      To provide a national grain inspection and weighing system
   v. Food Safety and Quality Service
      To certify the grade, quality, or wholesomeness of certain agricultural commodities and products
   vi. Foreign Agricultural Service
      To regulate imports of agricultural commodities
3. Department of Health, Education and Welfare
   i. Food and Drug Administration
      To protect the public against impure and unsafe foods, drugs, and cosmetics, and to regulate hazards involved with medical devices and radiation

4. Department of Housing and Urban Development
   i. Office of Consumer Affairs and Regulatory Functions
      To regulate certain types of housing and real estate activities (that is, Mobile Home Standards; Interstate Land Sales Registration; Real Estate Settlement Procedures)
5. Department of Justice
   i. Anti-trust Division
      To administer and enforce antitrust, consumer protection, and similar laws
   ii. Drug Enforcement Administration
      To control narcotics and other dangerous drugs
6. Department of Transportation
   i. Coast Guard
      To enforce federal marine navigation laws
   ii. Federal Aviation Administration
      To regulate the nation's aviation system for safety and effectiveness
   iii. Federal Highway Administration
      To set highway safety standards and administer the federal aid highway program
   iv. Federal Railroad Administration
      To administer and enforce rail safety laws and regulations
   v. National Highway Traffic Safety Administration
      To set standards for motor vehicle fuel economy and emissions
7. Department of the Treasury
   i. Bureau of Alcohol, Tobacco and Firearms

Table 3.1 (continued)

To enforce laws and regulations governing the legal flow of firearms, explosives, and alcoholic and tobacco products
ii. Customs Service
To enforce regulations governing international traffic and trade
8. National Transportation Safety Board
To promote transportation safety on land and in the air

Job Safety and Other
Working Conditions
1. Department of Labor
i. Employment Standards Administration
To administer and enforce various employment standards
ii. Labor-Management Services Administration
To regulate employee welfare
iii. Mine Safety and Health Administration
To protect the health and safety of U.S. miners
iv. Occupational Safety and Health Administration
To develop and enforce worker safety and health regulations
2. Equal Employment Opportunity Commission
To enforce antidiscrimination provisions of the Civil Rights Act as regards discrimination based on race, sex, color, religion, or national origin in hiring, promotion, firing, wages, testing, training, apprenticeship, and all other conditions of employment
3. National Labor Relations Board
To administer laws relating to collective bargaining between companies and labor unions
4. Occupational Safety and Health Review Commission
To review the appeals made on directives issued by the Occupational Safety and Health Administration (OSHA)

Environment and Energy
1. Council on Environmental Quality
To administer the environmental impact statement process and to develop and recommend to the president policies for protecting and improving environmental quality
2. Department of Defense, Army Corps of Engineers
To protect the nation's rivers, shores, and other navigable waters
3. Department of Energy, Economic Regulatory Administration
To regulate the supply, pricing, and distribution of crude oil, natural gas liquids, and petroleum products, and to manage coal conversion programs
4. Department of the Interior
i. Fish and Wildlife Service
To preserve and protect fish and wildlife resources
ii. Office of Surface Mining Reclamation and Enforcement
To regulate the strip mining of coal
5. Environmental Protection Agency
To protect and enhance the physical environment
6. Nuclear Regulatory Commission
To regulate the civilian uses of nuclear materials and facilities so that they are consistent with public health and safety regulations, environmental quality standards, and national security and antitrust laws

Finance and Banking
1. Department of the Treasury
i. Comptroller of the Currency
To license and regulate national banks
2. Farm Credit Administration
To supervise and examine the borrower-owned banks and associations that comprise the cooperative Farm Credit System
3. Federal Reserve System (Board of Governors)
To supervise and examine the Federal Reserve banks and the system's member banks

Table 3.1 (continued)

4. Federal Home Loan Bank Board
To regulate federally chartered
savings and loan associations
5. Federal Deposit Insurance Corporation
To regulate national banks, and
state banks that apply and are
qualified for Federal Deposit Insurance
6. National Credit Union Administration
To regulate and examine all federally chartered credit unions

Industry-Specific Regulation
1. Civil Aeronautics Board
To promote and regulate the civil
air transport industry
2. Commodity Futures Trading Commission
To regulate futures trading in agricultural and other commodities,
including lumber and metals
3. Federal Communications Commission
To regulate domestic interstate
and foreign communications by
radio, wire, television, cable,
and telephone
4. Federal Energy Regulatory Commission
To regulate interstate aspects of
the electric power and natural gas
industries
5. Federal Maritime Commission
To regulate the waterborne foreign
and domestic offshore commerce
of the United States
6. Interstate Commerce Commission
To regulate interstate surface
transportation carriers

7. Renegotiation Board
To determine and eliminate excessive profits on defense and
space contracts and subcontracts

General Business
1. Council on Wage and Price Stability (NR)
To monitor the economy as a
whole, and to examine the effect
of government policies on inflation
2. Department of Commerce
   i. Domestic and International
      Business Administration
      To regulate aspects of international trade relating to imports and foreign trade zones
   ii. Patent and Trade Mark Office
       To administer laws governing the granting of patents for
       inventions and the registration of trademarks
3. Federal Election Commission
To regulate the financing of political campaigns for federal office
4. Federal Trade Commission
To ensure "vigorous, free, and
fair competition in the marketplace"
5. International Trade Commission
To identify and eliminate "dumping" and other unfair practices
on the part of importers
6. Cost-Accounting Standards Board
To set accounting standards for
defense contractors
7. Securities and Exchange Commission
To protect the investing public
against malpractices in the
securities and financial markets

Classification by Wallace and Penoyer (1978), updated by Chilton (1979).
See note 2 for citation.

Federal occupational health, safety, and working condition regulation is extensive, and in this area the federal government plays a dominant role relative to state governments. However, in industry-specific regulation, although the federal role is broad, it is also shared with broad state government coverage. This is in contrast to financial regulation, where, although there is a prominent federal role, it is much narrower than that played by state governments.

The pattern of division of regulatory authority between the federal government and state government evidences the concurrent nature of regulation in the United States. In many areas both the federal and state governments regulate the private sector. In many areas there is a considerable degree of overlap or duplication, for instance, in environmental protection and health. In others there are parallel but separate federal and state legal jurisdictions, such as in transportation, consumer protection, and financial institutions.

Another measure of regulatory impact is the effort of enforcement. In some areas where regulatory law is extensive, the consequences of regulation may be slight due to lack of enforcement effort or unenforceability of the law. Much regulation, in fact, may not be enforced. Because measuring enforcement effort in general is somewhat difficult, this task is best approached through study of individual regulatory agencies and programs. However, one measure of regulatory enforcement effort is the magnitude of expenditures on the salaries, materials and services, office space, legal fees, and other to administer and enforce regulatory programs. It may be argued that this is the most adequate measure of general enforcement effort readily available. Still, reservations must be expressed with regard to differences in the scale and complexity of activities subject to regulation and their influence on enforcement effectiveness at various levels of expenditure. These complexities and others may confuse attempts to define enforcement effort through comparison of the administrative expenditures of regulatory agencies and programs.

To enable comparison of regulatory expenditures as a measure of enforcement effort, we have employed the same general methodology used by the Center for the Study of American Business (CSAB) to estimate federal expenditures on regulation.[3] Using CSAB categories we have grouped expenditure data by broad program area for the fiscal years 1970/71 and 1977/78 according to two expenditure classification systems, as shown in Table 3.2. Classification 1 conforms to the method used by CSAB to locate expenditures by area. Classification 2 differs from 1 in that it transfers the economic (price/output) regulatory expenditures of the Department of Agriculture from Consumer Safety and Health (CSH) to Industry Specific Regulation, Antitrust Division expenditures from CSH to General Business, and Bureau of Alcohol, Tobacco and Firearms and the Customs Service

TABLE 3.2

Federal Regulatory Expenditures, 1970/71 and 1977/78
($ million)

Area of Regulation	Classification 1		Classification 2		Percent Change 1970/71-1977/78	Percent Annual Average Change[a] 1970/71-1977/78
	1970/71	1977/78	1970/71	1977/78		
Consumer Safety and health	$593 48.5%	$2,255 46.3%	$332 27.2%	$1,810 37.2%	545%	78%
Job safety and other working conditions	104 8.5%	496 10.2%	104 8.5%	496 10.2%	477%	68%
Environment and energy	146 11.9%	1,296 26.7%	146 11.9%	1,296 26.7%	888%	127%
Finance and banking	123 10.1%	273 5.6%	123 10.1%	273 5.6%	222%	32%
Industry-specific regulation	151 12.4%	297 6.1%	375 30.7%	430 8.8%	115%	16%
General business	105 8.6%	245 5.0%	142 11.6%	557 11.4%	392%	56%
Total	$1,222[b] 100%	$4,862 100%	$1,222 100%	$4,862 100%	398%	42.5%

[a]Simple average change over 1970/71 base, not compounded change each year.
[b]Federal expenditures for regulation in 1969-70 were $886 million.

Source: Kenneth Chilton, "A Decade of Rapid Growth in Federal Regulation" (St. Louis: Washington University, Center for the Study of American Business, March 13, 1979), Table 1 for Classification 1. Data in Classification 2 are our estimates. Also note the following changes were made from Classification 1 in representing the data for 2: transfer of the economic (or price and/or output) regulatory aspects of the Department of Agriculture from "Consumer Safety and Health" CSH to "Industry-Specific Regulation," shift of the Antitrust Division from CSH to "General Business," shift of the Bureau of Alcohol, Tobacco and Firearms and the Customs Service from CSH to "General Business."

from CSH to General Business. The general effect of our revisions is to decrease the importance of the CSH category and to increase that of the Industry-Specific and General Business categories. We believe the transfers make the comparisons more meaningful than do the data provided by CSAB in that the actual regulatory activities undertaken by these agencies fit more appropriately with their new categories. These are not the only reservations we have about the CSAB system. [4]

Table 3.2 indicates that federal regulatory expenditures have grown at a remarkable rate during the 1970s. For the seven-year period shown, expenditures virtually quadrupled. The average annual increase was $520 million over the 1970 base of $1,222. Even when these figures are adjusted for inflation using the consumer price index, the comparison in constant 1970 dollars is $1,222 million for 1970/71 and $2,894 for 1977/78, or a $239 million average increase in constant dollars per year (19.5 percent simple annual average increase). Note that while the magnitude of this growth is great, regulatory expenditures still comprised only approximately 2 percent of total federal expenditures.

Using classification system 2, the 1977/78 data reveal that Consumer Safety and Health (CSH) is the area in which federal regulatory expenditures were highest, followed by Environment and Energy (E&E) regulation, General Business, Job Safety and Work Conditions, Industry-Specific, and Finance and Banking regulation. Table 3.2 also indicates that the areas having the greatest growth in expenditures, and consequently as a percentage of the total over the seven-year span of the data, were CSH and E&E regulation. The percentage of increase over the 1970/71 base for Environment and Energy of 888 percent, or 127 percent annually on average, and Consumer Safety and Health of 545 percent, or 78 percent annually, are impressive. Growth in expenditures in these two areas has been very great, even when compared with still large annual average increases in Industry-Specific and Financial regulation of 16 percent and 32 percent, respectively. Even when viewed in constant dollars, growth rates in all the categories, except Industry-Specific and Financial regulation, are somewhat overwhelming. From another perspective, as a percentage of the total federal budget, although the increase in regulatory expenditures in the years shown may appear to be small, it still was $3,640 million, or $2,166 million in constant 1970 dollars.

With regard to relative growth between categories of regulatory expenditure, predictably we find Environment and Energy and Consumer Safety and Health to have gained a greater proportion of federal regulatory expenditure growth in the 1970s, whereas rates remained relatively stable for Job Safety and Working Conditions and General Business regulation. Proportional gains in E&E and CSH were made at the expense of Industry-Specific and Financial regulation, which show proportional reductions of 22 percent and 4.5 percent of total regulatory expenditures, respectively.

Analyzing the growth in Consumer Safety and Health and Environment and Energy in more detail, according to William Lilley and James Miller, growth in CSH reflects the great increase in social regulation passed by Congress in the late 1960s and early 1970s.[5] Environment and Energy regulation expenditure increases are explained by increases in citizen and, consequently, federal concern over environmental protection, pollution abatement, energy supply and associated risks, and general threats to the health of the natural environment in the United States. As a portion of total growth in this area, expenditures for the Environmental Protection Agency increased from $125 million to $885 million, and those of the Nuclear Regulatory Commission grew from $16 million to $271 million during this period.[6]

The relative decline in expenditures for Industry-Specific regulation may be explained in part by the absolute drop in spending on the marketing of agricultural products, which fell from $224 million to $122 million, and slowed rates of growth for the Civil Aeronautics Board, the Federal Communications Commission, the Federal Maritime Commission, and the Interstate Commerce Commission.[7]

Additional measures of growth can be found by examining federal employment[8] for regulatory agencies and programs and other data provided in Table 3.3. Increases in regulatory expenditures grew much more rapidly than total federal expenditures, gross national product, constant dollar GNP (1972 base), and U.S. population.[9]

These measures indicate that federal regulatory effort is substantial in terms of total expenditures and employees committed, even if the percentages of expenditures and employees in regulatory programs are only a small portion of total federal spending and employment. However, even more impressively the data show how rapidly regulatory effort expanded during the 1970s. Indeed, Lilley and Miller have characterized this growth as indicative of "the explosion in the scope and pervasiveness of federal regulation that occurred between 1970 and 1975."[10] Regardless of the measure used, the growth in federal regulation in this period was dramatic: The number of pages published annually in the Federal Register more than tripled;[11] the number of pages in the Code of Federal Regulations increased by a third; and the number of major regulatory agencies increased by 35 percent. Thirty important regulatory laws were enacted by Congress, a summary of which is shown in Table 3.4. As a result of the passage of new regulatory laws and budgetary

appropriations to implement them, federal regulatory expenditures
had grown to $3,268 million by 1975/76. Modifying our comparison
base by one year, expenditure growth in the five-year period 1969/70
to 1975/76 was 271 percent, whereas the growth from 1975/76 to
1977/78 was 49 percent in total (noninflation-adjusted) dollars.

TABLE 3.3

Measures of Resource Commitment to
Regulation for 1970/71 and 1977/78
($M = Million, $B = Billion)

Measures	1970/71[a]	1977/78[a]	Percent Increase
Federal regulatory expenditures ($M)	1,222	4,862	298
Federal regulatory employment[b]	28,919[d]	77,643[e]	168[d]
Total federal expenditures ($B)	211,425	450,836	113
Total federal employment (1,000)[c]	2,597.2[e]	2,499.8[e]	-4
GNP in current dollars ($B), 1970, 1977	982.4	1,887.2	92
GNP in 1972 dollars ($B), 1970, 1977	1,075.3	1,332.7	24
Population (M) July 1970, 1977	204.8	216.9	6

[a]The federal fiscal year in 1970/71 extended from July 1 to
June 30; in 1977/78 the fiscal year was October 1 to September 30.
[b]Permanent full-time positions (source Wallace and Penoyer,
1978, p. 101; see note 2.
[c]Permanent full-time employment.
[d]See discussion in text and note 9.
[e]Estimated.

TABLE 3.4

Major Federal Regulatory Legislation, 1970-75

Year Enacted	Title of Statute
1970	Clean Air Amendments
	Occupational Health and Safety Act
	Poison Prevention Packaging Act
	Securities Investor Protection Act
1971	Economic Stabilization Act Amendments
	Federal Board Safety Act
	Lead Based Paint Elimination Act
1972	Consumer Product Safety Act
	Equal Employment Opportunity Act
	Federal Election Campaign Act
	Federal Environmental Pesticide Control Act
	Federal Water Pollution Control Act Amendments
	Noise Control Act
	Ports and Waterways Safety Act
1973	Agriculture and Consumer Protection Act
	Economic Stabilization Act Amendment
	Emergency Petroleum Allocation Act
	Flood Disaster Protection Act
1974	Atomic Energy Act
	Commodity Futures Trading Commission Act
	Council on Wage and Price Stability Act
	Employee Retirement Income Security Act
	Federal Energy Administration Act
	Hazardous Materials Transportation Act
	FTC Improvement Act
	Pension Reform Act
	Privacy Act
	Safe Drinking Water Act
1975	Energy Policy and Conservation Act

Source: Lilley and Miller (1977). See note 5.

Our concern up to this point has been to gain perspective on the extent and growth of federal regulation. However, in terms of its effect on the economy a more important measure of regulatory extent may be found in defining the proportion of economic activity subject to regulatory control. One way to make this comparison is to analyze the amount of the economy affected by direct market entry or price controls. This effort is complicated by the fact that, in addition to federal controls, state and local governments also have authority to regulate price and entry over a number of industries and private sector economic activities. In the data available for analysis it is not always possible to determine which portion of a given industry is subject to regulation by a given level of government. In addition, the distinction in practice between price and output controls is frequently blurred. Often, price controls are imposed to moderate or influence the consequences of supply controls. Barriers to entry are frequently erected to preserve publicly mandated price schedules.[12] Consequently, our analysis is somewhat more limited and qualitative than is optimal.

To determine the scope of price and/or supply controls, we first identified the contribution to real domestic product made by each industry or activity in the United States, as shown in Table 3.5. Next we identified all industries subject to price and/or supply controls and attempted to estimate the proportion of industry output subject to these controls. In addition, we made a qualitative judgment as to the predominant type of control exercised with respect to each industry or activity. Finally, these estimates were summed to produce an estimate of the proportion of total economic activity (gross domestic product, or GDP) subject to direct economic regulation. (The appendix to this chapter provides greater detail on our methodology.) The results are shown in Table 3.5.

The most frequently cited estimate of the size of the regulated sector is that made by Richard Posner of 17 percent of GNP (rather than domestic product), originating in seven industries: agriculture, transportation, communications, power, banking, insurance, and medical services.[13] If one uses GDP at factor cost rather than GNP, these industries account for 18 to 20 percent of the total economic activity. In this instance, the difference between the estimate shown in Table 3.5 and an estimate of 18 to 20 percent primarily reflects the fact that Posner's estimate ignores a number of industries and activities that are subject to price and supply controls of greater or lesser severity than those included in his list. Consequently, on reflection, the 25.7 percent of gross domestic product in our estimate appears to be reasonable.

TABLE 3.5

Proportion of Gross Domestic Product Subject to Price and Supply Controls, 1978

Industry of Origin	Percentage of Real GDP by Industry of Origin, 1976	Percentage of GDP Subject to Some Form of Direct Regulation, about 1978
Agriculture	3.520	.700[c]
Forestry	.290	—
Fishing and trapping	—	.276[b]
Mines	1.189	(**)
(Petroleum, natural gas, and so on)	(.460)[4]	
Manufacturing	25.700	.870
(Food and beverages)	(1.892)	(**)
(Petroleum and coal products)	(1.127)	(**)
Construction	5.341	—
Transport	3.949	2.454
(Rail)	(.867)	(.867)[a]
(Local and interurban passenger)	(.246)	(.246)[a]
(Trucking and warehousing)	(1.657)	(.994)[d]
(Water)	(.282)	(.226)[a]
(Air)	(.648)	(.032)[b]
(Pipeline)	(.089)	(.089)[a]
Communications[1]	2.767	2.767
(Telephone and telegraph)	(1.856)	(1.856)[a]
(Radio and TV broadcasting)	(.222)	(.222)[d]
(Post office)	(.690)	(.690)[a]
Public utilities	1.749	1.749[a]
Trade	15.518	—

Finance, insurance, and real estate[2,3]	11.403	9.122[d]
Business and personal services[1]	7.096	1.100[d]
(Services to business management)	(2.820)	(**)
(Personal services)[1]	(1.991)	(**)
Community services[1]	6.293	6.70*[d]
(Education)	(.88)[5]	(**)
(Health and welfare)	(5.383)[5]	(**)
Public administration and defense	15.035[6]	—
Total	100.0%	25.7%

Key: ( ) indicates subtotal; * indicates primarily health services; ** included in sector total due to small size or inability to disaggregate. Totals may not add due to rounding.

[1] Industry subgroups subject to some degree of regulation detailed below.

[2] Includes banking, credit agencies other than banks, security and commodity dealers, brokers and services, real estate, and holding and other investment companies.

[3] The real estate subgroup represents 7.7 percent of GDP in the United States under this definition.

[4] Includes coal.

[5] Private sector only.

[6] Less Public Education and Public Health and Welfare Services, this industry group represents 7.0 percent of GDP.

[a] Price and entry controls.

[b] Primarily price controls.

[c] Primarily output controls.

[d] Primarily entry controls.

Source: The National Income and Public Accounts of the United States, 1929–1974, Statistical Tables (Washington, D.C.: U.S. Government Printing Office, 1975), p. 189. For domestic product and salaries, 1977 data were used. Note that these data are based upon aggregations of firm data classified according to the primary product of the firm. However, this treatment should not materially affect our estimates. Services and goods that are produced and consumed internally are seldom subject to regulation. More details are provided on the derivation of these data in the appendix to this chapter.

The initial conclusion to be drawn from this statistic is that the amount of economic activity affected by regulation is high, both in comparison to Posner's estimate and in an absolute sense. In terms of the extent of price and entry regulation by area, the private health services and education industries, communications, and public utilities are the most highly regulated in terms of the percentage of their real GDP subject to some form of control. Approximately 80 percent of the finance, insurance, and real estate industrial segment GDP is subject to direct regulation by our estimates, and in dollar terms this area is the most affected by regulation as a percentage of total GDP (9.122 percent). The transportation industry is also subject to comprehensive price and entry control as reflected by this measure—62 percent of its GDP is regulated—whereas agriculture and mining are less regulated at 20 percent and 22 percent of their GDP, respectively. The manufacturing industry is only slightly affected by price and entry controls, and forestry, fishing, construction, trade and public administration, and defense industries are not subject to price and entry controls to any significant extent.

Based upon these comparisons, an additional conclusion that may be drawn from the data presented in Table 3.5 is the degree of variation in the application of direct economic regulation across the segments of industry. Whereas price and entry controls apply to virtually all economic activity in some segments, such as private communications and utilities, other segments are subject to very few regulatory controls of this type. Although these variations may, for the most part, be explained by the characteristics of production, operation, competition, and other factors that differ across industries, in some instances the differences are the result of a legacy of federal control—the rationale for which may have been persuasive at the time when regulation was first imposed but now appears inconsistent and, in some cases, out of date in terms of the balance of economic costs and benefits derived from regulation.

Finally, we should also note that although the levels of federal expenditure for regulatory administration and enforcement and percentage of gross domestic product subject to control are important measures of the extent of regulation, the total economic impact of regulation on the private sector is much greater than is reflected in the data we have presented. Even though federal outlays on regulatory activities comprise less than 2 percent of total federal expenditures, some estimates place the private sector's cost of complying with federal regulation at 20 times greater than federal expenditures, or in the range of $95 to $100 billion annually.[14] Although not all of these compliance costs are direct costs to society—they include transfer costs, for example—these estimates make us aware that the social costs of regulation far exceed the administrative and enforcement costs represented in the federal government's budgeted expenditures.

CONCLUSION

This chapter has provided perspectives on the extent of federal economic regulation. It has demonstrated not only the pervasiveness of regulation but also the rapid rate at which regulation has grown over the past decade. The growth has been explained as having resulted not only from public demand for more protection, for example, in the environmental area, but also as a result of congressional efforts to control the implementation of statutes by regulatory agencies and interpretation of laws by the courts. Indicators of the extent and growth of economic regulation provided in the chapter include a summary of federal regulatory department and agency functions and jurisdiction, an assessment of regulatory enforcement effort as reflected in federal expenditures by broad program area, including analysis of areas where growth has been greatest (Consumer Safety and Health and Environment and Energy regulation), and growth in regulatory agency employment. Federal regulatory expenditures grew from $1.22 billion in 1970/71 to $4.86 billion in 1977/78. Other measures noted were the number and length of federal statutes in the Federal Register and the Code of Federal Regulations, the growth in the number of major regulatory laws passed by Congress, and the number of major regulatory agencies in operation. In the period 1970-75 alone, 30 important new regulatory acts were approved. The chapter also presented and analyzed data on the magnitude of price and entry regulation across major industrial segments, finding that approximately one-quarter of the gross domestic product of the surveyed industries to be subject to these types of economic control.

Although indications of the extent of regulation may be found in federal administrative and enforcement expenditures and amount of gross domestic product subject to economic controls, the costs of compliance with regulation incurred by the private sector, the efficiency-loss costs of industry, and other social costs of regulation are much higher than is reflected in these measures. Some estimates of the true social and economic costs of regulation range as high as $100 billion annually. And it is likely that costs have risen since this estimate was made, perhaps to as high as $125 billion or more annually. This is a significant amount, given, for example, that total annual research and development investment made by U.S. business and industry is presently about $25 billion to $30 billion per year.

NOTES

1. Buhler gives the following figures on pages in the Federal Register: 1965, 17,206; 1970, 20,036; 1971, 25,447; 1972, 28,924; 1973, 35,572; 1974, 45,422; 1975, 60,221; 1976, 57,072, 1977, 65,603. Warren Buhler, "The Origins and Costs of Regulation," in The Dialogue That Happened: Proceedings of Workshop on the Private Costs of Regulation, ed. G. David Hughes and E. Cameron Williams (Cambridge, Mass.: Marketing Science Institute, 1979), pp. 45-55. The number of pages in the U.S. Code of Federal Regulations, as given by James C. Miller III, has grown as follows: 1970, 54,105; 1971, 54,487; 1972, 61,035; 1973, 64,852; 1974, 69,270; 1975, 72,200; 1976, 73,149; 1977, 75,000 (est.). The Economist, August 12, 1978, p. 61. James C. Miller III, "Prepared Statement Before the Subcommittee on Consumer Protection and Finance and the Subcommittee on Oversight, U.S. House of Representatives" (Washington, D.C.: American Enterprise Institute, October 24, 1979).

2. This comparison is based on the classification by Marcia B. Wallace and Ronald J. Penoyer, "Directory of Federal Regulatory Agencies" (Washington University, Center for the Study of American Business), as reprinted in Cost of Government Regulations to the Consumer, Hearings Before the Subcommittee for Consumers of the Committee on Commerce, Science, and Transportation, U.S. Senate, 95th Congress, 2nd Session, November 21, 22, 1978, pp. 99-171, as updated by Kenneth Chilton, "A Decade of Rapid Growth in Federal Regulation" (St. Louis: Washington University, Center for the Study of American Business, March 13, 1979).

3. Chilton, op. cit. Much U.S. regulatory activity is organizationally independent of other kinds of government activity. Hence, it is not necessary in most cases to ask which portion of an organization's budget supports regulatory activities and which does not. Where this is not the case, however, Wallace and Penoyer did not always allocate expenditures to functions. In some cases the entire organizational budget was either included or excluded from their estimate. This approach is not wholly satisfactory, but owing to the small number of organizations involved, it is unlikely that their estimates are greatly in error as a result. Wallace and Penoyer, op. cit.

4. The following criticisms of the CSAB classifications are appropriate: (1) CSAB includes in the Consumer Safety and Health category all of the expenditures of the Bureau of Alcohol, Tobacco and Firearms of the Department of the Treasury. In our view such expenditures are associated primarily with tax collection and should be omitted. If they are to be included, they should be placed in the

General Business category. (2) CSAB places a fraction of the total expenditures of the Customs Service (the regulatory component) in the CSH category. They should be classified as General Business. (3) There are other misclassifications in our view. For example, the Agricultural Marketing Service, Agricultural Conservation and Stabilization Board, and the Federal Grain Inspection Service are included in Consumer Health and Safety. Surely these agencies are concerned primarily with price or production controls and with establishing economic grading standards. Their main objectives do not concern the health and safety of consumers. Hence, they should be classified as Industry-Specific regulation. The Antitrust Division of the Department is classified under CSH rather than under Industry-Specific regulation. Although both concentrate on safety, they do relate to a single industry, unlike, for example, the Occupational Safety and Health Administration.

5. William Lilley III and James C. Miller III, "The New 'Social' Regulation," The Public Interest, Spring 1977, pp. 49-61.

6. Chilton, op. cit., p. 8.

7. Ibid., p. 9.

8. Wallace and Penoyer, op. cit., p. 101.

9. Ibid. Wallace and Penoyer show an increase in federal regulatory employment from 28,919 in 1970/71 to 47,623 in 1971/72. Most of this difference is accounted for by the Animal and Plant Health Inspection Service of the Department of Agriculture, which was established in April 1972. Wallace and Penoyer (p. 145) report its 1971/72 employment as 14,080 but report 1970/71 as zero despite saying "APHIS assumed the inspection duties of the Consumer and Marketing Service" of the Department of Agriculture. However, no figures are given for the Consumer and Marketing Service. The Budget of the United States Government, Fiscal Year 1971 (Washington, D.C.: U.S. Government Printing Office, 1970, p. 249), reports estimated expenditures of $149.2 million in 1970/71 for the "consumer, protective, marketing and regulatory programs" of the Consumer and Marketing Service. Therefore, we estimate 1970/71 employment to be 14,000. Similarly, no employment figures are given for the EPA in 1970/71, while the number for 1971/72 is 5,062 (Wallace and Penoyer, p. 123). By interpolation of the expenditure figures, we estimate the EPA's employment figure for 1970/71 to be 4,500. On a similar basis, we estimate the employment of the Nuclear Regulatory Commission, recorded as zero, to be 300. Conversely, Wallace and Penoyer (p. 111) report 2,807 employees for the Patent and Trade Mark Office in 1970/71 but zero (that is, not available) for 1971/72. We would estimate 2,850 for that year. Therefore, our estimate of U.S. federal regulatory employment for 1970/71 is 47,719, not 28,919 as reported in Table 3.3. Further-

more, Wallace and Penoyer's figure for 1971/72 should be 50,473, not 47,623.

10. Lilley and Miller, op. cit., p. 49.

11. Buhler, op. cit., p. 49.

12. We note that in some cases prices are not set directly but are the result of a constraint placed on the rate of return.

13. Richard A. Posner, "The Social Costs of Monopoly and Regulation," Journal of Political Economy 83, no. 4 (August 1975): 818-19.

14. Murray L. Weidenbaum and Robert De Fina, "The Cost of Federal Regulation," Reprint No. 88 (Washington, D.C.: American Enterprise Institute, 1978). However, it should be noted that Green and Waitzman have challenged Weidenbaum and De Fina's methodology and results. See Mark Green and Norman Waitzman, Business War on the Law: An Analysis of the Benefits of Federal Health/ Safety Enforcement (Washington, D.C.: Corporate Accountability Research Group, 1979). In turn, Miller has criticized Green and Waitzman's analysis; see Miller, op. cit.

APPENDIX: DERIVATION OF THE PROPORTION
OF GROSS DOMESTIC PRODUCT SUBJECT TO
PRICE, ENTRY, SUPPLY, AND OUTPUT CONTROLS
BY REGULATORY AREA (1978)

The following summarizes the steps followed in defining the
broad industry groups shown in Table 3.5.

1. Agriculture: Although there are 26 agricultural products
that are subject to acreage allotment controls or marketing quotas
in the United States, only 19 percent of 1976 farm cash income was
made from sales covered by these programs. For the most part,
these programs are aimed solely at restricting supply. The key exception is federal milk marketing orders (and state marketing orders
in California), which seek to control both price and output. See P. A.
MacAvoy, ed., Federal Milk Marketing Orders and Price Supports
(Washington, D.C.: American Enterprise Institute, 1977).
2. Forestry: Supply, entry and price are not directly controlled in this industry. However, it should be noted that much of
the timber harvested comes from public lands and is cut under license
and, consequently, a number of contractual restrictions apply.
3. Mines: No portion of this industry is subject to output controls. However, the wellhead price of about 80 percent of output of
natural gas and oil is controlled. That 80 percent represents less
than 60 percent of the value added to real domestic product by this
industry.
4. Manufacturing: For the most part this industry group is
free of direct price and supply controls. However, there are several
exceptions to this generalization: Petroleum refining is subject to
price control, and milk processing is subject to price and entry control.
5. Construction: This is a particularly difficult case to classify. We know that building contractors are licensed by local jurisdictions. The same is true of architects and civil/construction engineers. Furthermore, many states sanction self-regulation on the
part of craft unions. Finally, it is not uncommon for these groups
to set prices or job rates or to employ sanctions (formal or informal,
sometimes illegal) to deter price cheating. However, to our knowledge no jurisdiction at any level sets prices, and evidence that these
constraints effectively reduce supply is limited. One may point to
substantial grey markets in some areas, the growth in self-construc-
tion (residential and industrial), or in some jurisdictions long lines
of individuals seeking either to enter training or apprenticeship programs or to obtain contractors' licenses. But the most that might
be concluded is that this evidence is episodic and suggestive. Consequently, we have excluded this industry group from our estimates.

6. Transport: Most of this industry group is subject to price and/or output (that is, entry) controls. However, these controls are not uniform. In the United States, rail, most interstate trucking, interstate water, transport, and interstate pipelines are subject to both price and entry controls, as is most local and interurban bus service and taxicabs. In addition, the majority of states regulate intrastate trucking, water, transport, and pipelines. However, local trucking, the transport of some commodities, warehousing, and freight handling are largely free of direct price and supply controls. We would estimate that less than 60 percent of this industry is subject to price and/or supply control. Owing to the nearly complete deregulation of the air transport industry, at the federal level, we conclude that little if any portion of it is subject to entry controls and only about 5 percent of the industry operating in regulated intrastate markets continues to be subject to price controls.

7. Communications: Telephone and telegraph and the post office are subject to both entry and price controls. In addition, entry into the broadcasting industry is controlled through spectrum allocation and control of cable TV operations.

8. Public utilities: Price and entry are controlled. The regulatory function is also exercised at the local level.

9. Trade: Largely free of price and supply controls.

10. Finance, insurance and real estate: Three kinds of controls are relevant: regulations designed to insure financial responsibility; licensure of insurance and real estate agents; and rent controls. Also, in a number of instances the regulating authorities regulate prices (interest rates paid and charged and premiums). Real estate and insurance agents are licensed by states. It is not clear to what degree this restricts entry. However, real estate brokerage fees and insurance commissions are remarkably standardized. Finally, rent controls are levied by cities and they apply to 10 to 20 percent of the rental stock. Consequently, we have estimated that about 80 percent of this industry group is subject to direct regulation and judged that this is primarily of the entry control variety. But it should be understood that this is a very rough generalization.

11. Business and personal services: A large number of occupations and professions are subject to restrictive licensure. The average number of occupations licensed per state was 42 based upon a sample of 15 states. See Ronald L. Martin, "Will the Sun Set on Occupational Licensure," paper delivered at a conference on Occupational Licensure and Regulation, American Enterprise Institute, February 22-23, 1979. These include both fully regulated professions/occupations, such as architects, barbers, chiropractors, embalmers, hairdressers, lawyers, professional nurses, optome-

trists, pharmacists, physicians, veterinarians, etc., and partially regulated professions/licensed occupations, such as accountants or engineers. In addition, various jurisdictions license masseurs, court reporters, social workers, sex therapists, TV repairmen, and so forth. This industry group, however, excludes health professionals and technicians. Consequently, we excluded these groups and estimated the value added by the other professions/licensed occupations based upon reported incomes of self-employed lawyers, notaries, engineers, architects, accountants, barbers, embalmers, and repairmen. This represents 1.1 percent of GDP in our estimate.

12. Health services: Health care expenditures amounted to 8.6 percent in the United States in 1976. Health care services, however, represent 6.6 percent and entry is almost wholly regulated.

It must be stressed that the results shown in Table 3.5 are fairly rough estimates. Their accuracy may be influenced by the fact that, in some cases, certain types of firms within the regulated portion of an industry group may be excluded from regulatory controls, that is, small firms or firms selling in the intrastate market. Furthermore, in some cases, controls are not applicable to all the products produced by firms in the regulated industry. The exact proportions of domestic product generated by these firms or activities are not known.

4

THE OBJECTIVES OF REGULATION

As noted in Chapter 3, government regulatory activity is pervasive. Though the nature and scope of government regulation vary widely across the different sectors of the economy, no industry is exempt from its influence. In many industries this influence is important and in some it is growing. What are the consequences of these activities? Are they beneficial or detrimental? These are not idle questions. Many people believe that most of the presumed benefits of regulation are not benefits at all, but simply transfers from one group to another.[1] They imply that the sole purpose of regulation is the redistribution of income to specific groups. They further imply that the gains from regulation will tend to go to a small fraction of the community, that most others will be excluded from these gains, and that they will come at the expense of economic efficiency. In turn, these claims rest on the belief that such groups are at an advantage in dealing with the public goods problems that militate against interest group formation and on the assumption that only the losers or potential losers in competitive private market transactions are likely to seek redress in the political arena.

Moreover, these claims are no longer made only with respect to controls on price and entry, but have been directed at the new social regulation as well. Proponents of this position argue that if one looks at the "new social regulation" as it is in practice and, in particular, at the flaws in the design of the regulatory apparatus or errors in the choice of institutional arrangements, one finds the same kinds of bias that are found in the "bad old direct regulation." Here, too, they note that efficiency is a public good and argue that, as is the case with many public goods, it appears to be all too frequently undersupplied.[2]

This is not the place to refute such claims. Indeed, they are not totally without merit. Certainly, they cannot simply be rejected as incompatible with the facts of political conflict, which by its very nature involves a broader public in the determination of outcomes and not merely that portion of the public having an immediate or exclusive interest in them.[3] This is because an exclusive interest can triumph by disguising itself in such a way as to obtain the support of the broader public. Those who would deny the benefits to be gained from regulation imply that, in this instance, income redistribution has succeeded in its masquerade, deriving a power from the garb it has contrived to wear that it could never justly claim. Furthermore, they hold that the growth of regulatory activities has occurred because this masquerade has reached new levels of sophistication and effectiveness.[4]

Fortunately, it is not necessary to refute these claims to make a case for regulation. One may grant that regulation frequently serves exclusive interests, that the justifications presented on its behalf in public forums are more often than not mere political rhetoric, and still conclude that regulation can and often does produce real benefits. Furthermore, these benefits may be measured using the standard yardstick of traditional economic analysis, that is, aggregate willingness to pay. Regulation may produce economic benefits in at least four instances:

When it promotes effective competition.

When it permits the public to enjoy the economies of scale or scope that are associated with monopoly supply.

When it compensates for divergences between private and social costs, that is, where private market transactions have consequences in third parties. Such divergence may be caused by other government actions that modify relative prices and not only by so-called market failures.

When it reduces the number of mistakes made by parties to private market transactions by standardizing product or service attributes or working conditions.

However, to say that regulation can or even that it often does produce these benefits is not to say that it will necessarily produce benefits or that benefits will be produced in excess of costs. On this issue, unless the "what" and, especially, the "how" of regulation are clearly specified, it may be best to be agnostic. Moreover, other forms of government action or inaction may produce the same or similar benefits. Indeed, some critics have claimed that, in each of the instances cited above, the benefits produced by regulation may be obtained more efficiently by means of alternative government actions.

In this chapter we seek to explain in a systematic fashion the economic rationale underlying various government regulatory policies, to analyze the major issues and problems involved in measuring their costs and benefits, and to assess the circumstances under which regulatory as opposed to other kinds of policy instruments are likely to be best suited to achieve the ends of public policy.

The chapter is divided into two major sections. The first begins with a brief discussion of various ways of understanding and classifying governmental regulatory activities. After choosing a particular classification scheme as most appropriate to our purposes, the second proceeds to explain the various classes or regulatory policies, focusing on the objectives of each and on the costs and benefits associated with it. Where possible we allude to empirical studies regarding these costs and benefits and we consider the various conceptual, methodological, and measurement problems that arise in evaluating the costs and benefits of regulatory policies. The second part of the chapter, therefore, seeks to assess the relative merits of regulation as compared with other institutional arrangements and policy instruments, with a view to pointing out policy areas and circumstances where regulation has or does not have an apparent advantage.

CLASSIFICATION OF REGULATORY ACTIVITIES

In order to get a conceptual grip on the numerous and diverse activities that fall under the rubric of government regulation, it is useful to attempt a classification. It should be noted at the outset that there are some problems of overlap in any scheme for classifying regulatory activities, as some activities simply do not fit neatly into one category. The classification schemes we present are no exception.

For some purposes it is useful to classify government regulatory activities according to the objects of regulation. At the broadest level, classification can be based upon the objects of regulatory strictures—producers or employers (for example, price and entry regulation, occupational health and safety regulation); consumers (legal limits on quantities of particular goods that may be purchased, for instance, gasoline rationing, or on postpurchase disposal of property); or factors of production (regulation of labor unions, land use controls).

Similarly, regulatory policies can be classified according to beneficiaries. Some regulation may benefit consumers: regulation of monopolistic and oligopolistic industry behavior, product safety regulation, truth-in-advertising laws. However, quite a number of important regulatory efforts are directed at protecting employees (occupational health and safety regulation), groups of producers (prohibitions on price discrimination among competing suppliers, occupational licensure, various protections for small business and certain farmers), or the public at large (environmental pollution regulation, land use controls). Of course, particular kinds of regulation can be cross-classified by object and beneficiaries.

Another approach is to classify regulatory measures or activities according to whether they affect only particular industries, or, on the other hand, the entire economy. Industries affected by particular regulations may be specified (automobile, air travel, petroleum) or types of regulation that affect the economy may be subdivided, for example, environmental protection, occupational health and safety, product attributes (quality, hazards) information provision and fairness, and intellectual property (see Figure 4.1). As government regulatory activities have moved into new spheres in recent years, lines have been drawn between the "old" or "traditional" areas of government regulation—public utilities, telecommunications, land use, agriculture—and the "new regulation" that is not limited to specific industries and unconcerned with such things as environmental protection, hazardous product management, occupational health and safety, and standards of fairness applicable to many seller-consumer and employer-employee relationships.

As noted in Chapter 1, a closely related distinction may be made between "economic" and "social" regulation, the latter often termed the "new social regulation." This typology is typically represented as the "old" and the "new" regulation with long-standing controls on prices, entry, rate of return, price discrimination practices, and terms of service designated as "economic regulation," whereas the regulation of pollution, hazardous products, and occupational health and safety are termed "social." As noted, however, the economic/social distinction, drawn along these lines bears little relation to any accepted analytical definition of these two terms. This is generally admitted even by those who have used it; their and our purpose in using it has been essentially descriptive rather than analytical.

For purposes of this chapter, we choose to employ a classification scheme, by no means original, with more analytical substance, one that will assist in understanding the benefits of regulation and in pointing out where it is likely to be more and where less effective. As we have stressed, all regulation is "economic" in that it implies government-imposed constraints over the allocation of resources and/or the distribution of income that would occur in its absence. The first key to understanding and evaluating the disparate activities called regulation is to understand the different kinds of

FIGURE 4.1

Variations in Federal Regulation of the Private Sector

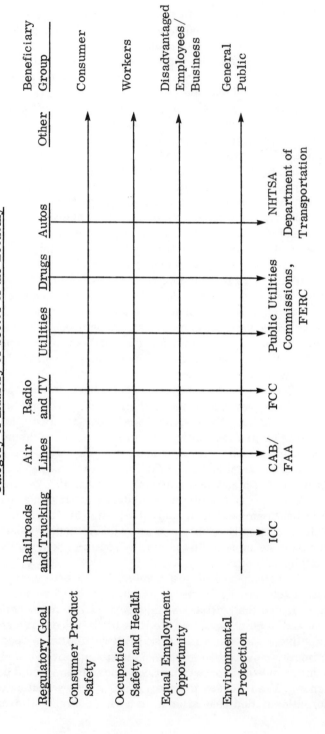

shortcomings associated with the allocative outcomes resulting from unregulated social arrangements. Regulatory instruments in this view are one type of attempted remedy applied to certain kinds of perceived problems, that is, allocative outcomes that are economically inefficient. This view helps us to conceive of and place in proper context alternative types of remedies, including "nonregulatory" approaches, to the perceived problems. The typology we use to begin the discussion of regulatory policies is based upon what might broadly be termed a "market failure" approach to the understanding of the various types of perceived problems and allocative outcomes that may be corrected by regulation. [5]

Using this classification scheme, then, we consider broad types of government regulatory policies. These are regulation of oligopoly and anticompetitive practices, controls on price and entry, regulation aimed to cope with external effects, and regulation to deal with markets in information. The array of regulatory policies applied in any one industry may remedy more than one of these types of problems.

REGULATION OF OLIGOPOLY AND ANTICOMPETITIVE PRACTICES

The theoretical notion that the absence of competition in an industry leads to static/allocative and dynamic/technical inefficiency is a very old one, as propositions in economics go. The general policy prescription of economists as far back as Adam Smith has been to promote competition by regulating practices believed likely to result in monopolization or cartelization of an industry. There are several justifications for this prescription. The most plausible begins with the assumption that the social control functions of the market are most efficient when firms face a hostile, threatening environment—one in which they are constrained to compete in terms of product and price in order to earn the positive profit required to ensure solvency, liquidity, maintenance of plant and equipment—in other words, to survive. Such an adequately threatening environment is supposed to ensure allocative efficiency and to motivate managers to strive for technical efficiency.

Regrettably, many, or perhaps most, managers would prefer a less threatening environment, one in which prices are always high enough to guarantee a "fair" profit and market shares are stable. For most firms the search for a safe haven is a vain one, realizable only through enterprise (for example, the identification of an unexploited product/market niche) or under the umbrella of the police power of the state (we have more to say about this in the next chapter).

However, where economies of scale in production, marketing, or finance are significant relative to the size of the market, and barriers to successful entry into the market are high, firms may find shelter and managers may gain the benefits of quiet life, insulated from pressures arising from changes in consumer tastes and preferences or technological and entrepreneurial innovation. This possibility arises because the firms participating in the market are few in number; consequently they can, and very likely will, cooperate to secure and maintain a benign environment. Moreover, if the number of firms in the market is small enough, cooperation need not be overt or formally enforced. Finally, in such markets, dominant firms can frequently enforce the status quo through predatory behavior.

Economists term markets that have these characteristics "oligopolistic," that is, relatively few firms (less than 20) account for the bulk (more than 50 percent) of total sales. [6] In the United States, a large number of markets meet this definition. In most of these markets the major means of regulating firms' behavior is that complex of laws and policy instruments known as antitrust policy. Antitrust policy operates chiefly by statutorily restricting certain practices of firms—such as price fixing, "predatory" pricing to eliminate competition, refusal to deal, tied selling, and other such tactics that are anticompetitive or potentially so. Antitrust policy is presently jointly administered by the Antitrust Division of the federal Department of Justice and the Federal Trade Commission. For the most part, it consists of the administration and enforcement of the Sherman and Clayton acts. The objective of antitrust policy is to make it harder for firms to collude than to compete. If successful, the benefits of this form of regulation will be realized in terms of increased output and/or a more optimal mix of products and product attributes, including greater certainty of product/service availability.

We would stress that the benefits to be gained from a more vigorous competition policy are likely to be extensive. Using fairly simple assumptions, David Schwartzman has estimated that a fully effective and costless antitrust policy would produce an allocative efficiency gain equal to 5 percent of GNP and, according to W. S. Comanor and Harvey Leibenstein, a technical efficiency gain of up to 7 percent of GNP. [7]

However, it must be noted that a perfectly effective competitive policy is neither possible nor desirable. This is because promotion of competition in oligopolistic markets is not costless. A rational competition policy would incur costs up to the point at which the marginal benefits from increased competition are equal to marginal cost of enforcing the antitrust laws (the sum of the costs borne by both government and firms). [8] This is illustrated in Figure 4.2. Here, the marginal cost of promoting competition is represented by the curve OC. BA shows the marginal benefit of the increase in competition resulting from enforcement at various levels. OBA is just equal to the welfare gain implied by Schwartzman (or Comanor and Leibenstein). This is the efficiency loss that would obtain if competition policy were unavailable. In Figure 4.2, marginal cost and marginal benefit are equal at point C; therefore, enforcement efforts are in equilibrium at K. The optimal efficiency loss under competition policy is, therefore, OCA.

FIGURE 4.2

The Costs and Benefits of Antitrust Policy

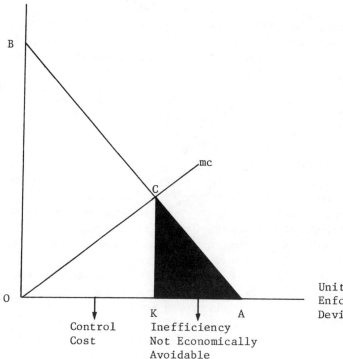

Cost and Benefits
of Promoting Competition
in Oligopolistic Markets

Recognition of these costs leads us to ask whether or not competition can be promoted in oligopolistic markets by other means. There are at least three alternative actions that could be taken by government that would produce benefits similar to those obtainable from a vigorous competition policy. First, it is likely that a substantial reduction in tariff and nontariff barriers to trade would eliminate the bulk of the potential benefit to be gained from antitrust policy. Second, the government could acquire control of participants in various oligopolistic markets and direct them to behave "competitively." In the short run, this direction could take the form of a mandate to increase revenues or market share subject to a profitability constraint. The resulting implied threat of a takeover could also influence dominant firms in other markets to behave more competitively. [9] Third, government can and does intervene directly—regulating entry, price, and product attributes. The concern that antitrust policy is inadequate to prevent monopolization or cartelization of the market by the most powerful firm or firms is a key justification for close control of the firms in several oligopolistic markets (finance, transport, and so on) by specialized regulatory agencies.

Of course, these alternatives to antitrust policy are also not costless. Rational choice requires that we obtain the benefits of increased competition at the least cost. Clearly, more vigorous competition should be beneficial, but it is not certain that antitrust policy is the best way to secure these benefits. That is to say, there is no clear, widely applicable policy prescription for dealing with oligopoly. The most that can be said is that appropriate policy choices are highly situation-dependent (see, for example, the three-volume work on antitrust policy by Phillip Areeda and D. F. Turner[10]).

REGULATION OF PRICE AND ENTRY

The benefits pursued via competition elsewhere in the economy are in some industries sought by means of direct regulation. Viewed as a transactional or institutional arrangement, direct regulation is a stable, self-perpetuating, continuous (but arms' length) relationship between a public agency, usually a regulatory commission, and a good or service producer in which liability is shared. [11] The regulatory commission prohibits competition among sellers in a specified market or service area in exchange for the right to control good or service provision variables through a review process. The variables that regulatory commissions frequently concern themselves with include price, return in investment (and its measurement), price discrimination practices, refusals to serve, conditions of service and service quality, and decisions on capital investments and generating expenses.

Advocacy of direct regulation by economists is not a recent phenomenon. And for some time, its theoretical justification, if not the performance of the regulators, was considered beyond reproach. This, however, is no longer the case.

The oldest justification for price regulation widely acknowledged by economists was formulated in the last quarter of the nineteenth century, evidently by Henry Carter Adams. The key to this formulation is the notion of "natural monopoly." The natural monopoly argument goes something like this: Given a single firm producing a single, homogeneous product, technological factors may result in constantly decreasing average total cost, at least up to the size of the market.[12] In such a situation, neoclassical theory holds that the normal economic advantages of competition may very likely be outweighed by the scale economies accruing to single firm production and supply. This natural or technical monopoly argument has long been thought to apply empirically to most situations in which users are connected physically to suppliers—for example, the distribution of electricity, water, gas, and telephone services—and where, after large initial capital investments, additional customers can be served at decreasing average total costs—for example, electrical power generation and railway and pipeline services. This latter occurs as high capital-related fixed costs are spread over many users and per-unit variable costs are low relative to fixed costs.

However, from the standpoint of the natural monopoly argument, the benefits of single firm supply may only be realized when the price charged by the producer is somehow made to approach that which would obtain if competition were practical, thereby inducing the producer to bring output closer to the socially optimal level.[13] Hence, given a natural monopoly, the nearly uniform policy prescription of economists has been government regulation of price (or return on investment).

However, despite the theoretical consensus supporting this policy prescription, regulatory practice has never precisely conformed to theory. In the first place, regulatory authorities have seldom restricted their attention to controlling price. In particular, their attention to control of entry into the regulated industry has always conflicted with the natural monopoly argument. In the second place, regardless of the presence of the supposedly critical technological factors, the natural monopoly argument has seldom been enforced with respect to services the provision of which has not been deemed vital in some sense or to firms providing services for which there were close and easily available substitutes.

Recognition of these discrepancies between theoretical justification and regulatory practice, together with increasing dissatisfaction with the performance of regulated industries and firms, evidently inspired a growing uneasiness among economists about both their diagnosis and their prescriptions. Thus, in an area of regulatory policy where economists have long agreed upon the nature of the problem and the appropriate regulatory response, there is now no consensus. Critics advocate deregulation and increased competition; proponents of traditional approaches either ignore criticisms or continue to search for evidence to bolster their position.

The considerable body of criticism of the natural monopoly justification for regulation developed in recent years is analyzed more fully in Chapter 5 within the context of the political feasibility of reform. Briefly, they may be summarized as follows: (1) There is little empirical evidence to indicate the effectiveness of regulation of natural monopoly. (2) Regulated monopoly firms have little incentive to be efficient or innovative because they are protected from the healthy pressures of competition. (3) Unregulated monopolists would increase profits in the short run by being technically efficient and would be induced by the threat of potential competition to keep prices down and output up and, in the long run, would either innovate or be replaced by an innovative competitor. (4) Virtually no regulated firm produces a single homogeneous product or service as the theory assumes.

It may be argued that natural monopoly and its regulation may still make sense if economies of joint production make a single firm the most efficient market structure even when several products or services are involved. However, analysis of interactions among product-specific scale economies, economies of joint production, and interproduct substitution effects on the demand side is extremely difficult. When the complexities of the regulatory environment are introduced, both theoretical and empirical analysis generate ambiguous, but largely negative, conclusions about appropriate regulatory policy. Moreover, it is difficult to see how regulatory authorities would discern the true shape of multiproduct cost functions for the purpose of developing optimal regulatory policy, or, in potentially contestable markets, how they could produce outcomes substantially better than those that would obtain in the absence of price controls and entry barriers. [14]

Furthermore, it is now widely understood that, despite the ubiquity of entry barriers, a substantial amount of direct government regulatory activity is exerted in markets with a large number of competing firms. In a broad sense, the rationalization for this regulation is dissatisfaction with the outcomes that would presumably result from the operation of an unregulated market. Although the hypothetical outcomes that provide the rationale for regulating competitive industries vary considerably from industry to industry, the common thread that runs through these otherwise disparate cases is that regulation attempts to discourage competitive supply. In transportation and agriculture, for example, the nominal justification for regulation has been the prevention of excessive or destructive competition. It is argued that in the absence of controls on entry (franchises, licenses, fees), minimum prices of the characteristics and quality of service (routes served, frequency of service, condition of vehicles), the low natural entry barriers in these industries will cause inefficient and unfair competition. This will occur to an extent as a result of the constant influx and demise of numerous low-budget and unscrupulous competitors. It is alleged that such competitors often provide the public with inferior, unsecured, and unsafe service, cause instability in service availability by constantly entering and going out of business, engage in fraudulent behavior, and cause unstable and uneconomically low prices in their attempts to gain a share of the market. Uneconomically low prices are defined as those that produce profits too low to fund capital investment and technological innovation sufficient to permit a business to survive.

Destructive competition is also regulated to prevent the de facto organization of cartels that might engage in informal oligopolistic market domination. Regulation is thus intended to prevent domination of industry by the most powerful competitor or competitors. In addition to the disadvantages cited previously for monopoly and oligopoly in economic theory, in many industries characterized by many small entrepreneurs there is considerable sentiment against permitting small firms to be driven out of business by large firms that can afford to undercut prices for lengthy periods of time and that also enjoy marketing and production technology not available to smaller firms. Finally, some regulation to prevent destructive competition is intended to preserve the productive capacities of domestic industries when survival is thought to be in the national interest, as, for example, maritime transportation, agriculture, oil, and natural gas.

Economists, however, generally are quite skeptical of regulation to prevent destructive competition. Their opposition has been based in part on the belief that much regulation in this area constrains competition unnecessarily, providing protection to businesses and industries that do not merit it on economic grounds. From this view, regulators sympathetic to familiar but not necessarily efficient or innovative businesses and industries have been persuaded to establish rules by self-serving arguments about destructive competition. More generally, the skepticism about this type of regulation has roots in the theory of efficient competitive markets where anti-competitive constraints are not deemed necessary. Relatively few critics accept the position that low entry barriers prevent well-managed and dynamic firms from growing to sufficient size to be efficient and innovative. On the other hand, where exit costs are reasonably low, it is also recognized that size, per se, will be an insufficient deterrent to potential entrants.

Numerous empirical studies have been conducted on the effects of government regulation in the industries where the destructive competition argument is an important part of the rationale for control. In prefacing their review of the literature on regulation in industries with competitive market structures, Paul Joskow and Roger Noll observe:

> If economics has any scientifically settled issues, one is surely that price and entry regulation in perfectly competitive industries generates economic inefficiencies. . . . The contribution of the literature on regulating competition is that the data confirm the theory in several key economic sectors that nearly all nations attempt to regulate. Economic research has demonstrated price and entry regulation in agriculture (an industry we shall henceforth ignore, reflecting an ignorance about the research on it), transportation, and oil and natural gas production creates economic inefficiencies. Usually this inefficiency is manifested in higher prices, higher costs of production and slower technological progress than would occur without regulation. In a few instances, such as regulation of hydrocarbon fuels, the inefficiency is created by prices that are too low to clear markets, leading to inefficient patterns of commodity utilization. [15]

Nevertheless, empirical estimates are gross, and methodological problems involved in making such estimates are substantial. In some cases direct comparisons can be made between a regulated and closely comparable unregulated market, or between outcomes (prices, quantities produced, rates of technological innovation) immediately before and after regulation is imposed. [16] Joskow and Noll note that "In each instance, these studies find efficiency losses due to regulation that loom large as a proportion of total transactions in regulated markets."[17] However, in many circumstances it is not possible to find a comparable unregulated market for comparison with the regulated one, and the behavior of the hypothetical unregulated market must be simulated. Although ingenious analytical models of markets have been developed, they are based upon numerous assumptions especially with regard to how businesses and industries may be expected to react to particular economic circumstances.

Service quality is another issue that casts doubt on the magnitude of some of the empirical estimates of inefficiencies caused by regulation. Nevertheless, the theoretical and methodological problems involved in valuing quality are also formidable. It is difficult to derive unambiguous inferences about price-quality and quantity-quality trade-offs from evidence on market transactions or through theoretical analysis. This is particularly so where quality itself has several dimensions, some of them very difficult to measure, such as esthetic characteristics of a product or personalization of service. Nevertheless, when quality is a significant attribute of a product or service, it should be taken into account in estimates of the effects of regulation. This has not been done in many empirical studies, and because there is evidence to support the notion that service quality is often higher under regulation, it appears that the inefficiencies attributable to regulation may have been overestimated in some of the earlier studies.

However, despite all of these caveats, the general conclusion still stands: Regulation of contested and potentially contestable markets either has no effect or its costs exceed benefits. Furthermore, many regulated markets are contested; most may be potentially contestable.

Yet, there is a justification for regulation of price and entry in potentially contestable markets that has received greater support over the past few years than the destructive competition argument. The intellectual lineage of this justification may be traced back to the work of Edward Chadwick in the nineteenth century, but the increasing attention given it in recent years owes a great deal to the rise of the public choice perspective in economics and political science. The public choice approach holds that a key economic role to be played by government is a combination of tough purchasing agent and competitive service supplier. From this perspective, both public provision of goods and services and contracting arrangements with private suppliers may be economically efficient. Through central purchasing, transaction costs are reduced and, as a consequence, wasteful duplication can be avoided. Furthermore, countervailing monopsony power may be exercised in the presence of local monopoly.

Contracting arrangements have been shown to be, in certain situations, more efficient than either public provision or fully competitive private supply. [18] Competition for the market appears to be the dominant institutional arrangement for the provision of services where economic barriers to entry and exit are insignificant;

given that the franchise is usually coextensive with a community or even a neighborhood and user preferences may be assumed to be fairly homogeneous, a real natural monopoly exists at the service delivery level, for example, inefficient overlapping delivery or pick-up routes; and service quality is easily defined and monitored, for example, curbside trash pickups per week. When these circumstances obtain, the sum of supply and transaction costs may be minimized by means of straightforward bidding arrangements.[19]

The comparative advantages of public contracting vis-a-vis the more continuous contractual relationship associated with direct regulation is also evident in certain situations. It appears that the dominant institutional arrangement for taxi services, for example, combines free entry and a zonal/time-of-day/time-of-week rate structure as in Washington, D.C., or Seattle. A standard fare structure has the advantages of reducing transaction costs between passenger and driver, yet may be easily modified to ensure adequate supply. Furthermore, this arrangement may contemplate an unregulated limousine market in which services are usually provided for a per-hour fee to the customers who are willing to pay a premium for certainty. It should be stressed, however, that with respect to taxi service, quality considerations are not particularly problematic.

Finally, in the case of many of the services requiring a physical connection between users and service suppliers, transactional costs involved in controlling service quality may make it impossible to achieve a contingency contract awarded by bid that would protect consumers sufficiently over time. Oliver Williamson concludes that a reasonable contract, given an almost infinite continuum of service quality, would establish a process to mediate or arbitrate disputes, enable periodic inspection, and provide sufficient flexibility to deal with unexpected or unanticipated problems as they arise. This is, of course, the kind of institutional arrangement we described earlier as direct regulation.[20]

Even this narrowly circumstantial justification for direct regulation is not, however, necessarily an unambiguous endorsement of any particular regulatory regime. Realization of the potential benefits of this particular institutional arrangement is contingent upon each of the following:

Oversight performed by a regulatory agency permits costly mistakes that would otherwise have been made to be avoided, and analytical costs must be less than the costs of error.

Bargaining costs are reduced, and this reduction must more than offset the welfare losses imposed upon consumers as a result of excluding them from making bargains they otherwise would have preferred.

Benefits from an arms'-length relationship (that is, reduced welfare losses owing to the greater flexibility of the regulated firm to respond to changes in preferences and technologies) are not offset by the costs associated with creation of an exclusive franchise.

To ensure these conditions the regulatory agency must be vigilant, must possess considerable specialized knowledge, and must be politically effective. Unfortunately, the agencies that regulate monopolies generally have inadequate resources and mediocre talent.[21] Consequently, these conditions may seldom obtain in practice.

To summarize, then, we agree with Williamson that minimization of information costs can lead to the choice of the direct regulation alternative under prescribed circumstances. However, it appears that in practice this conclusion is contingent upon satisfactory performance of analytical tasks, that is, collecting, analyzing, and using information. Consequently, even the best case for direct regulation is none too strong.

Elsewhere, regardless of the historical circumstances that led to the choice of this institutional arrangement, technological changes, the use of substitutes, and even international competition have tended to eliminate any efficiency benefits that may once have accrued to direct regulation. For that reason, when we look at the performance of regulatory regimes erected in an earlier age, frequently all that is found to remain are wealth transfers. These exist, of that there is no doubt. Nor is there any doubt that they are substantial. But to say that, because that is all that we see now, regulation's purpose was merely to transfer wealth to the politically influential, is to commit the most serious kind of error in causal reasoning.

Other objectives sometimes tangentially pursued via direct regulation include consumer and worker health and safety, environmental protection, preservation of wildlife, equal employment opportunity, fair employee compensation, and safeguarding of professional service standards. A discussion of the justification for regulation in these areas is presented in the subsequent sections on regulation to compensate for externalities and to correct imperfections in the markets for information.

REGULATION TO COMPENSATE FOR EXTERNALITIES

A considerable amount of government regulation is based on the economic theory of externalities. Positive and negative ex-

ternalities, also called spillovers or external economies and diseconomies, may be defined as the consequences of events or ex-
changes that are not automatically compensated for in market prices.
In the case of negative externalities the parties to an economic transaction or set of transactions do not bear the full costs of their actions. Some costs, the external costs, are borne by third parties,
whose interests are not reflected in the market signals that attract
participants to the transaction. Left alone, some parties will produce too much of a commodity, such as toxic particles emitted into
the air, from the view of the general populace. Production, distribution, and/or consumption may produce costs that are overlooked
by the market. The typical example of consumption externalities is
the tragedy of the commons. In this example, grazers of sheep on
common lands collectively destroy the productive capacity of the
land trying to feed their sheep. From this perspective the enclosure
movement of the fourteenth and fifteenth centuries may be thought of
as an early and highly successful form of successful government intervention on behalf of the environment.

In the case of positive externalities, or external benefits, the
reverse is true. Because parties to a transaction cannot appropriate
all the benefits that result from it, they will ignore the benefits that
accrue to third parties in making their spending decisions. From
the view of society as a whole, the result will be that too few externality-producing transactions will occur.

Government regulates and provides subsidies to stimulate the
output of some commodities that are thought to have external economies associated with their production. For example, regulatory
policy and tax subsidies encourage innovative investments by industry and support public and private education. In the case of education there are elements of direct regulation by government related
to social welfare and service quality in that parents are required to
send their children to school. Also, education service distribution
is regulated professionally, geographically, and in other ways. An
important case of government regulation to support the production
of externality-creating outputs is the complex of regulations to protect intellectual property. Without copyright, patent, and related
laws, it is generally believed that the supply of new ideas in industry
and in the cultural sphere would be severely curtailed. Government
regulation attempts to remedy market failure in production and distribution of intellectual goods and services that would otherwise limit
production of these externality-creating outputs. Market failure in
this instance is a result of the fact that preventing distribution of intellectual products to other than paying customers is not feasible
without regulation.

Attempts to compensate for externalities encompass a wide range of government regulatory activity, and one that has increased in scope in recent years. In particular, environmental quality regulation has expanded rapidly, as we have noted in Chapter 3. Until the environmental pollution resulting from industrialization, rapid technological changes, and other factors became impossible to ignore, the assimilative capabilities of the air, water, and land were treated essentially as free goods. This was natural enough because producers and consumers of any particular commodity generally bore only a tiny fraction of the environmental costs associated with its production and use. Recognition of the dangers inherent in a laissez-faire policy has led inevitably to regulation to limit or prohibit environmental degradation. Environmental protection regulation is embodied in legislation such as the Clean Air Act and rules promulgated by regulatory agencies on the authority of legislative mandates.

Environmental regulation seeks to reduce harmful emissions by directly prohibiting them, by mandating reductions in emissions to a specified level (performance standards), or by requiring some corrective action (engineering standards, for example, requiring all new stationary sources to employ a specified but available emissions reduction technology). Because there is no doubt that air, water, and other types of pollution can cause demonstrable damage to public health and tend to reduce the quality of life, that environmental regulation produces real economic benefits is beyond question.[22] The problem with environmental regulation is that it is far from costless. In addition to the decision-making, monitoring, and enforcement costs associated with antitrust policy or direct regulation, not to mention the more subtle x-inefficiency losses, there are losses associated with regulation-induced politicization of an industry.[23] This form of government action can and does impose huge compliance costs on both firms and consumers. Of course, to an extent these costs are justified and unavoidable. The question is, To what extent? We should want to be sure that the benefits of environmental regulation exceed their costs and that emissions reductions are achieved at the lowest possible costs.

Unfortunately, owing to the incredible complexity of environmental regulations, it is not possible to uncategorically conclude that the benefits they produce are sufficient to justify the costs they impose on industry and on the economy in general. Indeed, any meaningful answer to this question must be highly disaggregated: Is a particular emissions-reducing technology efficient when mandated for a specific firm or plant, in a particular area, from the standpoint of a target pollutant? Nevertheless, ambitious attempts to overcome the formidable measurement and other methodological problems involved in evaluating the benefits and costs of environmental protection have been made in recent years. One example is the U.S. Environmental Protection Agency's analysis of the costs and benefits of compliance with the Clean Air Amendments of 1970. This study made numerous assumptions about how industries, governments, and consumers would respond to the ambient standards and timetables set by the law. The procedures and methodologies used in this analysis are instructive, if now somewhat dated. The EPA found that the benefits of meeting the Clean Air Act standards exceeded the cost of compliance by several billion dollars (constant 1970 dollars). Henry M. Peskin and several colleagues reanalyzed the EPA data after making various adjustments and filling in some information gaps[24] (one large data gap was the neglect of benefits resulting from auto emission controls by EPA; in addition, many EPA cost figures had to be revised upward). They found that estimated costs exceeded estimated benefits by about $20 billion. The research also divided that data by industry, finding substantial differences in the balance between costs and benefits across various industries. This suggested that air pollution control efforts, at least of the type the EPA envisioned at that time, would be far more cost-beneficial to some industries than to others.

In contrast with these results, after ten years of study of the research on the relationship between air pollution and human health, Lester B. Lave and Eugene P. Seskin concluded that, if EPA estimates of the costs of cutting particulate and sulfur oxide emissions from stationary sources to mandated levels were correct, realized benefits of such controls from reduced mortality alone would likely exceed total costs by some 70 percent annually.[25] However, the same study also concluded that, at the margin, the benefits of achieving current mandated standards for mobile sources of air pollution were less than the costs. This analysis suggested that a "two car" strategy—emphasizing strict standards and enforcement where pollution damages are worst—would achieve most of the benefits of a more uniform national program but would reduce costs measurably.[26] Indeed, most empirical analyses of the benefits and costs of environmental regulation agree on one point: When the objective of public policy is a reduction in emissions of a target pollutant, uniform standards (for example, mandating a uniform percentage reduction in emissions or the use of a single abatement technology) will not achieve an efficient result. In many cases, uniform standards imply compliance costs six to ten times greater than the minimum required to reduce total emissions to some target level.[27]

Recognition of these problems has led to reconsideration of previously rejected alternatives to regulation. In fact, economists have for some time argued that the most efficient institutional arrangement for reducing harmful emissions or other damage-producing externalities is an economic sanction or tax levied on residual emissions and set to equal the damage caused by increments to pollutant concentrations. Under this proposal, decisions as to where and how to reduce emissions levels would be explicitly delegated to firms. Damages or, if damage measurement presented insuperable problems, residual emissions would be continuously monitored and penalties would be directly proportional to emissions levels. Many economists argue that such a levy would minimize the cost, reducing total emissions to a target level.[28] In theory, an emissions tax would bring the polluter's cost-benefit calculus in line with society, and polluters would have, therefore, an incentive to invest in pollution abatement equipment up to the point where the costs and benefits of abatement are equal. Consequently, an emissions tax would "lead some to reduce pollution to a greater extent, some to a lesser extent, depending on the marginal benefits of polluting in each case."[29] European examples[30] and an extensive body of theoretical analysis[31] indicate that such an institutional arrangement could be extremely cost-effective in reducing emissions.

This approach is carried one step farther by J. H. Dales[32] (and others), who argues that, because the market failure here arises as a consequence of the absence of a market in the assimilative capacity of the environment, the solution is to create a market wherein rights or purchasable permits to pollute may be bartered among polluting firms. Under Dales's scheme, a pollution control agency would establish concentration standards for a region. It would then auction off the rights to contribute to pollution concentrations to the highest bidders. According to Fisher and Peterson: "if the costs and benefits of pollution, or pollution abatement are known to the control board, the pollution rights market can lead to the same (efficient) level of pollution as a tax."[33]

Dales's program has never been tried as proposed. Nevertheless, there are pollution rights markets throughout the United States. In these instances, the EPA has established regional non-degradation standards. Firms are expressly prohibited from adding to pollution concentrations except where they can secure an equivalent reduction in emissions elsewhere within the region. However, subject to other EPA standards (standby controls that are required to respond to changing weather patterns, and so on), they are granted the right to continue to generate emissions at existing levels or to transfer those rights to other firms in the region. With the help of state officials who have created inventories of these assets, this has led to the creation of active markets in pollution rights (or offsets).[34] Where pollution concentrations approach optimal levels, this seems to be a nearly ideal solution to the problem: It is straightforward, easily enforceable, and controlled by means of environmental impact statements. Furthermore, once such a market is established, it could facilitate the efficient transition to lower concentration levels in areas where concentrations of harmful emissions are excessive. In this case, all firms would be required to make uniform cutbacks in emission levels of a given amount (for example, 5 percent a year) or arrange for equivalent reductions elsewhere in the zone. Public intervention could facilitate the operation of such a market and would probably be necessary to police it. However, once established, market forces should be sufficient to ensure that the total reduction in emissions sought would be obtained at least cost. [35]

We may also note that the marketable rights approach can be applied in other areas to allocate scarce resources: airport landing and takeoff spaces, hospital services (beds or equipment), the electromagnetic spectrum (radio frequencies). [36]

In the last few years, particularly under the Carter administration and to some extent through the efforts of the U.S. Regulatory Council (terminated by Reagan in 1981), marketable rights and other innovative and market-oriented approaches to regulation have been given greater consideration. [37] In addition, economists have looked more closely at the very real problems of information availability and cost, uncertainty, and administrative feasibility that present obstacles to the implementation of market-oriented regulatory approaches. As noted by Joskow and Noll, "When economists have considered these factors, they have identified circumstances that lead to a preference for standards, even input standards, rather than decentralized market processes."[38] Similar conclusions have been reached based upon review of the effectiveness of emissions taxation schemes. [39]

In the first place, the proximate goal of pollution control is the reduction of pollutant concentrations, not simply the reduction of emissions. In some cases, of course, the effect of a reduction in emissions will be a corresponding reduction in pollution concentration. But this appears to be a rather special case. Generally, owing to the environment's capacity to assimilate certain pollutants, variations in meteorological conditions, proximity to populations at risk, and so forth, an individual firm's contribution to concentrations, let alone its contribution to hazard levels, cannot be assured to be directly proportional to its total emissions of harmful residues. This implies that, if a tax scheme were adopted, it would have to be modified frequently to maintain environmental quality. Consequently, a better strategy would likely include a mix of taxes and standards. [40] However, under a marketable permits scheme, a reasonably satisfactory solution might be to assign permits so as to reflect plant locations and meteorological conditions. For example, various classes of marketable permits could be issued that would be good only under conditions specified by local air quality managers, as in the following table.

Permit Class	Authorization
1	Good under all weather conditions
2	Good except during stage 3 alerts
3	Good except during stages 2 and 3 alerts
4	Good except during stages 1, 2, and 3 alerts
5	Good only when weather conditions are most favorable

Unfortunately, the more complex the permit process, the more costly are the monitoring and enforcement costs.

Also, many market- or performance-oriented institutional arrangements require continuous monitoring of emissions at the plant level, which is far more costly than is inspection of equipment or procedures. Furthermore, monitoring costs make no direct contribution to emissions reductions. In some cases, it may be that firms' personnel will be less competent to determine how best to meet emissions standards than are their counterparts in regulatory agencies. Finally, the fact of the matter is that we do not really know how responsive firms are to incentives, or how much a given tax would reduce emissions levels. Nor do we know how to design and manage a full-fledged market in pollution permits. The fact is that much of the discussion surrounding these alternative institutional arrangements is highly speculative (this is also true of regulation as well). While we believe these mechanisms have considerable potential, realization of that potential will be delayed until such time as the factual information upon which more effective policies can be based is provided. The best way to get this kind of information is through a systematic program of experimentation.

One other compelling institutional arrangement should also be mentioned here; this alternative emphasizes the influence of market incentives through tax expenditure rather than regulatory policy. Tax expenditures (tax revenues foregone by government) provide reductions in the taxes owed by business and industry in order to provide capital for investment in pollution abatement. In essence, use of tax expenditures to improve environmental quality depends on establishment of contracts between government and private firms to the effect that money left in the private sector will be used to meet quality objectives embodied in regulation. Tax expenditures are favored by industry because they leave decision on pollution control in the private sector; they appeal as well on the basis of limiting government expenditures on regulation. However, the effectiveness of this approach is dependent on the extent to which financial incentives actually produce the outcome desired in improved environmental quality. Thus, the role of government in setting overall environmental quality standards and evaluating the extent to which standards are met remains even though regulatory control is relaxed.

This is particularly evident under the tax expenditure policy changes enacted into law under the Reagan administration in 1981. These changes enable industry to buy and sell tax credits provided by government to satisfy a variety of objectives, including environmental quality. Creation of a market for tax credits implies even further that government must monitor the outcomes of tax espenditure policy so that private sector obligations to invest in pollution abatement technology, purchased by government through tax expenditures, actually result in desired improvements in performance. If the exchange of tax credits blurs responsibility for investment in the most efficient means for maintaining or improving environmental quality, then the objectives sought by tax expenditures as an alternative to direct regulatory control will not have been met. This would tend to support advocates of direct regulation, at the expense of tax expenditure policy. From a theoretical economic perspective, there are strong reasons to believe that a tax expenditure market will result in improved performance in the long run. Still, as we observe in so many areas of regulation, theory often does not encompass complexities of application that, in some instances, are significant enough to make theory invalid.

At present, there is little consensus on environmental quality taxation approaches, despite acknowledgment of their attractiveness as general alternatives to direct control through regulation. The need to define and resolve problems of information, uncertainty, instrument and institutional design, and others remains. Some of these problems are addressed subsequently in this chapter. In the meantime it makes sense to us to apply the net-benefit criterion (benefits minus costs) to help determine how policy should be set. This assumes the possibility of a shifting public consensus on the levels of acceptable environmental quality, without specifying the direction of the shift.

The environmental quality problem is by no means the only case of government regulation to deal with negative externalities. As noted, another important class of cases involves instances of depletable resources. When business and industry, groups of consumers, or a society depend on a common but exhaustible resource, market signals may not fully reflect the true value of the resource. Prices will reflect costs of production that may change as the resource is depleted, plus demand pressure, and other factors. But they will not be influenced automatically by the fact that exhaustion of the resource will cause economic and social dislocation. As discussed earlier under the tragedy of the commons example, in situations where the market price is as a consequence too low, government must intervene to ration the resource or to prohibit further depletion. Rationing may be accomplished through definition of legal rights to the resource and regulation schedules reflecting the relative priorities of various consumers, through prices or other means.

Another area in which government intervenes through regulation to stimulate production is in markets for information. In many cases firms have no incentive to provide information about product hazards, work-place safety or aspects of their operations that may be sufficiently valuable to consumers or workers to justify the costs of provision. In some cases government requires the provision of additional information beyond what would be supplied by the unregulated market. The next section of this chapter addresses the costs and benefits of information provision and alternative regulatory strategies in such situations. In addition, Chapter 7 provides perspectives on information, uncertainty, and related problems to indicate their importance in the regulation of worker health and safety.

REGULATION TO COMPENSATE FOR
IMPERFECTIONS IN MARKETS FOR
INFORMATION

Among the assumptions that must be met if unfettered market arrangements are to produce the most efficient allocation of society's resources is the assumption that economic agents (producers, consumers, workers) have sufficient information about the costs and benefits of their alternative choices to make rational decisions. [41] Alas, there are a wide range of situations where decisions must be made with very imperfect information, due to the fact that relevant information is either very costly or impossible to obtain.

The rationale for a considerable portion of environmental, health, and safety regulation is that unregulated market arrangements will not produce optimal levels of the information that economic agents need in their decision making. Consequently, prices, wages, product consumption levels, injury and accident rates, and so on will be different and less satisfactory than they would be if information were adequate. Producer firms, even if they possess such information, have little incentive to provide information to consumers that may reduce product sales or to provide information to workers about job hazards that may result in the need to pay higher wages or to make costly changes to reduce hazards. For that matter, they may have little incentive to obtain such information in the first place. Consequently, workers and consumers are often unable to obtain relevant information and may be unable to utilize it properly even if they do get it, often because it is difficult for the layperson to interpret. Our point is that, because information is not a purely private good, efficient quantities of it are unlikely to be produced by private entrepreneurs.[42] Thus there is an economic as well as a political rationale for government intervention in such areas as product and worker safety.

Government interventions in response to failures in information markets fall into several broad categories, based on the reasons for the shortages of usable information. In circumstances where consumers, workers, or others could presumably utilize information properly if it were available, and where the information in question can be developed at a cost that does not appear to exceed the expected benefits from its development, governments employ strategies that depend on individual economic actors to utilize information. Government may, for example, conduct or sponsor research on the nature, incidence and prevention of product or work-place hazards and disseminate this information free or at subsidized prices to potential users. The Consumer Product Safety Commission and the Occupational Safety and Health Administration (through the National Institute for Occupational Safety and Health) support millions of dollars worth of information-gathering and disseminating activities each year.[43]

Another approach, sometimes integrated with the first, is to require firms to collect and provide information about product or job hazards to consumers and workers. Consumers and workers may then use the information, along with data about prices, wages, and other relevant characteristics, to satisfy their preferences more efficiently than would be possible in the absence of the information.

A third approach is to structure economic incentives so as to ensure that costs associated with product and work-place hazards will be taken into account in economic decisions. Business and industry then have an incentive to develop the appropriate amount of information to utilize their costs, for example, about causes and preventions of occupational injuries or product-related accidents. When the hazard is limited entirely to parties to private market transactions, such an incentive may be created by making one party (usually the employer or the seller, as he is assumed to be the better informed party as to the level of hazard) responsible for compensating the other for damages incurred as a consequence of the transaction. This may be accomplished indirectly, via a body of tort law (by making it possible for the damaged party to sue for compensation on a case-by-case basis), through some form of no-fault compensation scheme (such as workers' compensation), or by some combination of the two. Also, it may be done by imposing a public tax on adverse health consequences and public compensation of the injured party. Problems of worker and product health and safety have been traditionally addressed through such mechanisms. But in their design and development, little attention has been given to the part they might play in providing firms with an incentive to reduce hazards. Instead, income maintenance and post hoc compensation have been emphasized. This may have unnecessarily reduced the effectiveness of these mechanisms as a means of promoting efficient hazard reduction decisions. [44]

For example, workers' compensation laws shift much of the liability of work-place accidents to employers. Employers are required to carry insurance to pay off claims that may arise under the program. In turn, the premium an employer pays is based upon his firm's accident record. This provides an incentive for reducing hazards. However, under most workers' compensation laws there is a fixed upper limit on the amount that can be paid to any given claimant. As Nina Cornell et al. observe:

> The compensation that would give producers proper incentives for prevention is the expected value of damages, whereas the process by which damages are actually compensated is primarily a mechanism for protecting workers against loss of income resulting from accidents. The former requires that compensation be systematically related to the probabilities that the hazard caused the damage and that a particular damage actually occurred, whereas the latter principle requires that the focus be on the magnitude of the loss of the damaged party. [45]

Thus, hazards that have low probabilities of causing severe damages are likely to be underprevented under such a scheme. On the other hand, overemphasis is likely given to preventing hazards that result in frequent but minor losses. Finally, firms are frequently made liable for outcomes over which they have no control, for example, injuries that occur on the way to the work place. However, it is one thing to say that it is inappropriate to address problems of income maintenance by means of workers' compensation (to do so distorts the proper purpose of these programs), and quite another to say how this objective ought to be pursued.

It should also be noted that the system of tort liability compensates, to a degree, for the limits placed on workers' compensation. If the firm can be shown to be negligent, the injured party may successfully sue for compensation. However, it is no simple matter to prove negligence. Moreover, litigation is costly and time consuming, and the existing liability system limits compensation in several ways, for example, a firm's maximum liability is its net worth. (This may be one explanation for the frequently observed phenomenon that large firms comply with regulations more readily than do small firms.) Consequently, except where events with certain causes are concerned and where the damages inflicted do not push against institutionalized limits to compensation, we cannot expect the possibility of legal action to be 100 percent efficient in leading firms to invest in preventing accidents or sickness.[46] Furthermore, there is reason to believe that the tort system may not ensure equitable compensation for injured parties.

The point of this discussion is that an economist would likely reverse the targets of employer liability and workers' compensation and provide for income maintenance by some wholly independent means. Legal accountability should be most effective where it is addressed to known hazards with known consequences—to situations where negligence is fairly easily demonstrated. Workers' compensation, on the other hand, should be targeted at open-ended losses, which result from partially indeterminate causes, and shared responsibility for hazards—in which case, premiums based upon the loss records of firms should provide a reasonably satisfactory guide to investment in hazard protection. Unfortunately, such a system would place overwhelming underwriting and actuarial burdens on private insurance providers. It is likely that few, if any, would choose to provide such coverage. Consequently, some economists have proposed a pure accident tax and public compensation scheme as an alternative to private insurance. Others argue for the efficiency of a system of strict consumer liability for product-related damages, but this model appears to contain unrealistic assumptions about consumer knowledge and behavior.[47] Indeed, one of the biggest concerns with any of the information-type strategies is the question of the intended users' ability and willingness to use information rationally.

Another broad class of circumstances that has compelled government intervention occurs where information about relevant product or job characteristics is inherently inadequate for some reason. This may be because the relevant causal relationships involved are poorly understood and not easily researchable. This may also occur because the information that can be produced is too technical and probabilistic in nature to be utilized properly by the layperson. In such cases, information provision alone may not be a viable strategy. Governments may sponsor research to improve the information base but, for periods of time, important information may be unavailable or inadequate. In such circumstances, governments have not been hesitant to set product, process, and performance specifications, to establish permissible standards for work-place contaminants, and to promulgate outright bans on particular products and materials. Although such regulatory interventions have been subjected to substantial criticism, the ideas supporting them often make good economic as well as political sense.[48] Where information is complex and processing costly and individual risk preferences do not vary too widely in the relevant population, government is likely to be in the best position to carry out whatever analysis is possible and to establish efficient standards for society as a whole.

A third set of circumstances that has stimulated government regulatory control is characterized by information that is at least potentially both adequate and interpretable—thus there is no market failure—but where at least some individuals choose to ignore it. Here, regulation often attempts to protect people from themselves, that is, from the consequences of their own actions. Examples would include mandatory seat belt laws, mandatory motorcycle helmet laws, and prohibitions on the use of psychoactive drugs the effects of which are known. Of course, regulation of this type also seeks to protect society from some of the external effects that unregulated behavior would cause and also may serve as an information function by making it clear that society regards the behavior in question to involve substantial risk. However, there is clearly an element of government paternalism behind most of this type of regulation.

Unfortunately, but not surprisingly, it is difficult to evaluate the benefits of either information-provision or standard-setting strategies, especially after the fact. Isolating the effect of improved information and demand for the products and services affected for the purpose of comparing the resultant increases in welfare at the prevailing market price to the costs of providing the information is likely to be very difficult in most cases.[49] Accurate evaluation of both costs and benefits is usually problematic where standard-setting regulation is involved. Most of the costs of this type of regulation are borne not by the public but by producers and consumers. Methodology has been developed for calculating some of these costs, but the costs associated with long-term shifts in production, consumption, and other behavior patterns are very hard to assess.[50] The difficulties on the benefit side are usually even greater. If good information about the relationship between the amounts consumed of the regulated activity or product and costs or benefits could be developed, it would probably be unnecessary to regulate with the standard-setting approach. Information-provision or market incentive approaches would appear to be more efficient.

EVALUATING THE RELATIVE EFFECTIVENESS OF REGULATION

In recent years, a number of attempts have been made to assess empirically the benefits and costs of regulatory standards. Studies of the benefits and costs of air quality standards were noted earlier. Perhaps the most interesting analysis of the effects of various intervention strategies to protect health and safety, including information provision and standard setting and enforcement, is Michael Lewis-Beck and John Alford's longitudinal study of coal mining fatalities. Their analysis looked at mine safety in four distinct periods:

1. 1932-41   No intervention
2. 1941-52   Federal mine inspectors gain access to all mine operations, powers limited to providing advice to mine operators and workers; safety recommendations not mandatory
3. 1952-69   Inspectors given broad powers to mandate safety measures aimed at preventing major disasters (10 percent of all coal mining fatalities); inspectors were excluded from mines employing fewer than 15 miners (80 percent of all mines) and evidently prohibited from offering unsolicited safety advice to either operators or workers.
4. 1969-76   Enforcement powers of federal inspectors much expanded, and a detailed set of health and safety regulations made mandatory for all mines

During the first period, coal mine fatality rates were higher and stable. During the second they fell substantially. They stabilized again during the third period and fell dramatically in the fourth.[51]

We would submit that these results demonstrate the potential effectiveness of both information-provision and regulatory strategies. The effectiveness of nonmandatory safety recommendations is very probably explained by the prior ignorance of both operators and workers. Both were likely unaware of a substantial number of specific hazards in the work place and, even more important (particularly where small operators were concerned) did not know how to correct them. Furthermore, once workers were informed of hazards in the work place they could (and very likely did) bring economic pressures to bear on their employers to correct these hazards when it was in their interest to do so.

It should also be noted that, under information provision, productivity increases in below-ground mines were realized at roughly the same rate as in preceding and following periods.

Comparing periods three and four, the most salient outcome is the reduction in fatalities following a substantial increase in regulatory effort, scope, and coverage. However, unlike in the 1941-52 period, this benefit was achieved at a very substantial cost. According to one estimate, deep mining costs (in constant dollars) more than doubled as a result of the implementation of the 1969 mine safety legislation.[52]

In other areas, a model of drug industry regulation has been developed to derive hypotheses about the patterns of demand for drugs after the 1962 amendments to the Food and Drug Act.[53] This research argued that regulation under the 1962 amendments raised innovation costs, reduced the number of new drugs on the market, and caused a net welfare loss to society. Studies have analyzed Consumer Product Safety Commission (CPSC) regulation.[54] They argue that the data base maintained by the commission is inadequate, and due to other factors it is impossible to measure the impact of most CPSC regulation. Cases are noted where product hazard regulation was clearly successful—crib safety regulation, for example—but the conclusion based on limited evidence available is that most CPSC regulatory standards have higher costs than benefits.[55]

A number of studies of auto safety regulation have appeared in the last few years.[56] Although it is difficult to sort out the effects of the various safety devices and of the other changes that may affect accident trends—reduced speed limits, smaller cars, changes in road conditions—the evidence is clear that seat belts are cheap and, when used, are effective in reducing deaths and injuries. On the other hand, air bags and other automatic passenger protection devices are viewed to be costly and uncertain in their benefits. Some analysts argue for mandatory seat belt laws such as those that prevail in some provinces of Canada, promotion of the benefits of seat belt use, and improvements in their design as an alternative to requirements for mandatory automatic devices as proposed by the National Highway Traffic Safety Administration (NHTSA). It should be noted that this analysis ignores the inconvenience cost to the seat belt user. Furthermore, nonusers have proven to be

strongly resistant to marketing programs designed to increase voluntary seat belt use. Given that the seat belts are somewhat inconvenient and that it may be very costly to persuade people to use
them, a fairly strong case may be made for mandatory provision of
passive restraints.[57]

The Occupational Safety and Health Administration (OSHA) has
also attracted considerable attention from researchers. Unfortunately, a new data system on industrial industries was established
at the birth of the agency, so that before-after comparisons of OSHA
impacts are limited. In particular, workers' compensation data on
injuries appear to have serious flaws.[58] There is a great deal of
work yet to be done, much of it basic scientific research, on occupational health hazards. Good benefits estimates are generally hard
to develop, and the problems of cost assessment associated with
shifts in production, consumption, and other behavior patterns remain. Empirical studies to measure the overall impact of OSHA
standards on industrial accidents have thus so far been unable to
discern any impact. Benefit-cost analyses of specified OSHA standards attempted by the U.S. Council on Wage and Price Stability
generally estimated costs to exceed benefits, using plausible assumptions about the value of various attributes of benefits.[59]

These findings do not indicate necessarily that regulation in
this area is a failure. Several recent studies have pointed to ways
in which OSHA, or its watchdogs in Congress, could improve performance. One step would be to increase the expected costs to
firms of noncompliance with OSHA standards. Fines are currently
so low and inspections so infrequent that compliance for most firms
is irrational in economic terms.[60] Other studies make persuasive
cases for a shift in priorities for OSHA to long-term occupational
health problems, where the tools at OSHA's disposal are likely to
have a larger net impact (see Chapter 7).

As in other areas of regulatory policy, evidence suggests the
effectiveness of decentralized strategies such as provision of job
hazard information to workers and the use of injury taxes to induce
employers to invest in safety.[61] Problems related to the efficiency
of an injury tax have been identified,[62] but sound reasons remain to
explore further the applicability of decentralized regulatory approaches, especially in light of the unattractiveness of coercive
bureaucratically administered standards and the steady accretion
of knowledge regarding the impact of hazards. Indeed, Cornell,
Noll, and Weingast argue that substantially increased investments
in research may have the highest payoff among options open to occupational safety and health regulatory agencies.[63]

An increase in knowledge about relationships between worker
health and safety and the effects of government to correct imperfec-

tions in markets for information would seem necessary in order to proceed further in this area. On one hand it is appealing to believe that provision of information is a sound alternative to regulation. On the other, we must acknowledge that in many cases the provision of information can be more costly than regulation, yet may produce similar results. If a public agency is able to collect, evaluate, and disseminate information more efficiently than the market, there appears to be sufficient justification for public provision of information. It should also follow that if it is less costly to set a standard or to ban a product than to inform people, then regulation is preferable to information provision. We may cite an example of just such a situation in the Consumer Product Safety Commission's mandatory standards for baby cribs:

> In 1968 a presidential commission discovered that the spacing between the slats of baby cribs was so wide that, under certain conditions, the entire body of a baby could slip between the slats until stopped by its skull. The baby would then strangle as it hung outside the crib.
>
> The crib problem had two features. First, no one was collecting data that would make the government or the industry aware of the problem, and accidents were too infrequent for the press and consumers to have become alerted to it. Second, once the problem was recognized, no one knew what kind of a safety standard would deal with it effectively.
>
> The problem was next addressed by the trade association of crib manufacturers. Without benefit of any systematic analysis, the manufacturers voluntarily adopted a standard of 3.25 inches between slats, but a little less than the former 3.5 inches. Next, the Bureau of Product Safety of the Food and Drug Administration—a precursor of the CPSC—commissioned a research project to measure the size of babies' buttocks as part of a larger project of various aspects of infant anthropometry. The study estimated that the buttocks of 5 percent of infants could be compressed by the pressure of their own weight to a diameter of 2.375 inches or less, nearly an inch smaller than the industry standard. In April 1973 a mandatory spacing standard of 2.375 inches was adopted. [64]

In this instance, there was misunderstanding on both sides of the market. Once the hazard was identified, prospective parents could have been informed of it, or manufacturers of cribs with slats spaced more than two inches apart, for example, could have been required to warn buyers that their product was hazardous. Either of these strategies would have involved substantial costs. On the other hand, mandating the standards was practically costless. Had prospective parents been informed, few if any would have chosen a defective crib. Furthermore, except for the costs of transition to a new design, it would cost no more to manufacture a safe crib than one that was hazardous.

The implication of this case is that the more costly it is to inform people, the greater the likelihood that regulation will be more efficient than information provision. Consequently, the question becomes: When is it more costly to inform people? The initial answer is that it will be more costly whenever more information is required. However, it is somewhat tautological to specify that more information is required to deal with complex decision problems. It may clarify the search for an answer if we clarify the definition of a complex decision problem. First, a decision problem involves a choice between alternative actions, each of which will produce different outcomes. The decision maker wishes to obtain the most preferred outcome. Second, the greater the uncertainty about the elements of the decision problem (that is, uncertainty about the status quo, the range of alternatives, the relationship between alternative actions and outcomes, and the utility of alternative outcomes), the greater the complexity of the decision problem. Therefore, to note that we lack information is to indicate that we are less certain.

Given this understanding, government may reduce the complexity of the decision problem facing individuals in private market transactions in one of two ways: by ensuring that individual consumers or decision makers understand the relationships between actions and outcomes, or by eliminating alternatives from consideration. If government chooses the former, the cost of that choice may be measured in terms of resources used to collect, evaluate, and disseminate information to the public. If government chooses to regulate, part of the cost of this choice may be measured in terms of the resources used to establish and enforce regulations. However, a significant portion of the cost will result from reduced satisfaction on the part of some individuals, that is, those who would choose the prohibited alternative and would not err in this choice. An example of this is the cost borne in mandatory automobile seat belt regulation by consumers who would not wear belts without regulation and would not suffer adverse consequences from this choice, for example, where these consumers were not involved in injury-producing accidents. However, the benefits of regulation for these individuals must also include reduced taxes and other payments to support the provision of medical care to consumers injured as a result of not wearing seat belts, as well as reduced insurance payments. As illustrated by this example, determining the distribution and overall balance of costs and benefits of safety by regulation can be a complex undertaking.

Health and safety regulation attempts to reduce the incidence of outcomes that most people would choose to avoid anyway. But this fact alone does not justify regulation. Regulation that prohibits choices that would not be made is trivial. Furthermore, because individual preferences differ, it is often more difficult to determine which choices ought to be prohibited than it is to provide correct information. Consequently, a key to determining whether to regulate is identification of the cost of ensuring that individual decision makers understand the relationship between alternative actions and outcomes. These costs are likely to be highest where a high level of understanding is required to avoid mistakes. This claim has long served to justify professional licensure, despite the ambiguity of evidence on levels of understanding required in order for consumers to avoid mistakes, as in health care and physician selection.

There is one area in which it is documented that individuals err consistently: the assessment of risks and probabilities. The evidence suggests that people are simply not good natural statisticians.[65] People tend to be insensitive to differences in the probabilities of outcomes and the implications of sample size and predictability. Assessments of probabilities frequently are biased by the availability of data. In addition, errors are made in what is termed anchoring and adjustment—that is, people generalize between cases erroneously and fail to make adjustments for differences in circumstance. Furthermore, individuals tend to deal with problems sequentially, causing the proper relationships between low and high probability events to be ignored. Consequently, to ensure that individuals do not make mistakes when faced with choices involving probabilistic outcomes, it is not enough just to inform them of probabilities. In order to improve choice, decision makers must understand the implications of statistical decision theory. Furthermore, their understanding must be sufficient so that their choice reflects the knowledge of probabilities somewhat automatically. There is no assurance that consumers or workers will develop such understanding.[66] Even professional statisticians may not use their training in day-to-day problem solving.

A conclusion that may be drawn from research on decision making is that regulation is likely to be less costly than information provision where difficult probabilistic judgments are required to avoid mistakes. The general rule that regulation will be preferable to information provision where uncertainties are great and information costs are high also may be generalized to analyze problems of externalities and market organization.

In a formal sense, the structure of decision problems faced by the producer of externalities parallels the choice problem of the consumer noted above. Market incentives change the understanding of relationships between alternative actions and outcomes. Regulation is generally intended to remove certain production alternatives from consideration. Of course, regulatory standards and enforcement procedures may also be viewed in terms of their impact on an externality-producing firm's understanding of relationships between alternative actions and outcomes. Standards and enforcement procedures rely on sanctions to motivate behavior. The actions of the externality-producer may be influenced by estimation of the probability that violations will be discovered and by the penalty associated with such performance.

From this perspective we may speculate on the manner in which the production of negative externalities may be reduced. For example, the standards and enforcement approach could simulate the features of a charge for externalities. Other incentives could be set by basing frequency of inspection on violation records to increase the administrative and other costs to the firm of violation, or by setting the size of the penalty relative to the seriousness of the violation. Enforcement efforts could be directed to where the costs of compliance are lowest and/or where violations are most damaging. [67]

If it is assumed that either regulation or economic incentives (the analogue to information provision) could produce the same reductions in negative externalities, the choice between these approaches should be based upon minimizing the sum of search or design costs, bargaining and decision costs, and policing and enforcement costs. As noted, in consideration of these factors, researchers have identified circumstances under which regulation appears to be the least costly alternative. [68] In general, it appears to be more costly to develop appropriate uniform design standards than to identify appropriate charges, but design standards are less costly to police and enforce. Consequently, where the externality-generating process is fairly homogeneous across many firms, and high level of technical expertise is required to determine how best to reduce the output of the unwanted externality, a "best available technology" standard should be optimal. Paradoxically, where large numbers of small firms are involved it may also be cheaper to tell them what to do and how to do it than to rely on outcome-related incentives. This is because it may be relatively more costly for them to figure out how to respond to the incentive than to comply with a directive. However, even the first of these generalizations is subject to exceptions. Furthermore, given the arguments presented in Chapters 5 and 6 explaining how bureaucratic politics and administrative and budgetary policies condition the choice of regulatory strategies, the best practical solution in these cases may still be to rely on market incentives.

CONCLUSION

It should be obvious that, although we have employed a fairly traditional approach to market failures and believe this strategy is justified by its usefulness as a means of identifying potential remedies, we are fundamentally monists. That is, we are persuaded by Kenneth Arrow that the comparative advantage of markets or any other institutional arrangement may be reduced to a question of transaction or information costs and to the ability and willingness of those affected by these costs to recognize and bear them.[69] According to Arrow, any institutional arrangement has the potential to reduce welfare losses associated with another, but before any conclusion can be drawn with respect to the advantage of alternative institutional arrangements, it is necessary to balance information costs under the existing arrangement with those of the alternative systems under consideration.

The most plausible case for this proposition is made by Carl Dahlman. He argues that, although it may be useful for some purposes to distinguish between types of information cost—search costs, bargaining and decision costs, and policing and enforcement costs— these classes all reduce to a single one in that they all represent losses due to the lack of information. As he explains it:

Both search and information costs owe their existence to imperfect information about the existence and location of trading opportunities or about the quality or other characteristics of items available for trade. The case is the same for bargaining and decision costs: these represent resources spent in finding out the desire of economic agents to participate in trading at certain prices and conditions. What is being revealed in a bargaining situation is information about willingness to trade on certain conditions, and decision costs are resources spent in determining whether the terms of the trade are mutually agreeable. Policing and enforcement costs are incurred because there is lack of knowledge as to whether one (or both) of the parties involved in the agreement will violate his part of the bargain: if there were adequate foreknowledge on his

part, these costs could be avoided by contractual stipu-
lations or by declining to trade with agents who would
be known to avoid fulfilling their obligations. Therefore, it is really necessary to talk only about one type
of transaction cost: resource losses incurred due to
imperfect information. [70]

Furthermore, imperfect information may justify any form of
government intervention. For example, if some Pareto optimal ex-
changes do not occur because of ignorance, government intervention
may be justified—if government knows more than private parties do.
However, we may not merely assume that government knows better. [71] Furthermore, markets work well enough in most instances
that the burden of proof ought to rest with those advocating intervention. Unfortunately, the burden of proof usually rests with those
advocating a change, any change, away from the status quo.
  In contrast, Dahlman argues:

In the presence of transaction costs, liability assignments and ownership rights will have effects on the
allocation of resources. As a consequence, transaction costs may prevent the establishment of a desirable
allocation of resources, one that everyone would agree
is better than the one attained when transactions are
costly. In this case the Coase analysis implies one of
two corrective measures: (i) find out if there is a
feasible way to decrease the costs of transacting between market agents through government action, or
(ii) if that is not possible, the analysis would suggest
employing taxes, legislative action, standards, prohibitions, agencies, or whatever else can be thought of
that will achieve the allocation of resources we have
already decided is preferred. The implication of
status quo is simply not there; the theory says to find
practicable ways of diminishing transaction costs, by
whatever kind of action is necessary, including government action . . . instead of referring to an imaginary
global optimum, the Coase approach explicitly requires
dealing with marginal concepts in terms of opportunity
costs, and always keeps an eye open to the fact that
transaction costs are here to stay; the fact that we all
agree on the desirability of reducing some externality
guarantees that some government action indeed may be
desirable since we otherwise could get together and
price out of business the beast who creates the dis-

turbance. If the government can make the costs of
moving to a preferred allocation lower than the benefits of doing so, there is a guarantee that the result is
sanctioned by the Pareto criterion. Any economist
who is also a self-interested government consultant
ought to embrace the Coase analysis whole-heartedly,
for it would seem to call for more and better cost-
benefit analysis. [72]

Also, the first objective (not, as is too frequently the case,
the last consideration) of regulatory analysis ought to be the selection of the right institutional arrangement, that is, making the right
choice among alternative instruments of public policy, including
competition. The second objective, where regulation is found to be
the best or the least worst institutional arrangement, ought to be to
regulate right. This means combining regulatory targets, standards, and monitoring and enforcement strategies so as to achieve
the benefits sought by regulation at the least possible total cost.
For sake of convenience, we shall refer to the pursuit of these objectives as "substantive regulatory reform" and will distinguish between the former and the latter with the terms "comprehensive" and
"incremental." With respect to both of these objectives, we would
insist that insufficient effort has been given to the design and evaluation of alternative institutional arrangements. Nevertheless, we
would make the following generalizations.

Regulation may produce substantial benefits under four conditions:

When it promotes effective competition.

When it permits the public to enjoy economies of scale and to
avoid the exercise of monopoly power. From the standpoint of the
consumer, the benefits of regulation are realized in terms of lower
prices and a more optimal mix of service attributes, including
greater certainty of service availability.

When it reduces negative externalities, resulting in a cleaner
and safer physical environment. Here, the benefits of regulation
are reflected in a healthier and esthetically satisfied public.

When it reduces the number of mistakes made by parties to
private market transactions by standardizing product or service attributes or working conditions.

However, in only one of these instances, when antitrust regulation is used to promote effective competition, can it be unambiguously concluded that regulation is the best option. And in this particular instance, the use of regulation may reflect no more than the

failure to consider possible alternatives to antitrust actions. In
each of the remaining three instances, the benefits of regulation may
be secured by alternative government actions. Critics of regulation
claim that in each of these instances, the alternative is more likely
to be efficient than regulation.

We conclude that regulation is not an appropriate means by
which to achieve single plant or industry efficiencies. Either some
form of franchise and bidding arrangement or public provision of
goods and services usually dominates regulation. If it is assumed
that potential service suppliers better understand the demand characteristics of their market and the production and cost behavior in
their industry, and if they can be prevented from colluding, then a
competitive bidding arrangement should ensure the best supply arrangements possible in any particular market. If it is assumed that
the regulators are as informed or better informed than are managers
in the regulated industry, then private ownership has no significant
function or responsibility to discharge.

Under conditions of externality, we conclude that regulation is
inferior to the manipulation of market incentives and penalties as a
means of reducing externalities. Incentives may take the form of
charges (effluent taxes) or marketable rights. It is assumed that
where producers can determine better how to reduce externalities
than regulators, market incentives will outperform regulation.

Under the fourth of the conditions noted earlier, it is asserted
that public provision of information (or in the case of information
asymmetries, certification, reassignment of liability, or enforced
disclosure such as truth in packaging and labeling) will produce more
efficient outcomes than will a regulatory program that restricts the
range of goods and services made available, enforces standards of
quality, or establishes maximum levels of exposure to health and
safety hazards. Once again, if it is assumed that participants in
private market transactions err only because information is absent,
then public provision of information is preferable to regulation.
This follows from the observation that public provision of information can meet social and economic objectives without removing alternatives from the market that some consumers and workers would
prefer.

On the other hand, the information cost criterion leads to the
conclusion that regulation is likely to be less costly and more effective than information provision where difficult probabilistic judgments are required to avoid mistakes. Relationships between risk,
costliness of error, and consumer preferences provide perspectives
on the choice of alternative institutional arrangements in other circumstances as well. With respect to direct regulation, we have
specified some of the circumstances under which this institutional

arrangement may be appropriate. Unfortunately, because of short-comings on the part of the regulatory authorities, these circum-stances are rarely fully satisfied. Nevertheless, we would, at a minimum, insist that where there is a fair degree of jointness in supply and consumption (where individual preferences are similar), total costs are likely to be lowest when purchasing and negotiation of the terms of purchase are delegated to a public authority or agent. These inferences are also implicit in our treatment of externalities.

Therefore, with regard to the advantages of regulation versus information provision, we conclude that where the probability of a costly error, rather than outcome, is high and consumer prefer-ences are fairly homogeneous, provision of information is likely to be more costly than regulation. Likewise, where the probability of error is higher and remedies are similar, market incentives may be more costly than regulation.

If regulation has a comparative advantage relative to other government actions in certain instances, why is there so much criti-cism of it? One reason is distrust of government decision making in general. In turn, this distrust frequently reflects a distaste for interest group politics and its consequences, an appreciation of the short-term horizon that characterizes political decision making and cynicism toward the claims made about the public interest in politi-cal debate. Allegations of destructive competition, the desirability of a zero-risk environment, the infinite value of a human life, and the distributional benefits of regulation are all too often no more than disguises worn by special or exclusive interests.

A second reason is that the arguments presented here may not be entirely compatible with the static textbook models that most analysts (ourselves included) prefer. We suggest that models to take account of a wider variety of institutions, changing technologies and products, consumer preferences, and the implications of uncer-tainty for individual and collective decision making would better in-form public policymaking than do abstract debates about the relative merits of regulation and competition or regulation and information provision. Unfortunately, such models are difficult to construct. Furthermore, as we have seen, their use seldom produces definite qualitative conclusions.

Nevertheless, we would speculate that so far as the choice between regulation and other forms of government action is con-cerned, the economists' bias against regulation reflects a very real tendency of government to rely too much on regulation. Regulation is the instrument most familiar to lawmakers. It is also consistent with the legal approach to problem solving in other areas. As Paul Portnoy observes, "We do not tax robbers in the hope that they will find it economical to stop robbing."[73] Consequently, regulation is often the first solution to a problem that lawmakers choose. Also, the information available to influence government choice between alternatives is often biased in favor of regulation. Paradoxically, given the logic of our argument, in making the choice between alternative instruments of public policy, government decision makers may be using the information cost criterion. However, it appears that they use cost measures that are not only inaccurate, but biased in favor of regulation; that is, they tend to see only those costs that are captured in the government accounts. If only these costs are considered, programs that shift most of the costs from government accounts to private individuals, firms, and other levels of government will appear to be less costly than those that do not. In many cases, regulation results in such a shift. Furthermore, it seems likely that because the costs associated with the failure to choose the right institutional arrangement are not reflected in government accounts, whereas the costs associated with institutional and program design and development are so reflected, government tends to underinvest in analysis.

This chapter has provided an analysis of some of the most prominent objectives of regulation and the manner in which regulatory policy is designed to meet these objectives. It concluded in an attempt to indicate where regulation is likely to be most and least efficient in meeting objectives relative to alternative institutional arrangements. It also concluded that in many instances government relies too heavily on regulation, offering a few reasons to explain why this is the practice. Inquiry into the politics of regulatory decision making sets the stage for consideration of the manner in which regulatory policy might be reformed, the topic addressed in Chapters 5 and 6.

NOTES

1. This position is, perhaps most baldly stated in M. Trebilcock, L. Waverman, and R. Pritchard, "Markets for Regulation," Government Regulation (Toronto: Ontario Economic Council, 1978). See also George J. Stigler, "Comment," in Studies in Regulation, ed. Gary Fromm (Cambridge, Mass.: MIT Press, 1981), pp. 73-78.

2. See Bruce Ackerman and W. T. Hassler, Clean Coal/Dirty Air (New Haven, Conn.: Yale University Press, 1981); see also Robert A. Leone and J. T. Erickson, "The Political Economy of Federal Regulatory Activity," in Fromm, op. cit., pp. 231-70; and George Stigler, The Citizen and the State (Chicago: University

of Chicago Press, 1975). One important consequence of the expansion in the scope and domain of government regulation has been a remarkable politicization of business. Increasing numbers of firms are to be found seeking favors in Washington and the state capitols. Many firms have recently developed a capacity to deal with bureaucrats and politicians to influence the design and enforcement of regulatory standards. This capacity is reflected in increased government relations staffs, Washington offices, and the investment of millions of dollars in public affairs. Such an outcome is hardly surprising. When government tells firms where to locate and how to design products, organize production processes, and cope with waste and by-products, the advantage accruing to those firms that have the capacity to influence the shape and content of the regulatory regimes to which they and their competitors are subject may be overwhelming. It would also be surprising if the increased politicization of business did not frequently cause substantial efficiency losses. This is so not only because of the biases inherent in interest group politics but also because of the consequent diversion of managerial resources away from operational problems—production, finance, marketing, and so on—to legal and political problems. See Barry M. Mitnick, "The Strategic Uses of Regulation—and Deregulation," Business Horizons, March 1981, pp. 71-83; and Mitnick, "Myths of Creation and Fables of Administration: Explanation and the Strategic Use of Regulation," Public Administration Review, May/June 1980.

3. E. E. Schattschneider, The Semi-Sovereign People: A Realist's View of Democracy in America (New York: Holt, Rinehart and Winston, 1960); see also R. Bauer, I. deSola Pool, and L. A. Dexter, American Business and Public Policy (Chicago: Atherton, 1963).

4. Jean-luc Migué, Nationalistic Policies in Canada: An Economic Approach (Montreal: C. D. Howe Research Institute, 1979).

5. In particular, we were strongly influenced in the exposition by Paul Joskow and Roger Noll, "Regulation in Theory and Practice: An Overview," in Fromm, op. cit., pp. 1-65.

6. Any number of firms less than 20 in a market meets most definitions of oligopoly.

7. David Schwartzman, "The Effect of Monopoly on Price," Journal of Political Economy, August 1961, pp. 352-61; M. A. Crew and C. K. Rowley, "On Allocative Efficiency, X-Efficiency, and the Measurement of Welfare Loss," Economica, May 1971, pp. 199-203; and W. S. Comanor and Harvey Leibenstein, "Allocative Efficiency, X-Efficiency, and the Measurement of Welfare Losses," Economica, August 1969, pp. 304-9.

8. This analysis is based on Fred Thompson and W. M. Zumeta, "Control and Controls," Policy Sciences 13 (Winter 1981): 25-50.

9. See W. G. Shepard, "Public Enterprise: Purposes and Performance and Strategy and Structure," in Managing Public Enterprises, ed. W. T. Stanbury and Fred Thompson (New York: Praeger, 1982).

10. Phillip Areeda and D. F. Turner, Anti-trust Policy (Cambridge, Mass.: Harvard University Press, 1978); see also H. J. Goldschmidt, H. M. Mann, and J. Fred Weston, eds., Industrial Concentration: The New Learning (Boston: Little, Brown, 1974). One justification for antitrust policy not mentioned here is that economic power leads to political power and that concentrated political power is dangerous. Our reason for this omission is that the evidence is almost entirely negative, see Bauer et al., op. cit. Why this is the case isn't entirely clear. However, we would note that industrial concentration likely reduces the number of legislators attentive to the industry's interests. Moreover, only where the payoff to political activity exceeds the payoff to alternative uses of scarce resources are firms likely to invest in it. This is least likely to be the case for highly successful firms capable of dominating an expanding market.

11. This definition follows that of V. P. Goldberg, "Regulation and Administered Contracts," Bell Journal of Economics 7, no. 2 (Fall 1976):926-48. See also Oliver P. Williamson, "Administered Decision-Making and Pricing," in The Analysis of Public Output, ed. J. Margolis (New York: National Bureau of Economic Research, 1970); and his "Franchise Bidding for Natural Monopolies," Bell Journal of Economics 7, no. 1 (Spring 1976):73-104.

12. One of the better treatments of natural monopoly is Gary S. Becker, Economic Theory (Chicago: University of Chicago Press, 1971), pp. 95-98.

13. This issue was first dealt with by Ramsey, but was independently formulated and in a more general way by Boiteaux. See F. P. Ramsey, "A Contribution to the Theory of Taxation," Economic Journal, March 1927, pp. 47-61; M. Boiteaux, "Sur la question des monopoles public astreints a léquilibre budgetaire," Economitrica, January 1956, pp. 22-40, trans. by W. J. Baumol and D. F. Bradford as "On the Management of Public Monopolies Subject to Budget Constraints," Journal of Economic Theory, September 1979, pp. 219-40. See also W. J. Baumol and D. F. Bradford, "Optimal Departures from Marginal Cost Pricing," American Economic Review, June 1970, pp. 265-83, for a review of the literature on this issue.

14. The main papers are John C. Panzar and Robert D. Willig, "Free Entry and the Sustainability of Natural Monopoly," Bell Journal of Economics 67 (Spring 1977):1-22; J. C. Panzar and R. D. Willig, "Economies of Scale and Multi-Output Production," Quarterly Journal of Economics, August 1977, pp. 481-94; W. J. Baumol, Elizabeth E. Bailey, and Robert D. Willig, "Weak Invisible Hand Theorems on the Sustainability of Prices in a Multiproduct Natural Monopoly," American Economic Review 67 (June 1977): 350-65; W. J. Baumol, "On the Proper Cost Tests for Natural Monopoly in a Multiproduct Industry," American Economic Review 67 (December 1977):811-22; Robert D. Willig, "Multiproduct Technology and Market Structure," American Economic Review 69 (May 1979):346-51; R. D. Willig and W. J. Baumol, "Intertemporal Unsustainability," manuscript, 1980; and Elizabeth E. Bailey, "Contestability and the Design of Regulatory and Antitrust Policy," manuscript, 1980. See also M. A. Fuss and L. Waverman, "Regulation and the Multi-product Firm," in Fromm, op. cit., pp. 277-312.

15. Joskow and Noll, op. cit., p. 4.

16. Ibid., pp. 5-10.

17. Ibid., pp. 4-5.

18. E. S. Savas, The Privatization of the Public Sector (Chatham, N.J.: Chatham House, 1982); Robert L. Bish and Robert Warren, "Scale and Monopoly Problems in Urban Government Services," Urban Affairs Quarterly 8 (September 1972):97-122; and Robert L. Bish, "Commentary on 'From Plato's Philosophic King to Bish's Tough Purchasing Agent,'" Journal of the American Institute of Planners 41 (March 1975):67, 74-82.

19. Harold Demsetz, "Why Regulate Utilities?" Journal of Law and Economics 11, no. 2 (Spring 1968):55-66; and Mark Crain and R. B. Ekeland, "Chadwick and Demsetz on Competition and Regulation," Journal of Law and Economics 19 (April 1976):149-62.

20. Williamson, 1976, op. cit.; Goldberg, op. cit.

21. Clair Wilcox and W. G. Shepard, Public Policies Toward Business, 5th ed. (Homewood, Ill.: Irwin, 1975), pp. 347-48.

22. See Daniel L. Rubinfeld, "Market Approaches to the Measurement of the Benefits of Air Pollution Abatement," in Approaches to Controlling Air Pollution, ed. Ann Friedlander (Cambridge, Mass.: MIT Press, 1978), pp. 240-71. See also D. Brookshire, "Experiments in Valuing Public Goods," in Advances in Applied Microeconomics, ed. V. Kerry Smith (JAI Press, forthcoming). An up-to-date survey of efforts to measure benefits from air pollution control is found in the May 1981 American Economic Review. For information on the effects of exposure to pollutant concentration on health, see A. S. Whittlemore, "Air Pollution and Respiratory Disease," Annual Review of Public Health (Palo Alto, Calif.: Annual Reviews, 1981), pp. 397-430.

23. See note 2.

24. Henry M. Peskin and Eugene P. Seskin, eds., Cost Benefit Analysis and Air Pollution Policy (Washington, D.C.: Urban Institute, 1975).

25. Lester B. Lave and Eugene P. Seskin, Air Pollution and Human Health (Baltimore: Johns Hopkins Press, 1977).

26. Ibid.

27. See E. S. Mills, ed., Economic Analysis and Environmental Problems (New York: Columbia University Press, 1975).

28. A. C. Pigou, The Economics of Welfare (London: Macmillan, 1932), pp. 159-61; A. V. Kneese, Water Pollution: Economic Aspects and Research Needs (Washington, D.C.: Resources for the Future, 1962); A. V. Kneese and B. T. Bower, Managing Water Quality (Baltimore: Johns Hopkins Press, 1968); A. V. Kneese, The Economics of Regional Water Quality Management (Baltimore: Johns Hopkins Press, 1974); L. E. Ruff, "The Economic Common Sense of Pollution," The Public Interest 19 (Spring 1970):69-85; W. J. Baumol, "On Taxation and the Control of Externalities," American Economic Review 62, no. 3 (June 1972):307-22; W. J. Baumol and W. E. Oates, The Theory of Environmental Policy (Englewood Cliffs, N.J.: Prentice-Hall, 1975); E. J. Mishan, "What Is the Optimal Level of Pollution?" Journal of Political Economy 82, no. 6 (December 1974):1287-99.

29. Anthony Fisher and Frederick M. Peterson, "The Environment in "Economics: A Survey," Journal of Economic Literature.

30. A. V. Kneese, Pollution, Prices and Public Policy (Washington, D.C.: Brookings Institution, 1975).

31. S. E. Atkinson and D. H. Lewis, "A Cost-Effectiveness Analysis of Alternative Air Quality Control Strategies," Journal of Environmental Economics Management 1, no. 3 (November 1974): 237-50; D. Chapman, "Internalizing an Externality: A Sulphur Emission Tax and the Electric Utility Industry," in Energy: Demand, Conservation and Institutional Problems, ed. M. S. Macrakis (Cambridge, Mass.: MIT Press, 1974); J. M. Griffen, "An Econometric Evaluation of Sulphur Taxes," Journal of Political Economy 82, no. 4 (July/August 1974):669-88; J. M. Griffen, "Recent Sulfur Tax Proposals: An Econometric Evaluation of Welfare Gains," in Macrakis, op. cit.

32. J. H. Dales, "Land, Water, and Ownership," Canadian Journal of Economics 1, no. 4 (November 1968):791-804; J. H. Dales, Pollution, Property, and Prices (Toronto: University of Toronto Press, 1968). See also T. A. Ferrar and A. B. Whinston, "Taxation and Water Pollution Control," Natural Resources Journal 12, no. 3 (July 1972):307-17; David W. Montgomery, "Markets in

Licenses and Efficient Pollution Control Programs," Journal of Economic Theory 5 (Fall 1972):395-418.

33. Fisher and Peterson, op. cit.

34. Peter Nulty, "A Brave Experiment in Pollution Control," Fortune, February 12, 1979, p. 121.

35. A further advantage of this proposal is that, if it were fully implemented, communities, neighborhoods, or even individuals with especially high demands for environmental quality could satisfy this preference through the purchase of permits.

36. U.S. Regulatory Council, Regulating with Common Sense: A Progress Report on Innovative Regulatory Techniques (Washington, D.C., October 1980), p. 8.

37. Ibid.; U.S. Regulatory Council, Innovative Techniques in Theory and Practice (Washington, D.C., July 22, 1980); U.S. Regulatory Council, Regulatory Reform Highlights: An Inventory of Initiatives, 1978-80 (Washington, D.C., April 1980). USRC reports may be obtained from the Administrative Conference of the United States (ACUS), Washington, D.C. ACUS became responsible for information on USRC after the Regulatory Council was terminated in 1981.

38. Joskow and Noll, op. cit., pp. 21-24. In particular Joskow and Noll cite A. M. Spence and Martin Weitzman, "Regulatory Strategies for Pollution Control," in Friedlander, op. cit.; and A. M. Spence and Marc Roberts, "Effluent Charges and Licenses Under Uncertainty," Journal of Public Economics 5 (Spring 1976): 193-208. See also J. B. Stephenson, ed., The Practical Application of Economic Incentives to the Control of Pollution (Vancouver: University of British Columbia Press, 1977).

39. T. H. Tietenberg, "Specific Taxes and Pollution Control: A General Equilibrium Analysis," Quarterly Journal of Economics 87, no. 4 (November 1973):503-22; T. H. Tietenberg, "On Taxation and the Control of Externalities: Comment," American Economic Review 64, no. 3 (June 1974):462-66; T. H. Tietenberg, "The Design of Property Rights for Air Pollution Control," Public Policy 22, no. 3 (Summer 1974):275-92. See also D. Starrett and R. J. Zeckhauser, "Treating External Diseconomies—Markets or Taxes?" in Statistical and Mathematical Aspects of Pollution Problems, ed. J. W. Pratt (New York: Decker, 1974), pp. 65-84. See also R. T. Page, "Failure of Bribes and Standards for Pollution Abatement," Natural Resources Journal 13, no. 4 (October 1973):677-704; R. T. Page and J. Ferejohn, "Externalities as Commodities: Comment," American Economic Review 64, no. 3 (June 1974):454-59.

40. Baumol and Oates, op. cit.

41. In a market characterized by freely available, perfect information on worker and product hazards, responsibility for damages

would be assigned to workers and consumers. They would be expected to take this information into account in their decision making so that wages and prices would reflect the risks associated with various hazards. Hence, firms would have an incentive to take preventive measures whenever the cost of prevention would be less than the damages averted. It is assumed some form of insurance could be designed to deal with equity problems. However, information is neither free nor perfect. Consequently, a government could provide information on hazards or require firms to inform individuals likely to be affected by the firm's decisions of the possible consequences of those decisions. As Cornell et al. have observed: "a central role of regulators is to increase the amount of information available by undertaking research, supporting the research of others, and imposing informational requirements on industry" (p. 474). However, a proper information strategy would take account of existing regulations, insurance schemes, and liability laws. Again, quoting Cornell et al.:

> the market system plus insurance and liability laws
> are unlikely to generate sufficient incentives for pro-
> viding warranted hazard protection in at least two
> cases. One is when the risks of a hazard are either
> known or knowable but the costs of acquiring or under-
> standing information about it are high. The other is
> when either the full nature of the hazard or the chance
> of it occurring are uncertain. In both situations more
> information about health and safety hazards are likely
> to be especially valuable. (p. 474)

This is so, and because the provision of such information can lead individuals and firms to make better decisions regarding risks, and because it can help decision makers to assess better the effectiveness of alternative hazard reduction mechanisms: regulation, mandatory compensation, or the provisions of information. See Nina Cornell, Roger Noll, and Barry Weingast, "Safety Regulation," in Setting National Priorities: The Next Ten Years, ed. Henry M. Owen and Charles L. Schultze (Washington, D.C.: Brookings Institution, 1976), pp. 457-504.

42. O. A. Davis and M. I. Kamien, "Externalities, Information, and Alternative Collection Actions," in Public Expenditure and Policy Analysis, ed. Robert A. Haveman and Julius Margolis (Chicago: Rand McNally, 1970), pp. 82-104.

43. Cornell et al., op. cit.

44. See W. Y. Oi, "The Economics of Product Safety," Bell Journal of Economics and Management Science 4 (Spring 1973):3-28;

M. J. Hinich, "A Rationalization for Consumer Support for Food
Safety Regulation," Department of Economics Working Paper
(Blacksburg, Va.: Virginia Polytechnic Institute and State University, 1975); M. J. Hinich and R. Staelin, "Regulation and the U.S.
Food Industry," in Committee on Governmental Affairs, U.S. Senate (Ribicoff Committee), Study on Federal Regulation, Appendix to
Vol. VI, A Framework for Regulation (Washington, D.C.: U.S. Government Printing Office, December 1978); Department of Health,
Education and Welfare, Medical Malpractice, Report of the Secretary's Commission on Medical Malpractice, Pub. no. 73-88 (Washington, D.C.: U.S. Government Printing Office, 1973); Guido Calabresi, The Costs of Accidents: A Legal and Economic Analysis
(New Haven, Conn.: Yale University Press, 1970); Peter A. Diamond
and James A. Mirrlees, "On the Assignment of Liability: The Uniform Case," Bell Journal of Economics and Management Science 6
(Autumn 1975):487-516. See also Guido Calabresi, "Transaction
Costs, Resource Allocation, and Liability Rules," Journal of Law
and Economics 11 (April 1968):67-68; C. S. Colantoni, O. A. Davis,
and M. Swamithan, "Imperfect Consumers and Welfare Comparisons
of Policies Concerning Information and Regulation," Bell Journal of
Economics 7, no. 2 (Autumn 1976):602-15; and H. Leland, "Quacks,
Lemons, and Licenses," Journal of Political Economy 87, no. 6
(December 1979):1328-46.
45. Cornell et al., op. cit., p. 474.
46. Ibid.
47. Oi, op. cit.
48. Cornell et al., op. cit.; Colantoni et al., op. cit.
49. Joskow and Noll, op. cit.
50. Arthur Anderson and Company, Cost of Government Regulation Study (New York: The Business Roundtable, 1979).
51. Michael S. Lewis-Beck and John R. Alford, "Can Government Regulate Safety? The Coal Mine Example," American Political
Science Review 74, no. 3 (September 1980):745-56. Note that the interpretation of results reported in this article is our own and is not
entirely consistent with that of the authors.
52. Richard Newcomb, "The American Coal Industry," Cur-
ent History 74, no. 2 (1978):206-28; and Richard Gorden, "The
Hobbling of Coal: Policy and Regulatory Uncertainties," Science,
April 14, 1978, pp. 153-58.
53. Sam Peltzman, "An Evaluation of Consumer Protection
Legislation: The 1962 Drug Amendments," Journal of Political
Economy 81 (1973):1049-91.
54. Cornell et al., op. cit.
55. Ibid.

56. See H. G. Manne and R. M. Miller, eds., Auto Safety Regulation (New York: Norton, 1976); see also citations in R. J. Arnould and H. Grabouski, "Auto Safety Regulation: An Analysis of Market Failure," Bell Journal of Economics 12, no. 1 (Spring 1981): 27-48; and Robert Crandall and Lester Lane, eds., The Scientific Basis of Health and Safety Regulation (Washington, D.C.: Brookings Institution, 1981), pp. 21-69.

57. Arnould and Grabouski, op. cit.

58. Joskow and Noll, op. cit.

59. R. S. Smith, The Occupational Safety and Health Act (Washington, D.C.: American Enterprise Institute, 1976).

60. John Mendelhoff, Regulating Safety: An Economic and Political Analysis of the Occupational Health and Safety Policy (Cambridge, Mass.: MIT Press, 1979); also R. S. Smith, "The Impact of OSHA Inspections on Manufacturing Injury Rates," Journal of Human Resources 14, no. 2 (Spring 1979):145-70.

61. R. S. Smith, "The Feasibility of an 'Injury Tax' Approach to Occupational Safety," Journal of Law and Contemporary Problems 38 (Summer-Autumn 1974):730-44.

62. Spence and Weitzman, op. cit. See also G. B. Reschenthaler, Occupational Health and Safety in Canada: The Economics and Three Case Studies (Montreal: Institute for Research on Public Policy, 1979).

63. Cornell et al., op. cit., pp. 501-2.

64. Ibid.

65. Amos Tversky and D. Kahneman, "Judgement Under Uncertainty: Heuristics and Biases," Science, September 27, 1974, pp. 1124-31; and their "Intuitive Prediction: Biases and Corrective Procedures," TIMS Studies in Management Science 12 (1979):313-27. See also Howard Kunreuther and Paul Slovic, "Economics, Psychology, and Protective Behavior," American Economic Review 68, no. 2 (May 1978):64-69.

66. We would note, for example, that the evidence on compensating wage differentials is very unpersuasive.

67. Paul R. Portnoy, "Efficient Use of Standards and Enforcement: The Case of Pollution Controls," Policy Analysis 5, no. 4 (Fall 1979):512-24.

68. Spence and Roberts, op. cit.; Spence and Weitzman, op. cit.

69. Kenneth Arrow, "The Organization of Economic Activity: Issues Pertinent to the Choice of Market Versus Market Allocation," in Haveman and Margolis, op. cit.

70. Carl Dahlman, "The Problem of Externality," Journal of Law and Economics 23 (April 1979):148.

71. Ibid., pp. 155-56.

72. Ibid., pp. 160-61.

73. Portnoy, op. cit., p. 522.

5

THE POLITICS AND PROSPECTS
FOR REGULATORY REFORM

In the previous chapter we analyzed the objectives of regulation, showing how those objectives might be achieved. This analysis
also reveals the need for regulatory reform. In this chapter we
proceed to inquire whether regulatory reform is possible, and if so
what type of reforms we ought to seek. Our exploration of the
theory and politics of regulatory reform causes us to conclude that
significant reform of the regulatory process is not only desirable
but possible, given that we understand how the existing process
operates and how reform efforts in the past have failed.

In this chapter, and the two that follow, we attempt to clarify
the options for reform along two dimensions: incremental versus
comprehensive reform and procedural versus substantive reform.
In the first instance we inquire whether reform is best achieved
through marginal adjustments to existing policy or through comprehensive change and equilibration to new policy, concluding that the
latter course will be the more productive one. In the second instance we analyze alternatives to procedural reform (that is, procedures to improve the review of regulation) and methods for
achieving substantive reform, concluding that change in one comple-
ments change in the other. Options for procedural reform are
analyzed in detail in Chapter 6, and Chapter 7 explores methods to
improve substantive reform through more and better analysis.

THE ROLE OF GOVERNMENT AND ECONOMIC
ANALYSIS IN REGULATION

Within the past five years significant effort has been exerted
to review and reform federal economic regulation of the private

sector.[1] Achievements range from marginal or incremental adjustments to regulatory policy and administrative procedures to comprehensive changes in the role of government control of business
and industry. Examples of marginal adjustment may be found in the
reform of banking and communications regulation, the phased deregulation of natural gas, and more comprehensive change has occurred in deregulating the air travel industry.

The debate surrounding these changes, and our brief experience
attempting to interpret the consequences of reform, lead us to inquire whether, and under what circumstances, comprehensive reform is more appropriate than marginal adjustment. And the fact
that resolution of this issue requires evaluation of the rationale for
alteration of federal economic policy causes us to ask what role
economic analysis ought to play in improving regulatory decision
making.

This task compels us to speculate briefly on the role and performance of government in regulating the private economy. We
believe that the proper role of government is to ascertain and to
promote the common good, and that it should attempt to achieve
this end, however imperfectly. We also believe that improvements
may be made in the methods employed by government to ascertain
and to promote the common good. We recognize that government
may, and frequently does, err in setting economic policy, hence we
believe that the task of economic analysis is to help government
avoid and correct these errors.

However, some critics reject this view. They maintain that
the role of government in general, and of regulation in particular,
is necessarily that of arbiter among competing economic interests.
This position would appear to deny a normative role to economic
analysis. According to this second view, regulatory policy is no
more than a "fulcrum upon which contending interests seek to exercise leverage in their pursuit of wealth."[2] Regulatory policies may
be explained by "a theory of the optimum size of political coalitions
set within a framework of a general model of the political process."[3]
In this theory, the demand for regulation is a function of the benefits
to be derived from the use of government's power to improve the
economic status of groups. According to Sam Peltzman:

> The essential commodity being transacted in the politi-
> cal market is a transfer of wealth, with constituents on
> the demand side and their political representatives on
> the supply side. Viewed in this way, the markets here,
> as elsewhere, will distribute more of the good to those
> whose effective demand is highest.[4]

In other words, regulatory outcomes are predictable consequences of personal tastes and capabilities working through the political and administrative processes by which policy is formulated.[5] Furthermore, this view implies that regulatory initiatives that have survived the keen competition for votes must represent relatively efficient means of redistributing resources.[6] Consequently, carried to its logical extreme, this view implies that, under existing political rules and given information and transaction costs, the existing pattern of regulation is optimal. One is reminded of Pope's line, "Whatever is, is right." This leads us to inquire under which circumstances regulation produces desirable and predictable outcomes or undesirable and largely unintended consequences. We begin this inquiry by reexamining the rationale for and results of industry-specific regulation.

PREDICTABLE OUTCOMES OR UNINTENDED CONSEQUENCES IN INDUSTRY-SPECIFIC REGULATION?

Much economic regulation consists of the application of two conceptually distinct types of controls to specific industries: supply controls, including restrictions on the number of participants in a given industry and the specification of conditions of participation, as well as direct restrictions on output; and price controls. The latter may also include rate of return regulation.[7]

Until very recently, the logic underlying these types of regulation appeared self-evident. So far as most local regulations and all forms of supply controls are concerned, regulation clearly has been intended to transfer income from one group to another, other self-serving justifications notwithstanding. With some exceptions—local rent controls, for example—the pattern of transfer has been from the many consumers to producers or suppliers. In several instances, the origins of these controls can be traced to exceptional circumstances (the Depression, World War II), which created a temporary, albeit severe, disequilibrium in the market and hence a demand for controls. This explanation of the origins of supply controls traditionally has not been open to serious debate. However, as noted, over the last few years, the traditional explanation for price controls has been savaged. A number of economists now believe that the origins of price controls have much in common with the origins of supply controls. Certainly the existing array of price controls cannot be explained as a response to natural monopoly. Consequently, it has been proposed that the origins of these policies can be explained as having resulted from the actions of effectively organized interests operating through the political process to gain economic advantage (rents).

Public Utility-Type Regulation

As explained in Chapter 4, the traditional view of price controls is that they are supposed to protect society from the abuse of monopoly power. The logic underlying this view rests upon the notion of a "natural monopoly." A natural monopoly is said to occur when long-run average (and hence marginal) costs continue to decline over the range of total market demand. Under such conditions, a single firm can produce the required total volume of output at the lowest total social cost. Consequently, these markets will "naturally" tend to be dominated by a single firm. However, this "natural" state of affairs has two rather unpleasant by-products. The struggle for dominance in such markets can produce wide fluctuations in the price, quality, and quantity of the goods or services available. Depending upon the importance of the good or service in question, this can have a destabilizing effect upon a regional economy. Furthermore, the struggle for dominance may often be highly wasteful. Where one firm succeeds in driving its competitors out of the market, it will likely exploit its monopoly position to the detriment of consumers and potential consumers. Therefore, if it is accepted that price controls or public ownership can eliminate these by-products of the "natural" state of affairs, government regulation or ownership of major natural monopolies is justified.

The Critique of Price Controls

This view has been recently subjected to two fundamental criticisms: Most markets regulated in practice are potentially competitive in terms of their market structure, and government regulation or ownership may be, although not necessarily, somewhat more benign than private monopolization, but is also more likely to result in allocatively and technically inefficient outcomes. In a sense both criticisms are extensions of traditional assumptions about natural monopolies. If government regulation succeeds in controlling prices so that monopoly or "excess" profits are not made, it follows from these assumptions that there should be no need to regulate entry also. However, competitors persistently attempt entry into numerous regulated industries such as trucking, telecommunications, and retail electric power. [8] Therefore, the need to regulate entry implies at a minimum that there is either something wrong with the notion of natural monopoly or that the regulators are not doing their job.

As we have noted, much of the empirical analysis that has been done tends to support one or the other of these conclusions.

For example, if price regulation is intended as a check on monopoly power, it should cause prices and profits to be lower than they would be without regulation. However, with the exceptions of the wellhead price of natural gas and local rent controls, regulation does not appear to reduce prices. At the same time, there is little evidence to show that regulated firms earn exorbitant profits. This leads to the conclusion that regulation has no effect, or that it raises costs so that the profit potential of monopoly pricing is not realized. In turn, these observations have stimulated the development of a set of competing theoretical propositions about the origins of price regulation.

First came the "capture" theories. These assume that price regulation was created by legislators who genuinely intended to serve the public interest, but that over time the regulators gradually yielded to pressures from the regulated industry. One version of this theory holds that, together with the congressional committee responsible for oversight of the agency and the industry it regulates, the regulatory agency forms an "iron triangle" of mutual support. The members of the subcommittees that oversee the agency's program and budget get decisions from the regulators that contribute to their reelection and financial support from the regulated industry. The regulated industry gets protection from the rigors of competition, and the regulatory agency gets a larger budget and greater authority. Unfortunately, as the advocates of this theory note, the "proper" purposes of regulation are all too frequently sacrificed to the interests of the more active participants in the regulatory process.

Another more recent interpretation of "capture" holds that no such iron triangle exists, although it grants that regulatory decisions will tend to reflect the opinions of the members of oversight committees and to favor the interests of well-organized advocacy groups. Instead, this view assumes that regulators really try to serve the general public rather than the special interests but, because the success indicators that are used to assess their performance are somewhat perverse and because the information they get is systematically biased against unrepresented groups, they fail to do so. In part, they fail because they react rationally as bureaucrats to their perception of the system of incentives that operates in a highly politicized environment.

Then there are the radical theories of the origins of public utility regulation that hold that the mechanism was designed, proposed, and supported by business as a means of replacing competition with a legal cartel to the benefit of the regulated firms.[9]

However, none of these theories provides satisfactory explanations for the regulatory phenomenon in question. The earlier version of the capture theory is now generally understood to over-state the influence of the regulated industry on regulatory decision making. The fact is that regulatory agencies are not simply con-duits for the interests of regulated firms, but more often than not they try to accommodate a rather broad range of interests. The newer version of the capture theory seems to be more satisfactory. However, it is largely concerned with explaining the ongoing per-formance of regulatory agencies; it is silent on the origins of industry-specific regulation. How, then, does one account for the origin of regulation? Furthermore, how does one account for the persistence of an institution that produces apparently unsatisfactory outcomes?

The radical theory of the origins of regulation answers these questions. There is no capture; regulatory agencies were created with the purpose of serving a single economic interest. But this answer ignores the fact that price controls were generally sought by consumer as well as producer groups. Why should consumers support policies apparently contrary to their own interests?

General Theory of Economic Regulation

Peltzman has provided us with one set of answers to these questions in an expansion and generalization of George Stigler's theory of the demand for and the supply of regulation, the so-called "economic theory of regulation."[10] Peltzman claims that transfer of wealth through the political process reflects the dynamics of constituent demand for benefits and the ability of political actors to supply benefits where demand is greatest. From this view, there-fore, the demand for regulation is a function of the benefits to be derived from the use of public power to improve the economic status of groups. The supply of regulation is a function of the level of op-position to the regulatory proposal and the rules governing decisions about the use of public power.

However, support for or opposition to a regulatory proposal requires resources. Other things being equal, the larger the group, the more costly it is to organize to exercise effective political de-mand. Furthermore, group size also tends to reduce the size of individual benefits to be gained through the use of public power. Consequently, group opposition or support of a proposal may not be directly proportional to the group's potential stake in the outcome.

This factor clearly accounts for the disproportionate number of organizations representing producers' interests in Washington. Stigler and Peltzman also claim that it explains regulatory outcomes that are both contrary to the interests of large majorities and allocatively inefficient. For example, a numerically compact group made up of individuals having a substantial stake in the regulatory outcome, such as physicians, may effectively demand supply controls because it is neither easy nor worthwhile for the rest of us to organize to oppose them.[11] Furthermore, this factor helps to account for exceptions from the purported tendency of price regulation to favor the interests of producer groups, for example, local rent controls and regulation of the wellhead price of natural gas. Ownership of rental property is widely dispersed. As for natural gas, there are a large number of major producers and literally hundreds of small producers. Moreover, the intermediate consumers of their product, the pipeline companies, and the distributors of natural gas are small in number and well organized.

For the most part, however, the industries subject to price regulation have certain characteristics in common that guarantee substantial opposition to policies that wholly favor either consumers or producers. On the one hand, these industries usually form part of the infrastructure of the economy, for example, transportation or communications. Their behavior has substantial consequences for large numbers of consumers, many of which are other firms and are frequently well organized. On the other hand, production in these industries is typically highly capital-intensive, and capital investment is characterized by "lumpiness" and long-term planning horizons—characteristics associated with a high degree of market concentration.

Furthermore, these characteristics give rise to conditions under which either consumers or producers might seek public intervention on their behalf. Rapid increases in consumer demand could be expected to result in increased prices, short-run monopoly, or "excess" profits, as well as capacity expansion. Under these circumstances one could understand a demand from consumer groups to control prices. Conversely, a fall in demand, most frequently owing to a general slump in the economy, could be expected to lead to excess capacity, cutthroat competition, and demands from "industrial statesmen" that the government intervene to regulate prices to ensure a "fair rate of return" on invested capital.

However, so long as we accept the traditional view of natural monopoly, which necessarily requires that we treat the distributional consequences of government price controls as a zero-sum game between producers and consumers, it is not possible to conceive of a situation in which both would favor price controls simultaneously.[12] We are led, therefore, to question the zero-sum game assumption.

Here Peltzman steps beyond Stigler's argument by implicitly rejecting the traditional view of natural monopoly. In doing so, he is reflecting the most recent work in the industrial organization literature. It is now widely recognized that, if by natural monopoly we refer to a firm that produces a single homogeneous product using a single production technology, it is not at all clear that there are any natural monopolies, aside from those that have been created for the administrative convenience of regulators. Most regulated firms, indeed most large firms, employ multiple technologies to produce multiple outputs for sale in segmented markets. In addition, where product attributes are held constant, many firms face decreasing costs where the volume of output is increasing. This fact is not necessarily evidence of chronic market failure.

Under certain rather restricted conditions, it can be demonstrated that an unregulated market made up of firms with these characteristics will support the optimal number of firms, producing the optimal product mix, at optimal quantity levels and prices. This conclusion holds where nondecreasing returns to scale and production complementaries are strong enough to confer cost advantages to single firm production of the optimal product mix. In this instance, only the optimal set of prices and goods and services can guarantee a monopoly against competitive entry.[13] This conclusion holds a fortiori for industries characterized by ease of exit.

One implication of this perspective is that there is no reason to believe, based upon the logic of market failure alone, that price controls are appropriate to industries such as telecommunications or even the postal service, but not the automotive industry or the soap industry. The second implication is that, in any industry with these characteristics, some firms and some consumers stand to gain from regulation at the expense of others. Prices can be manipulated to benefit some consumers to the detriment of others and product differentiation suppressed, thereby reducing unit costs in the industry to the detriment of those firms seeking to exploit fully existing product/market opportunities. While Peltzman concentrates his attention on the first of these possibilities, cross-subsidization, the conclusions one might draw with respect to the second are identical. This is to say, that using the choice-theoretic, utility-maximizing assumptions of microeconomics, Peltzman identifies a regulatory equilibrium in which the costs and benefits of the different interest groups affected and the interests of selected officials able to establish regulation are equated at the margin.

It should further be noted that a minor extension of Peltzman's model permits a reconciliation of his perspective on the origins of regulation and the claims of the capture theorists. In Peltzman's model, elected officials are not distinguished from regulators. This is not the case, of course. Rather, regulators are in a sense the agents of the legislative branch. Regulators, however, may be expected to attend to a narrower range of interests. Consequently, one might anticipate a discrepancy between the expectations of elected officials and the behavior of the regulators and recurrent attempts on the part of the elected officials to revise the regulatory process so as to reduce or eliminate this discrepancy. This is precisely what one observes.

Finally, Peltzman offers an hypothesis to account for the application of price regulation to certain industries and not to others. He proposes that, because political equilibrium is at a point of tangency between the "profit hill" and a "majority curve," "Either naturally monopolistic or naturally competitive industries are more politically attractive to regulate than an oligopolistic hybrid. The inducement to regulate is the change in the level of the [iso-majority] curve occasioned thereby. For a monopoly with a price already intermediate between the competitive and monopoly price, the political gain from moving to [the point of tangency] will be smaller in general than if the one regulation price is either at the top or the bottom of the profit hill."[14]

This hypothesis is intuitively appealing. However, as we have seen, the utility of the Peltzman model is contingent upon the rejection of the existence of the notion of natural monopoly upon which this hypothesis rests. Furthermore, it implies that the political market is frequently not in equilibrium. Therefore, to accept this hypothesis is to question Peltzman's more general formulation.

As an alternative, it might be proposed that certain industries have been subjected to price regulation because the effects of rapid and unpredictable changes in their environment have widespread and undesirable effects upon producers and consumers. Over time, both might be better off if the industry were sheltered from these changes. In most cases, of course, most individuals are likely to be indifferent to the effects of such changes. Most of the costs are borne by producers; most of the benefits of such changes are passed on to consumers. However, as has been asserted, many of the industries subject to price regulation are particularly important to the economy and capital-intensive, and capital investment in these industries is characterized by "lumpiness" and long planning horizons. Because of these qualities, changes in the economic environment, particularly those associated with the business cycle, can be costly to consumers. These costs may be reflected in demands for public intervention. Indeed, there are situations in which a good case may be made for reducing business risk in such industries so as to promote more nearly optimal long-term levels of investment, the maintenance of plant and equipment during recession, and the prevention of unnecessarily steep price rises owing to capacity shortfalls during recovery. That these considerations are not the only ones that influence the demand for and supply of regulation is in no way inconsistent with acknowledgment of their importance.

Several other observations on Peltzman's theory should be noted: This theory of the demand and supply of regulation is general; unlike earlier models, it may be applied to an explanation of both the capture phenomenon and to the origins of both supply and price controls. And the theory is internally consistent and intuitively plausible, which is not to say it is all-encompassing and beyond legitimate criticism. However, as we have noted, Peltzman's general theory implies that under existing political process, and given information and transaction costs, the present pattern of regulatory policies is correct. It implies that regulations that have survived the keen competition for votes do represent relatively efficient means of redistributing resources. Consequently, if the outcomes produced in equilibrium are somehow unsatisfactory, the solution is to change the political rules. If this conclusion is interpreted to mean changing constitutional rules or somehow modifying the pattern of interest group representation, the prognosis for regulatory reform is dim indeed.

Furthermore, if the results of regulatory policy are predictable consequences of expressions of demand through the political process, where does this view admit the possibility of error? Where does it grant the relevance of economic analysis? The answer is simple in our view. If rational, utility-maximizing behavior is assumed, mistakes are clearly not possible ex ante. But regret, ex post, may necessarily occur. This is because people are assumed to maximize expected utility given the information available to them. However, additional information—provided by direct experience, a new awareness of previously available information, or the systematic acquisition of information—necessarily permits the revision of prior probabilities and may indicate that a different action should be or should have been taken. Consequently, although it may be theoretically correct to say that the existing pattern of regulation is optimal, which is another way of saying people do not make mistakes, this statement is almost wholly devoid of any practical meaning.

We prefer to view many of the outcomes of regulation, at least in part, as a series of avoidable mistakes. This is not to deny the thrust of Peltzman's argument. Existing decision-making processes do predictably, and perhaps necessarily, frequently produce unfortunate outcomes. One key to resolution of these two apparently contradictory viewpoints lies in a different understanding of what is meant by "existing decision-making processes." In the first interpretation, this term can be understood to mean political cal processes. In this case, as noted, fundamental constitutional changes would be required to avoid many predictably adverse outcomes.

Fortunately, changes in decision rules need not be so drastic. This is evident if one accepts the claim that among the relevant rules of the political system are those that have been adopted in response to the awesome complexity and uncertainty faced by political decision makers. Under almost any circumstance, it may be observed that one of the key uncertainties faced by decision makers has to do with the availability of information. This uncertainty leads them to adopt what Herbert Simon has called satisficing decision-making strategies. According to Simon, "Men satisfice because they lack the wits to optimize," but given information costs, such a strategy may be very nearly optimal. Its characteristics include limited search, which means that choice tends to focus on familiar alternatives that differ incrementally from the status quo; sequential attention to problems, which means that urgent problems are considered one at a time as they are brought forcibly to the attention of decision makers; and division of labor, which means that analysis and evaluation are socially fragmented—different groups are concerned with different consequences of a policy, and it is assumed that problems produced by a policy will be pointed out by the groups adversely affected.[15] Consequently, economic analysis that provides improved understanding of policy alternatives and their consequences is especially likely to be seen as useful if it permits decision makers to consider a wider array of alternatives or to seek better solutions.

Furthermore, it seems likely that economic and institutional analysis would be particularly valuable where regulatory issues are concerned. This is because availability biases, left uncorrected, can be expected to result in what will be seen ex post as an overreliance on regulation. In the first place, regulation is relatively more familiar than are alternative policy instruments. In the second, there are often no satisfactory alternatives to more regulation at the margins of current policy.

The Bias of Familiarity

In most instances, regulation is only one of a number of alternative policy instruments that could be used to modify undesirable outcomes produced in the marketplace. However, according to Henry Aaron, other alternatives are relatively unfamiliar, especially to U.S. legislators: "Most members of Congress are lawyers, more accustomed to dealing in mandates that require or prohibit behavior than they are to managing incentives that encourage or discourage behavior."[16] Furthermore, alternatives that involve incentives for performance change may seem indirect and may not have the appeal of an immediate "solution." Whereas, according to Robert Ball:

> Direct regulation is very appealing where matters do not seem to be going well. Regulation seems to be the approach that addresses itself most directly to the perceived problem. If prices are "too high," set rates; if desired services are not available in some areas or from some people, fix the responsibility on some institution or organization to see that they are made available; if the quality of service is too low, set standards.[17]

The appeal of direct regulation is not, however, unique to U.S. legislators. In most Western societies, situations "characterized by surprise, high threat to important values, and short decision time"[18] are likely to generate pressures for standardization, institution of controls, and centralization of authority.[19] According to D. J. Hartle, this is the way legislators react to problems. A law that directly prohibits or requires a certain behavior is the obvious instrument by which to "attack an evil" or "do good." Alternatives are seldom considered, nor are the indirect or longer term consequences of the law. As he puts it: "The thought that the government, by changing the relative cost or benefits associated with alternative actions, thereby induces changes in behavior is simply not contemplated."[20]

That governments turn first to regulatory instruments when confronted by a serious problem is hardly surprising. However, it also would be surprising if this propensity did not result, in a disproportionate number of cases, in regret after the fact. If so, additional ex ante information about the alternatives to regulation should be of particular value to government decision makers.

The Marginal Adjustment Trap

There is extensive literature endorsing the goal of moving from a regime of rigid government price and supply controls, including restrictions on the number of participants in a given activity and specification of conditions of participation as well as direct restrictions on output, to one of competition. Economists may not be able to provide precise estimates of the costs of direct regulation, but in a number of cases it is clear that these controls impose efficiency losses and that these losses are considerable.[21] However, there is also a developing literature to indicate that marginal changes in the direction of less comprehensive control can be expected to decrease efficiency. This leads to the following, rather counterintuitive proposition: If decision makers wish to increase economic efficiency, if they understand the consequences of their actions, and if they exclude from consideration all nonincremental alternatives to the status quo, movement away from regulatory control is not possible.

According to the new economics of scope and scale, where firms produce many products, use many technologies, and sell in many different markets, if prices are controlled but not entry, the consequence may be inefficient competitive entry.[22] In addition, these controls have to be extended to the full product or service line.[23] The same logic applies to product mix. If product characteristics are not specified, including aspects of use and selling, the regulated industry would again be threatened by excessive nonprice competition and inefficient product differentiation. If price and entry are controlled, product quality standards also must be set. To ensure that the regulated industry has capacity sufficient to meet demand at the regulated price, it is necessary for the regulators to determine the optimal production technology and to enforce its use. Ultimately, pursuit of efficiency may lead regulators to assume full responsibility for the management function. Of course, this logic applies only where the production and cost behavior of the regulated firms have certain, specified characteristics. However, many firms have these characteristics, including almost all of those that are subject to direct regulation.

What this means is that the logic of incrementalism directs governments toward ever more comprehensive control. This process is illustrated by the early history of the Interstate Commerce Commission (ICC). In 1887 Congress established the ICC, giving it the authority to hear complaints about railroads and to set maximum rates which would be "just and reasonable." However, the rates set by the ICC were evidently not considered just and reasonable by Congress, and in 1906 the Hepburn Act specified a rate-setting procedure. To offset "cream-skimming" and control nonprice competition, ICC authority was extended by the Hepburn Act to pipelines and water transport; in 1910, under the Mann-Elkins Act, to telephone, telegraph, and cable services; in 1913, to Pullman cars, lounge cars, and refrigerator cars; and in 1917, under the Esch Act, to railroad car pooling. In 1913, Congress stipulated that rates should be based on a fair return in relation to asset valuation. To determine asset value, it was necessary to make accounting rules uniform, and to provide the ICC with power to subpoena managerial information and to impose penalties. In the 1920 Transportation Act, ICC authority was extended to terminal management, securities issues, rail line abandonments, mergers, and construction. With the rise of trucking in the 1930s, the ICC assumed authority over interstate trucking with the ability to control entry and specify maximum tariffs.[24] As J. R. T. Hughes has observed:

> Even the briefest description of the ICC's early history
> demonstrates how a simple mechanism of nonmarket
> control quickly becomes complex and unwieldy. Such
> should not be surprising. Production and distribution
> of goods and services involve an infinity of decision.
> The market mechanism incapacitates these in price
> bargains . . . the ICC . . . was established in response
> to public clamor against the abuses. . . of the railroads.
> . . . It all seems logical when one reads the accounts
> of 1887 and before. But what followed acquired an ap-
> palling complexity, and fairly quickly too, as the non-
> market control . . . had to be extended over and over
> to be effective.[25]

Obviously, this short history does not prove that government decision makers pursue economic efficiency. Expansion of ICC authority may also be explained by the requirements of cartel management. The actions cited here may have been motivated by a desire to promote the interests of the railroads and, later, existing truck and barge lines. For that matter, some of the actions taken by the ICC appear to be contrary to the requirements of either economic efficiency or effective cartel management. In other words, it is not known for sure that government decision makers were interested in economic efficiency. But neither is it known that they were not.

DEREGULATION

The American experiments with deregulation in the 1970s stand in direct contrast to the tendency toward more comprehensive control. However, they in no way appear to challenge the notion that marginal change in the direction of less comprehensive control can be expected to result in decreased efficiency. In particular, decontrol of the wellhead price of natural gas indicates the implications of the piecemeal devolution of regulatory authority. In the airline deregulation experiment, knowledge of these pitfalls was carried to its logical conclusion.

Natural Gas Deregulation

The application of public utility regulation to natural gas production is particularly interesting because the chronic market-
failure argument simply cannot be applied to this industry. It is
clearly an increasing-cost industry and is structurally competitive.
There are many large producers and several hundred small producers of natural gas, and entry barriers are low.[26] Since the mid-
1950s, the regulators consistently have held the price of natural gas
in interstate markets below the price of equivalent alternative
sources of energy.[27] And since 1970, the rate set by the regulators
has been well below the market clearing price. In 1976-77 and
1977-78, shortages required substantial curtailment of use, causing
considerable hardship. Of course, these shortages induced a demand for further controls. In this instance, the regulators tried,
"to develop a set of standards that would automatically allocate gas
to those most in need."[28] In turn, this created additional problems
and demands for additional controls and more detailed standards.[29]
Furthermore, increases in the discrepancy between the regulated
rate and the market clearing price had the effect of increasing the
opposition of industrial and household users to deregulation. It is
not impossible that, if all natural gas production had been under
federal regulation, the outcome of this process would have been a
comprehensive system of rationing.

However, as it happened there was an extensive, unregulated,
intrastate market for natural gas. Indeed, there is considerable
evidence that transfers from the regulated, interstate market to the
unregulated intrastate market were, in part, responsible for curtailment of supply in some areas during the winters of 1976-77 and
1977-78. In order to obtain control over these supplies, supporters
of regulation of natural gas production were forced to agree to the
gradual decontrol of the price of new and high cost natural gas
supplies.[30]

At the time it was thought that if other states followed the
lead of California and New York in implementing inverted retail
rate structures, based upon the incremental cost of natural gas supplies, this compromise would work out rather well.[31] Decontrol
of wellhead prices on new and high cost gas would stimulate production and incremental pricing would constrain demand somewhat.
It was also thought that it would be very wasteful to force existing
users of natural gas, both residential and industrial, to convert
too rapidly to alternative fuel sources.[32] In many cases, alternatives were not available.[33] Consequently, it was thought that a
fairly good case could be made for more gradual, as opposed to
immediate, deregulation of the market for new gas.

It is difficult to evaluate this last argument. It is clear that the Natural Gas Policy Act (NGPA) of 1978 provides relatively little incentive to users to convert to alternate fuel sources. On the supply side, however, the NGPA does appear to be a market improvement over the previous regulatory regime. It is interesting to note that, although the NGPA is frequently described as a decontrol law, it substantially increases the scope and the domain of federal regulatory authorities. Not only is old intrastate gas now subject to price control but price controls have been greatly refined. Thirty-three separate tiers of prices are now set by regulatory authorities at the wellhead, based on nine different factors. Additional controls have been directed at pipeline operators and state-level regulatory authorities. W. J. Mead estimates that as a consequence administrative and direct compliance costs will nearly double under this program, to $4 billion per year.[34] While the NGPA may represent an incremental improvement over its predecessor, it can be argued that this improvement was realized by means of more regulation, not less.[35]

Airline Deregulation

Airline deregulation was preceded by the development of a substantial body of literature showing that the consumer would benefit from the increased price competition. This point was made by academics,[36] the Department of Transportation,[37] the General Accounting Office,[38] and a special staff study prepared by the Civil Aeronautics Board (CAB).[39] However, the single most persuasive evidence of the desirability of deregulation was the example of the less regulated air-travel markets in California and Texas. The experience of the California intrastate air carriers, not regulated by the CAB but by state authorities, implied that deregulation would reduce fares 30 to 50 percent, promote more efficient operations, and not threaten safety standards.[40]

In addition, it was demonstrated that very little cross-subsidization was taking place. Many small communities were, in fact, already being served by unregulated commuter carriers. The argument that deregulation would deprive small towns of air transport would not hold up. Some, but not all, airlines argued that deregulation would lead to chaos.[41] However, the example of the intrastate markets in California and Texas demonstrated that deregulation ought not to result in destabilizing, destructive competition.[42]

In this instance, the CAB and its staff took the lead in promoting deregulation. On April 8, 1976, John Robson, chairman of the CAB, testified before the Senate aviation subcommittee that the CAB had unanimously concluded that more price competition, easier entry, and less regulation were in the public interest.[43] President Carter's appointees to the CAB pushed support for deregulation even further, using its discretion to permit greater fare flexibility and multiple route entry.[44] Indeed, it is likely that in achieving de facto deregulation, the CAB under Robson's successor, Alfred Kahn, probably exceeded its legal authority. Kahn, of course, argued publicly that the board's decisions would stand judicial scrutiny.[45] However, it was widely believed that the CAB pushed deregulation as far as possible, hoping that its benefits would be made manifest and that, therefore, Congress would ratify its actions, making moot any possible legal challenge.[46]

If this was the strategy, it appears to have worked. Congress passed the Airline Deregulation Act of 1978, reaffirming and furthering the CAB's policies. And in the short term, nearly every prediction made by the advocates of deregulation, but few if any of the industry's predictions of reduced service or destructive competition, have resulted. For the purposes of our study, perhaps the most interesting insight to be gained from this experience is Kahn's discovery of the possible distortion effect of gradual deregulation. As he explains:

> The theory of the second-best tells us that if we want to go from point A to point C, it is not necessarily efficient to go part of the way. . . . I originally thought that we ought to move very cautiously, examining the results every step of the way, in the hope of minimizing the disruptions and distortions of the transition; my present conviction is that it means we must make the act of faith and move as rapidly all the way to C.[47]

The problems faced by the CAB include the calibration of changes in pricing and entry, balancing price and nonprice competition, and ordering entry on a route-by-route basis—all without creating handicaps or advantages for present and potential competitors. Predictably, the discovery was that it simply couldn't be done this way. The practical solution to these conundrums was as follows. Kahn said,

> make the transition rapid; move quickly on as broad a front as possible to permit all carriers to slough off the restrictions that limit their operating flexibility, to leave the markets they find it uneconomic to serve, to enter the markets they want to enter.[48]

Consequently, he concluded: "I have as a result been converted to the conclusion that the only way to move is fast. The way to mini-mize the distortion of the transition, I am now thoroughly convinced, is to make the transition as short as possible."[49]

Obviously, one way out of the marginal adjustment trap is via a nonincremental move. Moreover, Kahn claims that airline de-regulation is proof that such moves are possible. Does it also tell us when and where? Perhaps. If decision makers avoid abrupt policy changes because of uncertainty about their consequences, it follows that they might intentionally make a nonincremental move if they were confident that economic analysis had provided them with satisfactory information as to its possible consequences. What was remarkable about the airline deregulation decision was the amount and kind of information available to policymakers.

CONCLUSIONS ON INCREMENTAL VERSUS COMPREHENSIVE REFORM

One conclusion to be drawn from our review is that much more formal analysis—and political support, we might add—is required to move away from a regime of control than is required to move toward more complete control. We believe this perspective ought to be important to government decision makers so that they may understand why it often appears easier to achieve reform through a comprehensive change in institutional arrrangements, for example, through deregulation or by radically reducing the number of controls in use. It should be stressed that this conclusion does not assume that legislators are interested in economic efficiency. It observes merely that government decision makers frequently behave as if economic efficiency were an important objective. Given this be-havior, and regardless of their motivation, analysis in some cases may make them better off by expanding their ranges of choice to include alternatives that produce higher payoffs than those that would otherwise be chosen.

However, we make a stronger claim: Government decision makers can and sometimes do pursue economic efficiency. This claim explicitly challenges Peltzman's general theory of regulation as well as other explanations of policy outcomes that rely on inter-est group theory. At a minimum we would insist that many of those who have expounded on the politics of regulatory reform have re-lied far too uncritically on interest group theory and too little on political experience. Certainly, interest groups play an undeniable role in policy formulation and implementation.[50] But it is simply wrong to assume that interest group politics is the only politics. In many cases, it is not even the dominant politics.

Indeed, it is incredible that anyone would seriously question this assertion given the successes of recent reforms described in this volume. The facts are quite straightforward. Total or substantial deregulation has occurred in such areas as air freight, passenger air travel, securities brokers' commissions, fair trade legislation, broadcasting and cable television, oil and natural gas pricing and allocation, and trucking. Weighed against the overall scope and domain of government regulation of economic activity in the United States, these reforms are, perhaps, not very significant. But weighed against the predictions of the interest group theory of regulation, they are very surprising.[51]

In drawing attention to these "surprises," it is not our intention to discredit interest group theory. We merely wish to indicate that it has definite limits. Clearly, interest group theory is a powerful tool of political analysis. It is powerful precisely because the everyday politics of Congress is interest group politics. Indeed, the general utility of the interest group theory of congressional politics is so palpable that students of the legislative process seldom ask why it is that legislators are so responsive to the demands of exclusive interests.

CONGRESSIONAL VERSUS PRESIDENTIAL POLITICS

On reflection, it is clear to us that the responsiveness of legislators to interest group demands is somewhat problematic. Interest group theorists generally begin with the assumption that legislators are vote maximizers (that is, they behave as if the first rule of politics were to get elected and the second to be reelected). Interest group politics, however, is a selective process. Perhaps 90 percent of the electorate is outside the interest group system. It should be stressed that interest groups are concerned with issues and policies. Yet most voters pay no attention to, have no knowledge of, and are unaware of the consequences of particular policies.[52] Consequently, at the macro level, national elections—congressional and presidential—appear to be little more than referenda on the management of the economy. The inference one might draw from this is that the self-interested legislator ought to be concerned with the effective management of the economy in general and efficient performance of government in particular.

That American legislators are quite tolerant of inefficiency in government, on the one hand, and highly responsive to interest group demands, on the other, is largely explained by the system of geographic representation.[53] Furthermore, the consequences of geographic representation are reflected in and reinforced by the internal organization and decision-making rules of Congress.

Geographic representation results in an orientation toward the specific interests of constituents. Because activities on behalf of efficiency generally produce benefits that are widely diffused, the direct payoff to the individual legislator from such activities tends to be small. That is, the individual legislator cannot hope to get credit for influencing the welfare of his or her constituents in any significant way by improving the performance of government and the economy in general. What she or he can do is secure benefits for identifiable groups of constituents, reward supporters, and trade favors with lobbyists. Not surprisingly, that is, for the most part, what is done by rational legislators. Indeed, inefficiency in government offers the enterprising legislator extensive opportunities to provide highly valued services to influential constituents, by cutting through red tape or obtaining relief from niggling, arbitrary rules or regulations.[54]

In addition, certain characteristics of the American legislative process reinforce the legislators' propensity to respond to interest group demands. First, party discipline is weak. Second, legislative decision making is highly decentralized. The everyday business of Congress takes place in committee, where logrolling and vote trading are highly visible. This means that the individual legislator can take personal credit for grants made to identifiable groups by his or her committee or subcommittee(s). At the same time, it is equally difficult for legislators to avoid individual responsibility for denying grants to special interests. Specialization in Congress, therefore, tends to promote special interest legislation. Third, with some obvious exceptions, ideological commitments are either weak or widely shared by members of Congress. This means that most issues are viewed as negotiable.

Hence, the granting of favors to special interests in exchange for political support is a characteristic of much legislation. It seems to us, however, that the value of the favors conferred by regulation is often unusually high. If so, this may be attributable to the haste with which so much of the regulatory legislation was enacted—a particular characteristic of the new social regulation. It may also be due to the fact that, where grants are provided to special interests through regulation, Congress cannot easily or gracefully withdraw them simply by not appropriating funds to support everything promised in the authorizing legislation.

In any case, congressional politics is usually interest group politics, and interest group politics is usually inimical to economic efficiency. The Ford/Carter administration's efforts on behalf of deregulation and regulatory reform, however, should remind us that the president and the bureaucracy may act on behalf of the unorganizable many. Furthermore, if the president leads, Congress may follow. Indeed, when the president is heading in the right direction, it is nearly always in the interest of a majority of Congress to follow. Of course, Congress must be persuaded that the president is, in fact, going in the right direction.[55]

Our point is that presidential politics is party politics. Ultimately, the perceived performance of government is what party politics is all about. To the extent that the president is interested in reelection and in the success of his party, he ought to be interested in promoting allocative efficiency. As Elmer Schattschneider observed some time ago, interest group politics serves us well only when it is subordinated to and disciplined by the broader politics of party. It is not and ought not to be treated as if it were the only, or even the most important, politics. Unfortunately, this point is frequently lost on those who are caught up in the day-to-day (interest group) politics of "business as usual."

The observation that the president has an interest in promoting efficiency or that executive leadership may overcome interest group politics does not, however, explain why it is that the Ford and Carter administrations promoted deregulation so zealously. Nor does it explain why they were in several instances ultimately successful. And these questions must be answered before we can say whether or not the recent experience with deregulation is germane to the question of the political feasibility of further substantive reform.

EXPLAINING DEREGULATION

It appears to us that the necessary and sufficient conditions for the success of the Ford and, particularly, the Carter administrations' reform efforts include four factors exogenous to the political process and two endogenous to it. The four exogenous factors were the condition of the economy, technological change, the resurgence of promarket ideas, and compelling evidence that regulatory reform is in the public interest.[56]

1. Condition of the Economy: The dominant, intractable economic problem of recent years has been "stagflation"—inflation combined with slow growth. Regrettably, economists do not agree on how best to fight inflation; indeed, their recommendations are frequently in direct conflict. Yet the problem is so salient that government is compelled to take some action or at least be seen to be taking some action. And even if all economists are not persuaded that regulatory reform will reduce inflation, they generally agree that it will make most people better off. Hence, the American

government has chosen to fight inflation by fighting regulation. As Alfred Kahn observes:

> It was obviously not a coincidence that the deregulations of the last few years reversed legislation passed in 1933, 1934, 1935, and 1938—the Banking, Communications, Motor Carrier and Civil Aviation Acts. Both the governing statutes and the regulatory philosophy shaping these industries, more or less consistently, for the following forty-five years were forged during, and by, the Great Depression. Nor was it a mere coincidence that these deregulations were effected in an era of stagflation.[57]

Kahn's point is that, as a result of stagflation, we have rediscovered the economics of scarcity. In turn, this has promoted "the application of more rigorous tests and more efficient techniques to regulatory interventions, as well as subjecting regulations that suppress competition to much more careful scrutiny."[58]

2. Technological Change: The second exogenous factor that must be considered if we are to understand the changing climate for regulatory reform is the role of technology. Of course, as we have noted, the first response to technological change is to try to contain it by extending the scope and coverage of existing regulation. But, as we have also noted, technological change may not be contained indefinitely without subjecting a substantial proportion of the economy to direct government control.

The power of technology to erode regulatory boundaries is, perhaps, illustrated best by the communications industry, where it has rendered obsolete the distinctions drawn by legislators between written and voice communications, cable and satellite, video and telephone, data processing and communicators.

3. The Power of Ideas: The third exogenous factor is a change in the American conception of what constitutes "good public policy." Obviously, in Kahn's view, the condition of the economy and governing economic philosophies interact very closely. Yet the recent rediscovery of the virtues of the market certainly deserves special mention. Were not a good many American decision makers predisposed toward competitive market mechanisms, recognition of the drawbacks and problems associated with regulation of business might not have resulted in deregulation. Instead, government decision makers might have decided that outright public ownership was the best alternative to present regulations. Indeed, the argument that public ownership is the only system in which the incompatibility between profit and public values is resolved is not unheard in the United States. It simply isn't taken seriously.[59]

4. Compelling Evidence that Regulatory Reform Is in the Public Interest: Where deregulation is proposed, three kinds of information appear to be critical to its serious consideration. First, evidence is needed that competition would result in more satisfactory outcomes than would comprehensive regulation. Second, evidence must indicate that the costs of transition to a competitive regime would not effect gains realized by the move. For example, regulation frequently leads to excessive centralization, service standardization, and adoption of large-scale production technologies. If such facilities could not be adapted to respond to competitive market forces, the transition to competition could entail considerable cost. Third, evidence must show that adverse distributional outcomes would not occur. Of course, the definition of "adverse" is fraught with technical and political difficulties.

The story of airline deregulation illustrates the importance of hard evidence and shows how it can be used.[60] First, advocates of reform were able, on the basis of a substantial body of empirical research,[61] to demonstrate the adverse effects of regulation and to characterize the consequences of deregulation in such a way as to strengthen the political coalition in its favor. Supporters of airline deregulation, for example, repeatedly explained that price and entry regulation in the domestic airline industry had raised prices paid by consumers well above what they would have been had price and entry been determined by the market and, as Stephen Breyer has observed, "lower prices" are far more arresting than "more efficient use of aircraft."[62] Furthermore, this explanation was supported by highly plausible evidence. According to James Q. Wilson:

> If there was a single fact that was of crucial significance in making persuasive the argument that price and entry regulation had adverse effects on consumers, it was the comparison of rates charged by unregulated airlines (for example, those linking San Francisco and Los Angeles) with those charged by regulated interstate airlines (for example, those connecting Boston and Washington, D.C.). Even so it was necessary to look carefully for other factors besides regulation that might have affected prices (there were some, but they were not decisive).[63]

The apparent value of this further research should be stressed. It was needed (1) to explain both the original justification for regulating the industry and the objective it came to serve; (2) to understand the position of the major actors associated with industry and the effects deregulation would have on their positions, that is, to identify winners and losers; and (3) because "the detailed investigation [was] itself necessary to convince others that the proponents of reform [were] serious, thorough, and [had] made their case."[64]

As for the second and third points, the literature on the air travel industry reassured decision makers about such issues as destructive competition and consequent income redistribution. In retrospect, it may have overassured them. Still, before passage of the decontrol act, it was not sufficient for economists to show that there was nothing for competition to destroy, that the planes would still be there as would the trained personnel, and so on. It was necessary to show that deregulation would not result in destructive, destabilizing competition. The example of the intrastate markets in California and Texas also served to demonstrate this point. It was also necessary for the advocates of reform to show how to get from "there to here." It was not enough to show that regulation was inefficient. Proponents of deregulation had to develop a plan that appeared "practical and fair to allow a transition from the regulated regime to the new system."[65]

As to the distributional consequences of deregulation, it was demonstrated that there would be many winners but few losers. Most customers would benefit from lower prices, very few communities would lose service, and, overall, the airlines industry would benefit. This last conclusion was based on the observation that price and entry controls had not ended competition. They merely redirected it onto cost-increasing service rivalry. The results were high prices, high costs, and low profits for most carriers.

Several additional points should be made with regard to the costs of transition to a competitive state in general to follow up the observations noted on transition in the airline industry. In some industries it is possible that these costs might be quite high, and that significant adjustments in industry production capacity or industry structure might occur. As Paul Sommers has observed, citing the case of surface freight transport:

> The economic literature on surface freight transportation has devoted itself just to calculation of the costs of moving freight—by either truck or rail. . . . The weight of the (most recent) work suggests welfare costs attributable to intermodal misallocation on the order of $200-300 million per year. None of these studies attempted to calculate the costs of transition to preferred regime. Excess capacity would probably be created in one industry and different capacity in the other. Disposing of one set of capital goods and investing in another may result in social costs that would tend to offset the benefits of reorganization.[66]

The deregulation of industries with a small number of producers that are characterized by limited competition—such as the postal service, the telecommunications, or the broadcast industry— would likely involve substantially higher transition costs. Paradoxically, it appears that the transitional costs of deregulation are, in many cases, inversely proportional to the validity of the arguments for regulation. The greater the regulatory effort and the further the structure of the industry has been shifted from the competitive optimum, the more costly the transition.

More significantly, we would note that to a considerable degree, the kind of hard, credible evidence available for use by the advocates of airline deregulation, for example, is not now available to advocates of other comprehensive substantive reforms. To cite examples of effective alternatives to existing regulatory regimes, the proponent of incentive mechanisms, for example, must draw on evidence from outside the United States—from Great Britain or Scandinavia, as critics of the Food and Drug Administration do; from Canada, as supporters of accident taxes can; or from Europe, as supporters of effluent fees must. Unfortunately, these examples are, by the very fact of their "foreignness," unfamiliar and suspect to Americans. Finally, supporters of alternatives to current methods of regulation are not now able to put forward detailed, practical implementation plans. Faced with the costs of change and uncertain benefits, most people, including legislators, prefer to stay with "the devil they know."

These exogenous factors may promote a predisposition to regulatory reform. They do not guarantee it, however. Otherwise the successes of Ford and Carter administrations should have far outweighed their failures in this area. They didn't.[67] Recognition that they had both successes and failures leads us to ask what factors account for these different outcomes. Here two factors endogenous to the political process appear to be particularly significant: presidential leadership and the attention of Congress.

1. Presidential Leadership: Someone must initiate the process of regulatory reform, and it is likely that Congress can't or won't.[68] On the other hand, we have also claimed that the president has an interest in promoting economic efficiency (and good macroeconomic performance) in general. Under appropriate circumstances, that interest implies a particular interest in regulatory reform.

It is not sufficient, however, for the president to announce that he is in favor of regulatory reform, to order the bureaucracy to regulate better, or to shrink in size. Nor is it enough to "twist a few arms" (or "reason together") on behalf of regulatory reform legislation. Effective leadership must ultimately be aimed at the lawmakers in Congress. The president must adopt a plan of attack, including a list of targets and their priority, and a strategy of persuasion. So far as the Carter administration was successful, its success reflects a sequential attack on a limited number of targets, for example, airline deregulation and then trucking. Its failures, to a degree at least, reflect a failure to concentrate the resources of the presidency on a limited number of high-priority issues or to maintain a consistent definition of what it wanted done.[69]

One of the main lessons to be learned from the Carter administration is that appointments to regulatory bodies matter a great deal. If the president appoints advocates of special interests—business, labor, consumers, the environment—to senior policymaking positions in regulatory agencies, the agency in question will protect those interests. Economists, on the other hand, tend to be advocates of efficiency. Consequently, where the president wants allocative efficiency, he should probably appoint economists with prior records as advocates of efficiency—they are the "shock troops" with which to fight the battles of deregulation.[70]

A close scrutiny of the role played by Alfred Kahn and Elizabeth Bailey in achieving airline deregulation, or by Darius Gaskins in promoting greater competition in the surface freight industry, leads us to conclude that their major accomplishments lay in goading Congress to take legislative action. Given the right individuals, the right organizational roles, and, to be sure, the right external circumstances, experience suggests that economists can seek the attention of Congress and make the case for regulatory reform successfully. On the other hand, the Carter administration's failures are at least partially explicable by the absence of economists from key policymaking roles within the social regulatory agencies. It appears that if they are not in a position to influence regulatory policy from within, economists are unlikely to be effective lobbyists for efficiency.

2. <u>Getting the Attention of Congress</u>: The successful reform efforts of the Carter administration captured the attention of Congress. The unsuccessful ones did not. In both airline and trucking deregulation, a substantial number of legislators and particularly legislative leaders became interested enough in understanding the issue to pay attention to the arguments made on both sides.

In contrast, we would observe that most substantive reform proposals have not attracted the attention of the press or of Congress. It is probably true that increased efficiency, and regulation in general, are not in the abstract very arresting issues. Perhaps proponents of incentive mechanisms in such areas as health and safety regulation ought to pay more attention to characterizing the consequences of reform in attention-grabbing terms, such as saving the American auto industry. More important, we think, is the fact that, unlike Kahn or Gaskins, policymakers in other regulatory agencies have not, so far, sought by their actions to direct the attention of Congress to issues of substantive reform.

Consequently, where regulatory issues have been attended to by only a handful of committee members and their staffers (for example, the 1977 Clean Air Act Amendments), it is hardly surprising that legislative outcomes were dominated by "business as usual"—interest group politics. This meant that substantive reform was very unlikely. And the results were as expected (that is, special interest legislation favoring the eastern producers of dirty coal).

CONCLUSION

We conclude that comprehensive and substantive reform is likely to be more productive than the marginal adjustment approach in meeting the goal of government, industry, and society to improve the efficiency and reduce the cost of regulation.

The crux of our argument lies in the belief that unless we take nonincremental steps to reform economic regulation, we will never allow ourselves to discover better solutions to economic problems through trial and error and how to design new and less costly policies and implementation procedures. This is true also because the alternative to comprehensive reform is likely to be marginal changes in regulatory policy that lead to greater rather than less control. We wish this were not the case, but the lessons of many previous attempts to achieve reform are evident.

In review of industry-specific regulation and the deregulation of the natural gas and airline industries we have analyzed the basis for opposing macro-policy arguments on the manner in which changes in regulatory policy are achieved. This examination has led to the conclusion that although interest group theories of regulation are applicable to a point, a foundation for reform may be found through improved analysis, the development and use of better information on the outcomes and costs of regulation, and implementation of better procedures to evaluate regulation. However, we acknowledge that it is one thing to want improved analysis and a second to know how to do it.

In Chapter 6 we explore the options for procedural reform, and in Chapter 7, we return to the theme introduced in this chapter in order to demonstrate how we may obtain more and better analysis.

NOTES

1. Fred Thompson and L. R. Jones, "Fighting Regulation: The Regulatory Review," California Management Review 23, no. 2 (Winter 1980):5-19.

2. Sam Peltzman, "Toward a More General Theory of Regulation," Journal of Law and Economics 19, no. 2 (August 1976): 212-45.

3. Ibid., p. 212.

4. Ibid.

5. It should be stressed that even as a positive theory this view is, to say the least, incomplete. In the first place it tends to overlook the fact that the politics of pressure groups occur in the context of a broader system of party politics. Consequently, theorists tend to exaggerate the importance of positions and issues, what political scientists call positional or issue variables (because interest groups bring information on positional variables to the attention of political leaders and because human understanding tends to be biased by the availability of information, it seems likely that political leaders do too) and to ignore performance, or what political scientists call valence, variables. See below.

6. Gary Becker, "Comment," Journal of Law and Economics 19, no. 2 (August 1976):247. Also see Kenneth A. Shepsle, The Role of Institution and Structure in the Creation of the Policy Equilibrium, Working Paper No. 35 (St. Louis: Center for the Study of American Business, Washington University, September 1978).

7. In practice, of course, the distinction between these two kinds of controls is frequently blurred. Price controls are often employed to moderate or influence the consequences of supply controls. Barriers to entry are frequently erected to preserve publicly mandated price schedules. Nevertheless, the distinction remains a useful one, as it helps understand the what, the which, and the why of industry-specific regulation.

8. The logic here generally follows the argument advanced by Roger G. Noll, "The Consequences of Public Utility Regulation of Hospitals," in Controls of Health Care (Washington, D.C.: National Academy of Science, 1975).

9. Paul M. MacAvoy, The Regulated Industries and the Economy (New York: Norton, 1981); G. Kolko, Railroads and Regulation (Princeton, N.J.: Princeton University Press, 1965).

10. George J. Stigler, "The Theory of Economic Regulation," Bell Journal of Economics and Management Science 2, no. 1 (Spring 1971):3-20; Peltzman, op. cit.; see also Richard A. Posner, "The Social Costs of Monopoly and Regulation," Journal of Political Economy 84, no. 3 (August 1975):807-27.

11. Note, however, that under Peltzman's formulation, absolutely "pure producer protection" is only possible if marginal consumer opposition to higher prices is nil.

12. Two hypotheses have been proposed to account for such an outcome. Wilson suggests that it is more costly to organize larger groups and that this cost may be reflected in slower reactions to changes in the environment. Consequently, a consumer group might continue to support price controls for some time after the adoption of such a policy ceased to be advantageous to the members. This hypothesis seems to fit the facts in a number of instances, with the implementation of price controls occurring during a recession following a period of increasing demand for the product in question. However, the association of new regulation with industries where demand was growing rapidly (electricity and telephones in the early twentieth century, airlines in the 1930s, natural gas in the 1950s) has been common enough to reject the conclusion that this is the normal etiology of regulation; see James Q. Wilson, "The Politics of Regulation," in Social Responsibility and the Business Predicament, ed. James W. McKie (Washington, D.C.: Brookings Institution, 1974), pp. 135-68. More recently, Bruce Owen and Ronald Braeutigam, The Regulation Game (Cambridge, Mass.: Ballinger, 1978), have proposed that both producers and consumers are risk-averse and will cooperate to shelter one another from the unfortunate effects of rapid and unpredictable changes in an industry's environment or productive technology. They base their argument upon a set of case studies that show that regulation consistently favors the status quo. From this they conclude that voters prefer to minimize the risk of the market at some cost in terms of efficiency, viewing a process that gives some individuals and firms "legal rights to the status quo" as "fairer" than market determined outcomes (ibid., p. 28). However, while one might conclude that the political system is biased in favor of protecting the status quo, this does not mean that voters are risk-averse. As Elmer E. Schattschneider has explained (The Semi Sovereign People: A Realist's View of Democracy in America [Hinsdale, Ill.: Dryden, 1971]), only those who are losers in the marketplace are likely to turn to the political system for redress. Investment in restricting market forces must, therefore, necessarily promote the status quo. What all this proves is that sometimes losers in the marketplace have more political influence than winners or potential winners. Furthermore, it seems no more reasonable on a priori grounds to assert a generalized public interest in uncertainty reduction than it is to assert a generalized public interest in the goal of allocative efficiency.

13. This perspective joins two streams of economic thought: the benign view of the welfare consequences of monopolistic compe-

tition, propounded by economists at the University of Chicago and their colleagues, and the presupposition that cost schedules will be affected by a shift from uniform to discriminatory pricing urged by the advocates of the use of linear programming in economic analysis. The alternative perspective holds that, in the absence of regulation, entry will be excessive and all surpluses dissipated. The consumer surplus will be converted to profit and all supranormal profits dissipated by entry. Neither perspective implies that industries now subject to price regulation are somehow unique. But the first may be interpreted to mean that no industry should be subject to price and entry controls, while the second implies that most industries should be.

14. Peltzman, op. cit., p. 218.

15. David Braybrooke and Charles Lindblom, A Strategy of Decision (New York: Free Press, 1963), especially Chap. 5.

16. Henry J. Aaron, Politics and the Professors (Washington, D.C.: Brookings Institution, 1978), p. 162.

17. Robert M. Ball, "Background of Regulation in Health Care," in Controls on Health Care (Washington, D.C.: National Academy of Science, 1975), p. 7.

18. Charles F. Hermann, ed., International Crisis: Insights from Behavioral Research (New York: Free Press, 1972), p. 13.

19. Pradip N. Khandwalla, "Crisis Responses of Competing Versus Noncompeting Organizations," in Studies on Crisis Management, ed. W. T. Stanbury and C. F. Smart (Montreal: Institute for Research on Public Policy, 1978), pp. 147-74.

20. D. J. Hartle, Public Policy Decision Making and Regulation (Montreal: Institute for Research on Public Policy, 1979), p. 75.

21. Comments, Roger Noll, in Unsettled Questions on Regulatory Reform, ed. P. W. MacAvoy (Washington, D.C.: American Enterprise Institute, 1978), pp. 9-10. See, for example, C. T. Stigler and C. Friedland, "What Can Regulators Regulate? The Case of Electricity," Journal of Law and Economics 5 (1962):1-16; P. W. McAvoy, "The Effectiveness of the Federal Power Commission," Bell Journal of Economics and Management Science 1 (Autumn 1970):271-303; T. G. Moore, "The Effectiveness of Regulation of Electric Utility Rates," Southern Economic Journal 36, no. 4 (April 1970):365-75; M. E. Levine, "Is Regulation Necessary? California Air Transportation and National Policy," Yale Law Review 74 (1965):1416-47; P. W. MacAvoy and R. G. Noll, "Relative Prices on Regulated Transactions of the Natural Gas Pipelines," Bell Journal of Economics and Management Science 4 (Autumn 1973):114-57; P. W. MacAvoy, "The Regulation Induced Shortage of Natural Gas," Journal of Law and Economics 14 (April 1971):167-99;

Joel F. Brenner and H. M. Franklin, Rent Control of North American and Four European Countries (Washington, D.C.: Council for International Urban Liaison/Potomac Institute, 1977).

22. W. J. Baumol, E. Bailey, and R. D. Willig, "Weak Invisible Hand Theorems on the Sustainability of the Multiproduct Natural Monopoly," American Economic Review 67, no. 3 (June 1977):350-65. See also J. C. Panzer and R. D. Willig, "Free Entry and Sustainability of Natural Monopoly," Bell Journal of Economics 8 (Spring 1977):1-22; and R. D. Willig, "Multi-product Technology and Market Structure," American Economic Review 69, no. 2 (1979):345-51.

23. Avinash K. Dixit and Joseph E. Stiglitz, "Monopolistic Competition and Optimum Product Diversity," American Economic Review 67, no. 3 (June 1977):297-308.

24. J. R. T. Hughes, The Government Habit (New York: Basic Books, 1977), pp. 116-18.

25. Ibid., p. 118.

26. Alfred E. Kahn, "Economic Issues in Regulating the Field Price of Natural Gas," American Economic Review: Papers and Proceedings 70 (May 1960):506-17. However, see also O. S. Goldsmith, "Regulation of a Nonrenewable Resource: The Case of Natural Gas," Ph.D. dissertation, University of Wisconsin, 1976, University Microfilms Order No. 77-8786.

27. MacAvoy, "Regulation Induced Shortage of Natural Gas," op. cit. See also P. W. MacAvoy and R. R. Pindyck, "Alternative Regulatory Policies for Dealing with the Natural Gas Shortage," Bell Journal of Economics and Management Science 4 (Autumn 1973):454-98.

28. Curtailment Strategies Technical Advisory Committee, Federal Power Commission, "Natural Gas Survey Curtailment Strategies," NTIS, PC A19/MF ADI (March 1978); L. E. Buck, ed., Energy User's Law (Washington, D.C.: Government Institutes, 1977).

29. Natural Gas Pricing Proposals of President Carter's Energy Program (Part D of S.1469). Hearings before the Committee on Energy and Natural Resources, U.S. Senate, 95th Congress, 1st Session on S.256, a Bill to Regulate Commerce to Assure Increased Supplies of Natural Gas at Reasonable Prices for Consumers, and for Other Purposes (Washington, D.C., 1977); Behind-the-Pipe Natural Gas Reserves, Hearings before the Committee on Interstate and Foreign Commerce, U.S. House of Representatives, 95th Congress, 1st Session on allegations of withholding of Behind-the-Pipe Natural Gas Reserves (Washington, D.C., September 1977); Congressional Budget Office, Energy Policy Alternatives (Washington, D.C., January 1977); R. Lemon, "Critique of

Analyses of Natural Gas Pricing Alternatives," Energy Topics (April 10, 1978):1-6.

30. See S. Breyer and P. W. MacAvoy, Energy Regulation by the Federal Power Commission (Washington, D.C.: Brookings Institution, 1974); and P. W. MacAvoy, ed., Federal Energy Administration Regulation: Report of the Presidential Task Force (Washington, D.C.: American Enterprise Institute, 1977).

31. C. J. Cicchetti, "End User Pricing of Natural Gas," Public Utilities Fortnightly 101, no. 6 (March 16, 1978):11-15.

32. "How Large Gas Users Cope with Curtailment," Energy Users News, March 27, 1978.

33. T. E. Browne et al., Supply 77: EPRI Annual Energy Supply Forecasts (Palo Alto, Calif.: Electric Power Research Institute, May 1978).

34. W. J. Mead, "The Natural Gas Policy Act of 1978: An Economic Evaluation," in Contemporary Economic Problems 1979, ed. W. Fellner (Washington, D.C.: American Enterprise Institute, 1979), pp. 325-55. See also Alexander Stuart, "A Bad Start on Gas Deregulation," Fortune, February 12, 1979, pp. 86-91.

35. For another analysis of the costs and perils of gradualism in natural gas deregulation, see Peter R. Merrill, "The Regulation and Deregulation of Natural Gas in the U.S., 1938-1985," Harvard Energy and Environment Policy Center Discussion Paper, January 1981.

36. R. E. Caves, Air Transport and Its Regulators (Cambridge, Mass.: Harvard University Press, 1962); G. Douglas and J. C. Miller III, Economic Regulation of the Domestic Airline Industry (Washington, D.C.: Brookings Institution, 1974); G. Eads, "Competition in the Domestic Trunk Airline Industry: Too Much or Too Little," in Promoting Competitions in Regulated Markets, ed. A. Phillips (Washington, D.C.: Brookings Institution, 1975), pp. 13-54; and T. E. Keeler, "Domestic Trunk Airline Regulation: An Economic Evaluation," Report for U.S. Senate, Government Operations Committee, University of California, Berkeley, February 17, 1977. An expanded version is published by the Ribicoff Committee, op. cit., Appendix to Volume VI, Framework for Regulation, pp. 75-160.

37. The Transition to a Less Regulated Environment, 5 vol., prepared by Simot, Hillison, and Ecchner, Inc., Washington, D.C., for Office of the Assistant Secretary for Policy Plans, and International Affairs (DOT) (Washington, D.C., January 1977).

38. Controller General of the United States, Lower Airline Costs Are Possible in the United States and Could Result in Lower Fares (Washington, D.C.: GAO, CED, 77-34, June 3, 1977).

39. Civil Aeronautics Board, Special Staff, Regulatory Reform (Washington, D.C., July 1975).

40. The key study here is W. A. Jordan, Airline Regulation in America: Effects and Imperfections (Baltimore: Johns Hopkins Press, 1970), pp. 13-44.

41. See U.S. Congress, Senate, Subcommittee on Aviation of the Committee on Commerce, Science and Transportation, Hearings on S.292 and S.689, 95th Congress, 1st Session, 1977, 3 parts; and U.S. Congress, Senate, Subcommittee on Administrative Practice and Procedure, Oversight of Civil Aeronautics Board: Practices and Procedures, 94th Congress, 1st Session, 1975, 6 vol. Of the major trunk carriers, United and Pan Am were early supporters of deregulation.

42. Air Transportation Regulatory Reform (Washington, D.C.: American Enterprise Institute, March 1, 1978), pp. 18-19. See also Jordan, op. cit.

43. Paul Weaver, "Unlocking the Gilded Cage of Regulation," Fortune, February 1977, pp. 186-87.

44. Civil Aeronautics Board, Chicago Midway Expanded Service Proceedings, July 12, 1978; Domestic Passenger Fare Level/Structure Policies, September 5, 1978.

45. Alfred Kahn, "Applying Economics to an Imperfect World," Regulation 3 (January/February 1979):23.

46. Civil Aeronautics Board, staff interviews, August 1978. In short, the CAB had deregulated prior to October 28, 1978, but there was a threat of reregulation. The Airline Deregulation Act consolidated these changes, but at the same time the House of Representatives tagged on what could turn out to be expensive adjustment costs. These include direct subsidies to small communities and compensation payments to airline personnel who can be shown to have been laid off because of deregulation. It is also important to note that the deregulation measures related to the carriers. Yet the air transport industry also involves the airport sector and its services. The incumbent carriers often have considerable influence on the operation of the airports, and it is possible that they could use this influence to block the entry of new carriers. In San Francisco and San Diego, for example, incumbent carriers have pressed for the reduction of airport traffic as a means of reducing noise levels. The form of this reduction was interesting, for it in effect blocked new carriers from using the airports. See A. P. Ellison, "Deregulation: The U.S. Airline Experience" (Ottawa: Economic Council of Canada, Regulation Reference, January 1980).

47. Kahn (1979), op. cit., p. 21.

48. Ibid., pp. 22-23.

49. Ibid., p. 27. Despite the claims of Kahn that he speeded up deregulation, it would appear that lower international fares on the North Atlantic acted to accelerate the deregulation of domestic fares. Kahn's strategy may not have been as well planned as implied in this paper. See Ellison, op. cit.

50. See among others David Truman, The Government Process (New York: Knopf, 1951); V. O. Key, Political Parties and Pressure Groups, 5th ed. (New York: Crowell, 1965). More recent works on interest groups and lobbying include Terry M. Moe, The Organization of Interests (Chicago: University of Chicago Press, 1980); Richard Wagner, "Pressure Groups and Political Entrepreneurs: A Review Article," Papers on Non-Market Decision Making 1 (1969):151-70; and Norman Frohlich, Joe A. Oppenheimer, and Oren R. Young, Political Leadership and Collective Goods (Princeton, N.J.: Princeton University Press, 1971).

51. This point is made with great clarity by Barry Weingast, "Regulation, Reregulation, and Deregulation: The Political Foundations of Agency Clientele Relationships," Law and Contemporary Problems 44 (Winter 1981):147-77; and Michael E. Levine, "Revisionism Revised? Airline Deregulation and the Public Interest," Law and Contemporary Problems 44 (Winter 1981):179-95. One might also argue that efforts to deregulate natural gas failed, despite the fact that distributional consequences of deregulation would have tended to favor the few, while the costs would have been borne by the many. This outcome may also be interpreted as contrary to the predictions of what we have called the interest group model of politics. Examples, consistent with interest group politics, are provided by Levine, op. cit., p. 179. See also Bruce Ackerman and William Hassler, Clean Coal/Dirty Air (New Haven, Conn.: Yale University Press, 1981).

52. See Schattschneider, op. cit., p. 35, who states, "The flaw in the pluralist heaven is that the heavenly chorus sings with a strong upper class accent. Probably about 90 per cent of the people cannot get into the pressure system." Our point is that interest groups are concerned with issues and policies. Most voters pay no attention to, have no knowledge of, and are unaware of the consequences of most policies. Voting is largely retrospective, not prospective and performance or valence oriented. At the macro level, national elections—presidential and congressional—appear to be little more than referenda on the management of the economy.

53. See, for example, R. Douglas Arnold, "The Local Roots of Domestic Policy," in The New Congress, ed. Thomas B. Mann and Norman J. Ornstein (Washington, D.C.: American Enterprise Institute, 1981), pp. 250-87. See also Weingast, "Regulation, Reregulation, and Deregulation," op. cit.

54. Morris P. Fiorina, Congress: Keystone of the Washington Establishment (New Haven, Conn.: Yale University Press, 1977).

55. This argument was first advanced by Gerald Kramer, "Short Term Voting Fluctuations in U.S. Voting Behavior, 1898-1964," American Political Science Review 65 (1971):131-43. Kramer argued that: "If the performance of the incumbent party is 'satisfactory' according to some simple standard, the voter votes to retain the incumbent party in office to enable it to continue its present policies; while if the incumbent's performance is not 'satisfactory,' the voter votes against the incumbent" (p. 134). In other words, Kramer claims that elections are referenda on the economic performance of the governing party, and that voter expectations about future performance are positively correlated with recent performance. William Niskanen ("Economic and Fiscal Effects on the Popular Vote for the President," in Public Policy and Public Choice, ed. D. W. Rae and T. J. Eismeier [Los Angeles: Russell Sage, 1979], pp. 93-120) has provided a more rigorous formulation of the incumbency hypothesis in which voting is characterized as utility-maximizing behavior under binary-choice conditions.

These and other studies (see S. J. Lepper, "Voting Behavior and Aggregate Policy Targets," Public Choice 18 [Summer 1974]: 67-81; and Edward Tufte, "The Determinants of the Outcomes of Midterm Congressional Elections," American Political Science Review 69 [June 1975]:812-26) consistently show that the most powerful predictor of electoral success is the change in real per capita net national income. These results are not now seriously questioned.

However, the interpretation of these results is still being debated. For example, George Stiger ("General Economic Conditions and National Elections," American Economic Review 63 [May 1975]: 160-67) rejects the macroeconomic explanation of political behavior, and asserts that "the economic basis for political affiliation must be sought in the area of income redistribution" (p. 167). However, he has not presented empirical support for this assertion. Furthermore, Niskanen tested Stiger's proposition and found no evidence of a distributional effect on the popular vote for the president. Indeed, Niskanen suggests that standard cost-benefit analysis ought to be a sufficient guide for most decisions made by a president seeking reelection and that it should be "sufficient to explain most decisions of the Presidency, except when other groups, such as Congress, on which the President is dependent, are concerned about [distributional] effects" (p. 110).

Moreover, incumbents are evidently aware of the relationship between economic conditions and electoral outcomes and act accordingly, albeit sometimes in a wrong-headed manner. See William

Nordhaus, "The Political Business Cycle," Review of Economic Studies 42 (1975):160-90.

56. This discussion and the following two pages draw freely from Alfred Kahn, "The Political Feasibility of Regulatory Reform: Lessons from Economic Deregulation," in Reforming the New Social Regulation, ed. Leroy Graymer and Fred Thompson (Los Angeles: Russell Sage, 1982).

57. Ibid.

58. Ibid.

59. Contrast Alan Stone, Economic Regulation and the Public Interest: The Federal Trade Commission in Theory and Practice (Ithaca, N.Y.: Cornell University Press, 1977), with Robert Katzman, Regulatory Bureaucracy: The Federal Trade Commission and Antitrust Policy (Cambridge, Mass.: MIT Press, 1980).

60. A useful history of the process of reform can be found in Bradley Behrman, "Civil Aeronautics Board," in The Politics of Regulation, ed. James Q. Wilson (New York: Basic Books, 1980), pp. 91-120. See also A. P. Ellison, op. cit.; and Stephen G. Breyer, "The Genesis of Airline Deregulation: The Role of the Kennedy Hearings and Report," paper presented at the National Conference on Airline Regulation, Institute for Research on Public Policy and American Enterprise Institute, Ottawa, June 27, 1979. See also Stephen Breyer, "Analyzing Regulatory Failure: Mismatches, Less Restrictive Alternatives, and Reform," Harvard Law Review 92, no. 3 (1977):547-609; Alfred E. Kahn, "Applications of Economics to an Imperfect World," American Economic Review 69 (May 1979):1-13; and his speech to the New York Society of Security Analysts, Aviation Week and Space Technology, March 6, 1978, pp. 35-39, 39-42; Levine, op. cit.; Weingast, op. cit.; also Elizabeth E. Bailey, "Deregulation and Regulatory Reform of U.S.- Air-Transportation Policy," in Regulated Industries and Public Enterprise, ed. Bridger M. Mitchell and Paul R. Kleindorfer (Lexington, Mass.: Heath, 1980), pp. 29-56; Martha Derthick and Paul Quirk, "The Politics of Deregulation: A Preliminary Report," paper presented at the American Political Science Association meetings, September 4, 1981, New York; Anthony Brown, "The Politics of Civil Air Transportation Deregulation," paper presented at the American Political Science Association meeting, September 4, 1981, New York.

61. See, for example, Jordan, op. cit.; Levine, op. cit.; T. E. Keeler, "Airline Regulation and Market Performance," Bell Journal of Economics and Management Science 3 (Autumn 1972): 399-424; George Douglas and James E. Miller III, Economic Regulation of Domestic Air Transportation (Washington, D.C.: Brookings Institution, 1974).

62. Breyer, "The Genesis of Airline Deregulation," op. cit.

63. James Q. Wilson, "'Policy Intellectuals' and Public Policy," The Public Interest, Summer 1981, p. 41.

64. Breyer, "The Genesis of Airline Deregulation," op. cit., p. 4.

65. Ibid., p. 7. Potential "losers" (small cities who lost service and employees who lost their jobs) were provided with a "safety net" in the form of direct subsidy programs, although, to date the amounts expended have been far less than anticipated.

66. Paul Sommers, "The Economic Costs of Regulation: Report for the American Bar Association on Law and the Economy" (Yale University Department of Economics, November 18, 1977), p. 7.

67. Here we should note some of the failures of the regulatory reformers in the Carter administration. They range from the inability to place certain kinds of reforms on the presidential agenda—almost the full menu of proposals in the area of the new social regulation falls into this category—to embarrassment in Congress—deregulation of the wellhead price of natural gas and oil fall in this category. See Charles O. Jones, "Congress and the Presidency," in Mann and Ornstein, op. cit., p. 240.

68. This is not to say that individual Congress members have not introduced a large number of regulatory reform bills. Very, very few have been enacted. See, for example, Regulatory Reform: A Survey of Proposals in the 94th Congress (Washington, D.C.: American Enterprise Institute, 1976); Regulation and Regulatory Reform: A Survey of Proposals of the 95th Congress (Washington, D.C.: American Enterprise Institute, 1978); Government Regulation: Proposals for Procedural Reform (Washington, D.C.: American Enterprise Institute, 1979); Major Regulatory Initiatives During 1979 (Washington, D.C.: American Enterprise Institute, 1980); Major Regulatory Initiatives During 1980 (Washington, D.C.: American Enterprise Institute, 1981). See also the articles by Senator Ribicoff and Representative Brown in Regulation, May/June 1979, pp. 17-23.

69. See especially, Weingast, op. cit. See also Nelson W. Polsby, "Interest Groups and the Presidency: Trends in Political Intermediation in America," in American Politics and Public Policy, ed. W. D. Burnham and M. W. Weinberg (Cambridge, Mass.: MIT Press, 1978), pp. 41-52. Aaron Wildavsky and Jack Knott, "Jimmy Carter's Theory of Governing," in Burnham and Weinberg, op. cit., pp. 55-76, provide evidence for the conclusion that "Part of Carter's political theory, then, is to change everything at once. Comprehensive change enables one both to identify the public interest by considering the merits of opposing claims and to serve that

interest by making opponents fight on all fronts simultaneously,
thus diluting their forces while concentrating one's own. The bigger
the change, the greater the public attention and the more likely it
becomes that the public interest will prevail over private interests"
(p. 60). In the case of natural gas and deregulation, President
Carter apparently changed his mind as to what he wanted done.
See Malbin, op. cit.

     70. The outstanding examples are the appointments of Alfred
Kahn and Elizabeth Bailey to the CAB and Darius Gaskins to the
ICC. As Kelman explains, economists are effective in these situations, not because they are wiser or smarter than other people,
but because they have an intense, often irrational, commitment to
efficiency. See Steven Kelman, What Price Incentives (Boston:
Auburn House, 1981).

6

PROCEDURAL REFORM
ALTERNATIVES

What are the options for comprehensive reform of the process by which existing and proposed regulatory controls are evaluated? How may the process and procedures for review be altered to improve this evaluation? In this chapter we identify the major procedural reform options and attempt to weigh the merits of each against its liabilities. In order to understand the context for procedural reform, we also review the recent history of efforts made under three U.S. presidents to improve the evaluation of regulation, and the experience of a state government that has implemented a regulatory reform procedure worthy of note.

In an environment where many reform proposals are hotly debated as partisan political issues, it is necessary to define clearly what we mean by reform and to differentiate it from regulatory review. Regulatory reform is simply change in substantive regulatory policies and implementation measures, or change in the procedures employed to evaluate regulation and its effects. Substantive and procedural reform may be characterized relative to a magnitude of change criterion, that is, marginal or incremental adjustments to the status quo versus comprehensive change. Marginal adjustments to regulatory policy typically result in the imposition of new rules, although this isn't necessarily the case. Comprehensive change may result in either major additions or reductions in regulatory scope, coverage, and influence, for example, reduction through deregulation. Incremental substantive reform has been implemented in reducing U.S. government occupational health and safety rules and financial institution regulation; and comprehensive substantive reform may be observed in deregulation of the air travel industry and natural gas pricing. Marginal procedural reforms have been instituted under several recent presidential administrations, such as the institution of economic impact and benefit-cost analysis under Carter and Reagan. An example of comprehensive procedural reform discussed later in this chapter is the institution of a regulatory budget to consider the direct costs of government and the direct and indirect costs of regulatory compliance incurred in the private sector as costs to government.

Regulatory review may be defined as the process used to evaluate both the procedures and substance of regulatory policy. The purpose of this chapter is to identify and evaluate procedural reform options, that is, alternatives to the procedures presently employed to review regulation. In this task it is essential that we differentiate between procedures to review regulation and procedures to implement regulatory policy. Change in the former we term procedural reform, and alteration of the latter would constitute substantive reform.

The search for a satisfactory review process should be guided by a set of criteria that specify the manner in which review should be performed. Optimally, review would be manifest in a process that enables timely, systematic, and comprehensive evaluation of regulatory objectives, including the pertinence of prior justifications for regulatory policies and programs that, despite the best of intentions, seldom reach a sunset; the manner in which objectives are prescribed in legislation and are funded in the budget; the extent to which regulatory policy implementation conforms with legislative intent; regulatory benefits relative to costs; and regulatory outcomes. Regulatory review may concentrate only on existing rules or it may scrutinize both existing and proposed rules. It may evaluate purely economic regulation, social regulation with economic consequences, or purely social regulation. Review typically concentrates on government control of business activity, but may also consider government control of its own agencies or other levels of government.

The description of regulatory review rendered above is, of course, a better statement of what it might be than what it is in practice. This conclusion leads us to consider proposals to improve the evaluation of existing and proposed regulation. In considering alternatives we should bear in mind that the objectives of both regulatory review and reform are to improve regulatory decision making and its outcomes. Improvements may result from having better information upon which to decide, although we acknowledge that it is easier to define what information ought to be considered than it is to develop this information. In addition, we assume that simply having good information does not ensure that it will be used properly or that it will be used at all. If we agree generally on the purposes to be served by review, and if our other assumptions are correct, then what results should we expect from properly executed regulatory review?

The systematic evaluation of rules ought to clarify our understanding of relationships between the total benefits and costs of regulation, that is, net benefits. Perhaps more importantly it may cause us to weigh the distribution of costs and benefits more carefully. It may improve comprehension of the fact that exclusive concentration on either government administrative costs or private sector compliance costs will cause important distributional effects to be ignored. Regulatory review may improve decision making through clarification of implementation and enforcement strategies and their limitations. It may stimulate regulators to think more strategically about the limits to unilateral action by government, especially where compliance costs are borne by consumers rather than producers. Review may stimulate authors of government regulations to write rules in simpler language. Certainly, review should teach government analysts more about pitfalls in the uses of economic and cost analysis. Finally, regulatory review may improve decision making by causing reform of the political process within which regulation is authorized and funded.

In attempting to identify comprehensive procedural reform options to modify or replace the existing decision process, it is necessary to begin with a consideration of what is wrong with existing regulatory policy and how reform efforts have failed in the past. As noted in earlier chapters, some rather significant steps in federal regulatory reform have been made in the 1970s and early 1980s, including partial and complete deregulation in a number of industries.[1] Many of these results have been gained at the expense of the so-called "old regulation," such as industry-specific controls on prices, entry, and so forth. In many of these cases, it was demonstrated either that there had never been a valid justification for government intervention or that technological and market changes had rendered government intervention obsolete. Elsewhere, particularly so far as the "new regulation" (environmental, worker, and consumer health and safety regulation) is concerned, this is not the case. Government action can and usually does pursue valid, worthwhile social objectives. In these areas, the debate over reform has more to do with the effectiveness, efficiency, costs, and the appropriateness of the specific actions taken by the government.[2] Of course, in stating this we do not assume that all citizens or interest groups place the same value on social regulatory objectives (for example, standards for acceptable levels of toxicity). This is simply not the case. We do assume, however, that there is some agreement over broader social objectives (for example, that citizen health and safety is a worthy objective to pursue). We do not assume either that there is any fixed public consensus on the extent to which government versus the private sector should be responsible for pursuit of these objectives. The political process makes these determinations manifest over time, and public attitudes and preferences change.

In the area of social regulation, given the significant economic effect of many of the rules, in our view the issue is not that some regulatory policies are imperfect, inconsistent, ineffective, or inefficient. The new social regulation addresses real problems. Under the best of circumstances, mistakes in the design and execution of policies are bound to occur, but where regulation is involved, such mistakes appear to be more common than they are where other instruments of public policy are involved. Also, it appears that mistakes in the design and execution of both social and economic regulatory policies are less likely than others to be recognized and corrected.[3]

If regulatory outcomes are less satisfactory than other policy outcomes, this should not come as a surprise. Regulation has traditionally been subject to less comprehensive and continuing scrutiny than have alternative forms of government action. This has been the case not only because many regulatory agencies are independent of the executive branch, but also because existing executive and legislative review and control mechanisms are primarily oriented toward public spending. Over time, both the amount and quality of executive and legislative scrutiny given government actions tend to be roughly proportional to the levels of public expenditure required to carry them out. However, regulatory programs have consequences far in excess of and not directly proportional to the levels of public spending required to support them. Indeed, given the relative insignificance of the claims made by regulatory programs on the public fisc, it is frequently very difficult for regulators to get the attention of executives, budget authorities, and legislative finance committees even when they want it.[4]

Nina Cornell, Roger Noll, and Barry Weingast have argued that existing review processes not only fail to provide adequate scrutiny of regulatory programs but may increase the probability that mistakes in the design and execution of policies will occur. This possibility arises in at least two instances. First, when costs may be shifted to the regulatory industry or some other third party without threatening the core interests of the regulators or their clients, budget officers may approve such shifts or even encourage them. This occurs because budget officers are concerned primarily with restraint of public spending. Unfortunately, minimization of the public spending required to obtain a given regulatory outcome cannot guarantee the selection of the most efficient regulatory strategy. In some cases, it guarantees against the selection of the most efficient regulatory strategy.[5]

Second, when regulators must simplify or dramatize the case for regulation to obtain a hearing for their budget proposals, the result may be a distortion of regulatory policies. According to Cornell et al., to get the attention of Congress it is frequently necessary for regulators to stress well-defined, clear-cut problems that can be avoided in a straightforward manner, [6] to report tangible, easily quantifiable work-load measures, [7] and to explain problems in terms of heroes and villains, as if the principal causes of the problems addressed by regulation were "bad acts by unethical businessmen."[8] Unfortunately, this response, although perfectly understandable from the standpoint of the regulatory agency, has perverse procedural and economic consequences, particularly where health, safety, and environmental protection are concerned. They argue that in these areas regulation has the greatest advantage relative to other instruments of public policy where problems are not simple and well defined, where hazards cannot be avoided in a straightforward manner, where relationships between the behavior of firms and consequent damages are complex and uncertain.

All of the problems and dilemmas noted above point to the need for improvements in the process by which existing and proposed regulations are evaluated. To increase the scrutiny given government regulatory actions, a number of procedural reform options may be proposed, including straightforward budget cutting in regulatory agencies, policy and program termination, sunset review, legal and administrative review, economic impact analysis, zero-base review, federal assumption of compliance costs, and the regulatory budget. These proposals are not alternatives in the formal sense of that term; endorsing one does not imply rejection of the others. Indeed, it is possible that they may be linked together in such a way as to create a whole that is greater than the sum of its parts.

Each of these proposals insures increased scrutiny of government regulation, but increased scrutiny, per se, does not automatically ensure that regulatory decision making—and regulatory outcomes—will be improved. If regulatory decision making is to be improved, a review mechanism that will both facilitate and influence decisions must be installed. [9] By facilitating decisions, we mean ensuring that the kind of information needed to make better decisions—information on costs, benefits, distributional consequences— will be available to the decision makers before decisions are made. By influencing decisions, we mean motivating decision makers to use that information to make better decisions.

It is fairly easy to specify the kind of information that ought to be generated and considered before a decision is made, although it is frequently difficult to ensure that it will be used, and used in the desired manner. The principal design problem that must be solved in the development and installation of a satisfactory review mechanism is the provision of a set of incentives that will induce regulatory decision makers to make the "right" decisions, that is, decisions that result in the largest increase in net human and socioeconomic benefits.

In the following subsections we evaluate the potential value of a number of procedural reform options. Our conclusions are drawn relative to the criteria identified earlier and are based upon our understanding of how regulatory decisions presently are made in government. In turn, this view reveals our understanding of the motivations that operate within government to influence decision making.

BUDGETARY RETRENCHMENT AND POLICY TERMINATION

Initially, the most attractive reform alternative may be simply to cut the budgets of regulatory agencies and programs. The budgetary retrenchment reform alternative may involve little review of substantive policy. Reform of this type is often instituted on the basis of the ideological unacceptability of existing policy. Analysis of the effects of existing regulatory policy thus may be viewed as unnecessary. Where a change in executive administration has occurred, analysis may have been conducted prior to the point where administrations officially change places. This appears to have been the case between the Carter and Reagan administrations. Certainly this transaction provides an example of the dramatic consequences of a different value base and consequent ideological view of regulation on the part of a chief executive.

Under the budgetary retrenchment reform option, the executive may cut funds for regulatory activities across the board or target certain regulatory agencies for severe reduction. This approach is likely to involve direct and dramatic executive action, circumventing as much as possible the participation of upper- and middle-level government administrators and citizens. This approach may be effective in the short run as implemented through rescission and deferral of appropriations. However, it may run aground where legislative concurrence is not easily obtained, or where the "blitzkrieg" of executive action is delayed as a result of confrontation with conflicting and often mutually exclusive preferences of special interest groups.

The budgetary retrenchment approach may include zero basing the budgets of regulatory agencies or requiring budgets to be constrained by a fixed ceiling (for example, 80 percent of last year's appropriation). We shall consider the zero-base option subsequently. The elemental weakness of the budgetary retrenchment approach is that it may be long on budget recalculation and short on analysis of the effects of retrenchment on the achievement of regulatory objectives.

Under retrenchment, specific regulatory policies and their implementing programs and agencies may be targeted for elimination. This may result in partial or complete deregulation. Research in this area indicates that termination may be feasible where conditions are right, for example, where policy can be demonstrated to be harmful rather than merely ineffective, where constituent support can be co-opted, bought off, or otherwise reduced, where public opinion strongly supports reduction, and where some of the duties, obligations, and personnel of the targeted agency can be brokered to another agency. [10] The advantages of comprehensive reform under certain circumstances have been noted in Chapter 5.

Termination is compatible with budgetary retrenchment but differs in that often it will compel analysis that supports decisions to terminate on the grounds that a targeted regulatory policy or program is costly, ineffective, inefficient, unnecessary or wasteful and interfering with reform by preventing the consideration of better alternatives. [11] However, the actual rationale for termination in many cases may be the ideological unacceptability of existing policy as noted earlier. Because termination is best achieved quickly (Robert Behn warns, "Don't float trial balloons") and without the provision of alternative solutions ("Inhibit compromise"), this approach is not likely to involve broad participation by regulatory agencies, special interest groups, or the general public. [12] It may be criticized for its outcomes as well as for abridgment of government accountability norms and the democratic process. The evaluation that justifies termination may be more noteworthy for its use in "termination gamesmanship" than for its value in improving performance. [13] On the other hand, it may enable the elimination of regulation at the least cost for analysis.

SUNSET REVIEW

In principle, sunset review provides a means for implementing legislative review and oversight of regulation. It has been enacted ad hoc in a number of individual pieces of legislation. Further, some state governments (Colorado and Oregon, for example) have authorized comprehensive application of sunset review procedures across government agencies.

The sunset alternative is particularly attractive because it gives the appearance of being faultless and automatic. No one has to slip the noose over the neck of the regulatory program or policy. Rather, termination will occur at the end of a policy's life cycle.[14] Unfortunately, our experience with sunset indicates that it simply does not work out this way. In the end, sunsetted agencies live through to a new dawn because it is difficult to derive a powerful or willful enough group of decision makers to bite the bullet; arguments for continuation of agency mission are more compelling than those to allow a peaceful demise. Typically, only a few small, weak programs are permitted to sunset.[15] As has been noted in another context, "Some butterflies were caught, no elephants were stopped." In addition, sunset review is costly where permanent sunset review agencies are created to perform this function. The costs might be worthwhile if the benefits promised by sunset actually were achieved.

LEGAL AND PROCEDURAL REVIEW

This approach to regulatory review is less ambitious in one sense than the other approaches to reform considered here. It does not require development of expensive cost-benefit analysis or complex cost accounting systems. In fact, this approach generally does not include comprehensive review of either economic impacts or compliance costs. It would not concern itself with costs by and large, leaving this task to the Office of Management and Budget agencies, the Congressional Budget Office, and congressional policy and appropriation committees. Although less complex in implementation than many of the other alternatives, this approach is ambitious in terms of its comprehensiveness. As we have noted in Chapter 3, the breadth and length of federal regulatory statutes are enormous. Therefore, we would expect that in order for legal and procedural review to be successful, it would have to concentrate selectively on specific high priority regulatory statutes, agencies, and programs.

Legal and procedural review attempts to evaluate the pertinence of government regulatory activity against the objectives of regulatory statutes and legislative intent. It seeks to determine the extent to which regulatory agencies comply with legislative guidelines and whether objectives prescribed in the law are met. It also attempts to ferret out outmoded, obsolete, and unenforceable regulations. Regulatory agencies are required to prepare plans for review of existing regulations according to a common set of criteria. Amendments to existing regulations and new regulations are reviewed according to the same criteria. Finally, legal and procedural review attempts to improve self-evaluation capability by requiring development of long-term agency review plans.

On face value, the strength of this approach appears to be its directness and relative ease of implementation. Where this approach is supported by the executive and legislature, it is likely to exhibit more teeth and sunset and other types of review because it invests in one office the responsibility for eliminating ineffective regulations and preventing the enactment of inappropriate new regulations. An additional advantage of legal and procedural review is that it may be implemented without extensive training of specialists in benefits and costs and other types of economic analysis. And because it does not rely on these methods, the results of analysis are more likely to be understood in the executive and in Congress. Predictably, the potential weaknesses of this approach are that it may concentrate on benefits rather than on the relationships between benefits and costs, and it may tend to ignore the manner in which direct and indirect costs are distributed among citizens, industry, and the economy.

Merely stating the apparent advantages and disadvantages of legal and procedural review are not sufficient to enable evaluation of its effectiveness, a point that holds as well for the other procedures and reform options included in this chapter. For this reason, and because legal and procedural review is likely to appeal to state decision makers because of its evident simplicity and directness, we should be attentive to experience with this procedural reform option in state government.

To some, legal and administrative review may appear simply as accelerated administrative code and procedures review. Perhaps this is true in form but, as we shall note, in substance the tasks performed by the Office of Administrative Law (OAL) in California far exceed the activities normally undertaken in state government administrative code review. In 1979 the California legislature passed and Governor Jerry Brown signed Assembly Bill 1111 into law, thereby becoming the first state to establish an executive branch office with the mandate to review, control, and improve state regulation. [16] On July 1, 1980, the Office of Administrative Law became a functional reality charged with the mandate of assessing and rectifying the alleged problem of overregulation in the state of California.

The origins of Assembly Bill 1111 and OAL's mandate stemmed primarily from the professed belief of lawmakers and the governor that many administrative regulations were ineffective, inappropriate, and impediments to private sector initiative. The bill noted that there had been unprecedented growth in the number of administrative regulations in recent years (the California Administrative Code had more than doubled between 1974 and 1978); the language of many regulations was frequently unclear and unnecessarily complex; and substantial time and public funds had been spent in adopting regulation, the necessity for which had not been clearly established.[17] OAL was charged to reduce the number and improve the quality of existing and proposed regulations. The deadline for conclusion of OAL review, into which agency self-review was to be integrated, was set for December 31, 1984. Governor Brown proceeded quickly to shorten the original deadline for completion of review by two years to the end of 1982 to coincide with the conclusion of his second consecutive term in office. (California governors are limited to two consecutive terms in office.)

The Office of Administrative Law was provided approximately 40 staff positions to do its job. AB1111 authorized gubernatorial appointment of a director and deputy director, subject to Senate conformation. The director and deputy director were required to be attorneys, and their tenure was set to be coterminous with that of the governor. The director and his executives hired a staff composed of about one-third program analysts, one-third lawyers, and one-third clerical support personnel. The staff was divided into two functional arms: the Legal Division, responsible for overall regulatory review, and the Legislation Management and Analysis Division, designated to monitor and review new regulations proposed in the legislative process. OAL was budgeted $3.5 million by the legislature for its first year of operation, with 60 percent of this amount appropriated to cover agency costs incurred in complying with OAL mandates. State agencies reimburse OAL for the review it performs on their behalf. The enabling legislation established five criteria against which regulations were to be evaluated: necessity, authority, clarity, consistency, and reference. All criteria had to be met both by agencies reviewing their own regulations and by OAL in its independent analysis in order for regulatory measures to survive. The five standards were defined as follows:

Necessity: The need for a regulation as demonstrated in the record of the rule-making procedure. To help agencies demonstrate the necessity of a regulation, OAL clarified the standard by asking agencies to analyze regulations in response to the following two sets of questions: Should government be involved in the regulatory activity, and if so, why? What is lacking in private enterprise that requires government intervention? And do the benefits of the regulation outweigh its costs? Would an alternative approach be as effective and less burdensome?

Authority: The provision of law that permits or obligates the agency to adopt, amend, or repeal a regulation. An agency must demonstrate that it has been given clear authority by the legislature to issue regulations.

Clarity: Regulations must be written so that the meaning will be
easily understood by those persons directly affected by them.
Regulatory language must be constructed simply and directly,
using a minimum of technical jargon.

Consistency: Regulations must not be in conflict with or contradictory to existing law. Federal and state statutes, court decisions,
and other state regulations are considered as existing law by OAL.

Reference: The statute, court decision, or other provision of law
that the agency implements, interprets, or makes specific by
adopting, amending, or repealing a regulation must be identified.

Regulations were required to have a basis in existing statute or
court decision to ensure that they did not exceed the intent and scope
of such measures.

The standards of necessity, authority, and consistency have
provided cornerstones for the OAL review process. To meet the
test of necessity, it is required that regulations be more than a
repetition or rewording of existing statutory language. Where statutory language is self-executing or sufficiently specific, a regulation
may not be needed. When analyzing the authority standard, an agency
may not rely simply on general powers and authority to move into
new regulatory areas. The standards assume that the legislature
had not intended to grant broad authority to regulate to agencies unless clearly specified in enabling legislation. In meeting the consistency standard, agencies have been compelled to evaluate the extent to which their regulations might be at variance with those of
other agencies in order to reduce regulatory overlap and duplication.

Under AB1111, state agencies were required to develop and
submit a formal review plan document for approval by OAL. The
plan would outline procedures to be employed in self-evaluation of
all the regulations administered by each agency. Review plans were
required to include cost estimates for administrative implementation, review time schedules, and personnel requirements. Moreover, OAL requires that plans describe: how the agency would ensure adequate public participation, such as through advisory committees and task forces, public meetings, and the solicitation of
written comment; how the agency would coordinate with other agencies sharing regulatory responsibilities for overlapping or closely
related program areas; and how the review process would be administered to ensure an even flow of activities, for example, through
designation of an agency review coordinator, establishment of a
priority listing of regulations, and preparation of regulation issue
papers providing background information, complaints or problems
associated with a regulation, and costs and other data that might
assist in focusing the public review process. Agency review plans

were to be submitted to OAL by December 31, 1980. Approximately 65 of 123 proposed plans were submitted by this date, with the remainder filed by March. Proposed review plans were reviewed by OAL and negotiated with agency staffs, and a summary of all review plans approved by OAL was published as required by law on April 1, 1981.

As is evident by these deadlines, little time was allowed for foot-dragging by agency or OAL staff. It is somewhat remarkable that OAL was able to publish its nearly 200-page Master Plan for Regulation Review barely nine months after it began operation. In addition, OAL published a Comprehensive Index to the California Administrative Code providing 73,000 subject entry identifiers and a cross-reference of regulations to administrative statutes as required by AB1111. These feats are even more remarkable considering that while supervising, reviewing, and negotiating review plans, OAL also was occupied with analysis of amendments to existing regulations and new regulations proposed by agencies.

The process for review of proposed regulatory actions was also established in AB1111. In proposing adoption, amendment, or repeal of a regulation, agencies were required to give notice of a public hearing on the regulatory action. A statement of the reasons for the regulatory change along with a Notice of Proposed Regulatory Action (NPRA) was required to be filed with OAL 45 days prior to conducting a public hearing. Among the information required in the NPRA was a summary of existing laws and regulations relating directly to the proposed action; an estimate of the costs or savings in federal funding to the state, or in state funding to any state or local government agency;[18] and the name and telephone number of the state agency officer to whom inquiries concerning the proposed action would be directed. The statement of reasons for proposing a regulatory action was required to include the specific purpose of the regulation, the factual basis for the determination by the agency that the regulation was necessary to carry out the purpose for which it was proposed, and the substantive facts or other information (including the technical, theoretical, and empirical studies) upon which the agency was relying in proposing the change. The statement of reasons had to be made available to the public upon request and was to be updated before final agency adoption. It was to include citation of objections to the regulatory action and brief explanations of why any objection had been rejected.

In addition, every agency also was required to maintain a file of each rule making "which shall be deemed to be the record for that rulemaking procedure."[19] The rule-making file would include copies of petitions, public notices, factual information, studies and written comments, public meeting minutes, and other information required by law.

Following completion of all legal review requirements, the agency can adopt, amend, or repeal the regulation and transmit the change to the secretary of state for certification and publication in the California Administrative Code. Within 30 days OAL was required to either approve or disapprove the regulation that had been forwarded to it at the same time it was sent to the secretary of state. In conducting its review, OAL was to concern itself only with the proposed change, and not the existing rule, in the context of the record of the rule-making proceeding indicated above. If the agency met the provisions of the regulatory review process, and the proposed rule was found to be in compliance with the standards of necessity, authority, clarity, consistency, and reference, it would be approved by OAL and the secretary of state, and the agency and others would be so notified. If a proposed regulation was disapproved by OAL, the submitting agency could appeal to the governor, who, within 30 days, could overrule the decision.

An additional aspect of the system under which review has operated is that although agencies must secure OAL approval to create new regulation or to modify existing rules, they may repeal rules without consulting OAL. This feature permits agencies considerable flexibility in review of their own rules and establishes some incentive to reduce the number of rules in force.

AB1111 provided OAL with the responsibility for reviewing all regulatory legislation proposed in the California Senate and Assembly, including "emergency" regulations and those regulations that were proposed by agencies to be necessary, "for the immediate preservation of the public peace, health and safety or general welfare."[20] An agency or any other party proposing the adoption of an emergency regulation was required to submit the rule to OAL together with a written statement containing the information required in the Notice of Proposed Action procedure described above. OAL was to conduct its review of proposed emergency regulations within ten days of filing, and could repeal such regulation if it did not meet the five adoption standards. Emergency proposals reviewed by OAL were required to be accompanied by a statement that justified immediate action and specified the costs or savings to the state or local governments that were estimated to result from its passage. If approved, an emergency regulation would become effective at the date of filing or at a later time noted in the rule. An emergency regulation would be effective only for 120 days; after this period it would lapse unless continued as a result of approval through the regular review process during its four-month period of effectiveness.

It is interesting to note that under California law in force at this writing, emergency proposals to repeal existing regulations must be reviewed by OAL, while regular proposals to repeal existing regulations are not evaluated. Emergency repeal proposals are reviewed by OAL relative to their merit as weighed against the five review criteria. OAL has not been authorized to determine whether an emergency exists where agencies propose emergency repeal of existing rules.

The summaries of OAL actions over the first year of its operation provided in Tables 6.1 and 6.2 indicate that it has tended to be most critical of proposed emergency regulations; more than one-third of the emergency proposals reviewed were disapproved. OAL found that a substantial number of emergency proposals for new regulations did not need to be implemented immediately. In fact, OAL review has confirmed to an extent what many legislators and administration observers have long suspected: that in many instances the emergency enactment procedure is abused in order to secure quick approval of politically sensitive legislation. In 1980-81, OAL disapproved 41 of the 111 sets of emergency regulations submitted for its review, a disapproval rate of 37 percent. This compares to a 24 percent disapproval rate by OAL for regular proposals. In addition, 52 percent fewer sets of emergency regulations were submitted for filing in 1980-81, compared to the average of such proposals submitted for the previous three-year period.

TABLE 6.1

OAL Review and Disposition of Proposed Regulations,
July 1980–June 1981

	Type		
	Emergency	Regular	Total
Sets of regulations reviewed	111[a]	485[b]	596
Approved for filing	70	367	437
Fully disapproved regulations	41	101	142
Partially disapproved regulations	0	17	17
Percent disapproved	37	24	27

[a]Does not include 13 statutorily mandated emergency regulations. Where a statute mandates the adoption of a regulation as an emergency, OAL does not review it to determine whether an emergency exists (see Government Code Section 11346.1, Finance Code Section 5500.5, and Welfare and Institutions Code Section 114105).

[b]Does not include repeal only sections, as OAL does not review such repealers.

Source: Reprinted by permission of OAL from its first annual report, Slashing Government Red Tape, No. 82733-404 (Sacramento, Calif.: Office of State Printer, August 1981), pp. 4-5.

TABLE 6.2

Sets of Regulations Submitted for Filing,
July-June 1977-81

Year	Emergency	Regular	Total	Percentage Change
1977-78	254	691	945	
1978-79	265	687	952	+.74
1979-80	232	691	923	-3
1980-81[a]	120	511	631	-32

[a]Does not include resubmittals following OAL disapproval.
Prior to OAL, there were no resubmitted regulations.

Source: Reprinted by permission of OAL from its first annual report, Slashing Government Red Tape, No. 82733-404 (Sacramento, Calif.: Office of State Printer, August 1981), pp. 4-5.

In one instance, OAL determined that an emergency rule proposed by the Department of Social Service (DSS) to alter the cost indexing portions of the formula for determination of Aid for Families with Dependent Children (AFDC) grants violated the state Welfare and Institutions Code requiring fair public hearings of proposed rule changes. The effort of the DSS to avoid the financial and perhaps political costs of public hearings through enactment of an emergency statute was disapproved by OAL. Subsequent to this decision, the legislature passed a measure to implement the change in the law sought by DSS through the regular process of review without emergency designation.[21] The DSS case and OAL's approval record on proposed emergency regulations indicate that regulatory review may enforce greater discipline on the part of agencies and legislators over the use of emergency procedures.

Perhaps the most significant indication of the effect of OAL review is found in comparing the number of new regulations approved for filing in the California Administrative Code (CAC) during the first year in which OAL operated against the number of regulations approved before its creation. In the 1977-78 fiscal year, 668 sets of new regulations were filed in California (sets of regulations as defined by OAL vary in size from 1 to 300 separate regulations). The corresponding figures for 1978/79 and 1979/80 were 683 and 719:[22] In 1980-81, the first year in which OAL operated, only 437

sets of regulations that OAL was authorized to review were added
to the CAC, which represents an approximate 37 percent decrease
in new regulations approved for filing compared to the average for
the previous three-year period and a 39 percent decrease relative
to 1979-80. It is also significant to view the rate of proposal of new
regulation for this period. The number of sets of regulations proposed on average for the years 1977-78 through 1979-80 was 940,
compared to 631 for 1980-81. Of the 631 sets of regulations submitted, OAL reviewed 596, consisting of 485 regular submittals and
111 emergency submittals. Not included in the 437 sets approved
for 1980-81 and the 631 total sets reviewed were 13 statutorily mandated emergency regulations that OAL was not authorized to review.
In addition, the 631 figure for 1980-81 does not include resubmittals
following initial OAL review.

Among other things, these data indicate that fewer new regulations were proposed under OAL than were proposed in the past, a
reduction in 1980-81 of 33 percent compared to the average of the
previous three years. The extent to which this change may be attributed to AB1111 and OAL, or to general changes in social and
political attitudes toward regulation, is, of course, not reflected in
the statistics.

Although these findings represent a summary of OAL action
for only the first year of its existence, they may be instructive to
other states and to the federal government in setting the evaluative
agenda for regulatory review offices or agencies with missions similar to that of the Office of Administrative Law. It would be premature to attempt to draw conclusions with regard to the long-term
effectiveness of OAL, but preliminary findings indicate that it has
contributed significantly to a reduction in the number of new regulatory measures entered into law. Whereas the difference in the rate
of approval of new regulations by OAL in 1981 compared to the average for the three-year period 1977-78 to 1979-80 strongly suggests OAL effectiveness in reducing the number of regulations approved for filing, it is interesting to note that the overall disapproval
rate under OAL for 1980-81 was 27 percent compared to a disapproval rate of 33 percent of the total regulations proposed on average for the three-year period before its creation.

The most available measure of OAL effectiveness in review
of proposed regulation is the number of new regulations actually
filed in the California Administrative Code. With regard to how
this reduction was achieved during the first year of OAL's operation, it would appear that creation of the review office is a significant factor. However, longitudinal data imply that the primary factor explaining the decline in the number of new rules filed in the
CAC is the submission of fewer proposed rules by regulatory agen-

cies for OAL review compared to submissions to the review and approval process that operated between agencies and the California Department of Finance prior to the establishment of OAL. A secondary factor appears to be OAL's rate of disapproval of proposed regulations. It seems highly probable that the reduction in number of proposed regulatory filing by agencies is attributable to the creation of OAL. However, other factors appear likely to have affected the rate of proposal as well: the general public mood against regulation, media publicity indicating legislative and gubernatorial support for OAL, resistance of business and industry to rising compliance costs. The larger question is, therefore: Which contributes most to a reduction in regulation—the existence of a review procedure, the rate of disapproval of new regulations as an indicator of analytical rigor in the review process, or exogenous factors?

At present, partly owing to the limited time within which OAL has operated, it is not possible to provide an accurate assessment of the relative strength of these variables. To OAL, the governor, and the legislature this seems to be a somewhat moot point. From their view, the most important factor appears to be that the tide of regulatory filings has been turned. From the view of the taxpayers of California, and we suppose the California Legislative Analyst's Office, the best measure of the cost-effectiveness of OAL would be found by comparing the total appropriation of government funds for all OAL-related review activities to the costs avoided by the public and the private sector as a result of the reduction in the rate of approval of new regulations—a net-benefit criterion. Also, as we have noted, the second major element of OAL's mission is to shepherd the agency-based process to review approximately 30,000 pages of existing regulation in the CAC. Until this process has been completed and its effects analyzed, it is not possible to determine the extent to which long-term efforts to achieve regulatory reform through review have been successful.

Without such an analysis, and especially without the ability to include the effects of the long-term review of existing regulations in the calculation, we may speculate that OAL would be found to be worth its cost using the net-benefit criterion. Of course, whether the net cost savings to California is calculated on the basis of direct cost reduction (reduction of direct private sector compliance costs) or indirect cost reduction (total socioeconomic cost avoidance, including efficiency-loss costs) would make a significant difference in determining the cost-effectiveness of OAL and its cost-benefit ratio relative to the process that operated before its creation.

An independent analysis of OAL performance cites the following potential criticisms. Despite the fact that there was a decline in the number of new regulations enacted, the numbers do not indi-

cate the degree of effectiveness of OAL in reforming regulation or
reducing the "regulatory burden." A reduction in the number of
regulations proposed since OAL was created may have been the result of an increase in the rate of regulations proposed and enacted
prior to and in anticipation of OAL review. In the short run it is
not possible to determine how many of the regulations proposed and
rejected by OAL would be proposed and passed at a later date.[23]
In addition, while acknowledging that survival is not necessarily the
best measure of effectiveness, we must note that at present it is not
possible to say how OAL will fare in the transition to a new gubernatorial administration in January 1983. It is also significant that although the California legislature has authorized sunset provisions
into some laws, there is no sunset clause in the legislation authorizing OAL.

In the absence of data by which to evaluate the long-term effectiveness of OAL, we have employed circumstantial evidence of
performance. OAL established itself within the hierarchy and process of legislative and administrative review of proposed regulations.
It demonstrated further that it possessed the strength to disapprove
and to negotiate and the discipline to stay on schedule. The potency
of OAL has been due in no small respect to the continuing support
for the agency provided by the governor and the legislature. None
of the appeals made by agencies to the governor in the first year of
operation was successful in overturning OAL decisions. In fact,
few appeals were made at all, and OAL was not sued to overrule a
decision in this period. In a number of instances OAL battled small
and large agencies over sensitive policies and issues. It withstood
the scrutiny of political and media attention given to these conflicts,
and generally resolved disputes through negotiation rather than
through appeal to the governor. OAL was treated positively by the
press in its first year of operation, and there was no evidence to
suggest public displeasure with its performance. Only a few agencies were exempted from OAL review. However, exemptions granted
to the Public Utility Commission and the Division of Industrial Accidents were noteworthy. OAL executives have received informal requests from legislators and others to extend their review to "indirect" regulation, for example, state rules and administrative
guidelines over local government activities. OAL appears to have
reinforced discipline in the use of emergency designation for legislation. Certainly not the least in importance is that OAL won respect for fair and circumspect staff work and decision making from
many of the regulatory agencies with which it contended.

Finally, we may note that in order to evaluate OAL fairly relative to its mission, it is necessary to inquire not only whether it
reduced state regulation but whether its decisions have had any

marked effect on business-government relations or the role of government in regulating the private sector. One element of OAL's mission has been to reduce the "unnecessary" intrusion of state government into private sector economic activity and decision making. We do not know presently whether OAL decisions have increased, reduced, or not materially affected private sector costs of compliance with state regulation. Because OAL has not based its decisions on economic, benefit-cost, or purely cost criteria, we know very little about the effect of its decisions on specific businesses and industries or on economic efficiency in general.

Based on review of the experience of California's Office of Administrative Law, we may speculate on the effectiveness of legal and procedural review relative to some other types of regulatory review. In this analysis we may note differences that may apply to state versus the federal government. Legal and procedural review is perhaps the most easily implemented regulatory reform alternative because it employs criteria that most public administrators understand; is comprehensive in scope, applying both to proposed and existing regulation; is less costly to implement than many other approaches, partly because it causes agencies themselves to review existing regulations; concentrates on regulatory necessity, authority, clarity, consistency, and general goodness of fit with the law rather than on difficult to define costs and benefits; results in clear-cut decisions on the need for reform; and is comprehensive in that its evaluation is similar in application to that employed in normal analysis of proposed legislation and in administrative code review.

However, legal and procedural review has some distinct disadvantages: It does not consider costs relative to benefits, either for government or the private sector, and in this respect would appear to be inferior to the mandated cost assumption, regulatory budget, and other more comprehensive approaches to review; it may not be as aggressive in reducing the impact of government regulation on the private sector as would other alternatives; it ignores distributive impact of the regulatory burden to a considerable extent in almost exclusive concentration on the appropriateness and location of authority within government; and it may lead to reform on issues of lesser consequence while leaving high impact regulation untouched.

Legal and procedural review appears to offer great promise as an incremental addition to improve regulatory evaluation for state governments. Some states may wish to pursue more comprehensive, nonincremental approaches to reform such as the regulatory budget, where private sector costs of compliance are a primary consideration. For other state governments, assumption of compliance costs for intergovernment regulation may be more attractive. This option could permit state governments to assume a larger proportion of compliance costs where this change is politically feasible. In addition, we may assume that in the process of managing retrenchment, some states will selectively reorganize or terminate regulatory boards and agencies under the premise that deregulation is the alternative that best suits state needs to reduce expenditures and citizen and private sector desires for less regulation. However, in this regard it must be recognized that many state licensing boards and regulatory agencies exist to satisfy business and professional interests through control of labor supply, price, and professional standards. In other areas, regulation may be employed to generate revenues or to discourage consumption of goods that are thought to have negative socioeconomic spillover effects, as in alcohol price and supply regulation. Where protection is provided to satisfy special interests and state government revenue demand, and also as a means for implementing social values, strong support from the executive and legislative branches will be necessary in order for any approach to regulatory reform to be successful.

Regardless of which regulatory review procedure is employed, or whether one is employed at all, there are areas of regulatory activity that cannot be improved significantly through administratively guided regulatory review and reform. In many instances poor regulatory performance results from poor regulatory legislation. In such circumstances, regulatory review agencies at the state or federal level can do no more than point out legal inadequacies, placing the responsibility for reform with state legislatures, or the U.S. Congress, where it properly belongs.

Would legal and procedural review lend itself well to the evaluation of federal regulation, perhaps as a means for improving congressional oversight, for example? At the federal level, a principal advantage of this approach might be to place greater responsibility for review and reform with Congress. However, for reasons good and otherwise, Congress often has surrendered its review powers in this area to regulatory agencies, the Executive Office of President, and particularly to OMB.[24] This is unfortunate and might be corrected if Congress were to attempt regulatory oversight in earnest, utilizing a staff of lawyers and analysts to review high priority regulations. In addition, Congress would have to be willing to attend seriously to the strains generated in the political environment as a consequence of review. To an extent, this type of review takes place regularly in consideration and passage of new regulatory legislation. However, this review is not conducted systematically for existing regulation, is not performed centrally, and is not well coordinated, despite the efforts of the Congressional Budget Office, committee staffs, the General Accounting Office, and others. Comprehensive regulatory review proposals have not been greeted with enthusiasm by Congress, even though several major committee reports have recommended such a course. [25] Still, as noted by Antonin Scalia, in a situation where congressional power is split between parties and houses, comprehensive regulatory review proposals such as the one-house legislative veto appear more attractive to those wishing to block presidential action supported by the other house, for example, to Democrats in the House of Representatives during President Reagan's first year in office. [26]

Comprehensive review of existing regulation has been considered but not approved by Congress as of this writing. In the executive branch, under Presidents Ford and Carter, the Council on Wage and Price Stability, the Regulatory Analysis Review Group, the Regulatory Council, the Office of Regulatory Information and Policy in OMB, and others conducted comprehensive, albeit spotty and somewhat uncoordinated review of regulation. More recently, under President Reagan, the Office of Information and Regulatory Affairs (in OMB) and the Task Force on Regulatory Relief have attempted centralized and comprehensive review of regulation. Although these efforts have been criticized as noted earlier, systematic review of selected regulatory measures has taken place. [27]

From one view it may be acknowledged as inevitable and proper that the responsibility of Congress is to pass laws, leaving evaluation to the executive and the courts. However, this view will not suffice where Congress is required to amend and reauthorize existing regulatory law, as is the case with a number of major regulatory acts passed in the 1970s. In this circumstance Congress is likely to perform as it does in considering new legislation, separating out approval of policy from the appropriation of money to implement policy. For this reason a regulatory budget would appear to be useful to unify policy and appropriation decisions on proposed and existing regulations. Legal and procedural review might be attractive to implement centralized and comprehensive congressional review of existing regulation, but the enormity of the task detracts from its appeal. However, regulatory analysis that does not consider direct costs or economic consequences is likely to put Congress at a disadvantage to OMB and to regulatory agencies possessing the resources necessary to perform sophisticated economic and cost analysis.

An exhaustive study of regulation performed by the U.S. Senate Committee on Governmental Affairs from 1976 through 1978 concluded that responsibility for comprehensive legal and procedural review, combined with broader economic analysis and other activities, should be assigned to the Administrative Conference of the United States (ACUS). ACUS was reestablished by President Kennedy in 1961 following on the efforts of the Office of Administrative Pro-

cedures administered by Attorney General Brownell under Eisenhower and in response to administrative procedure reform recommendations made by the first and second Hoover Commissions and
others. [28] Under this proposal, ACUS would fulfill many of the functions performed by the Office of Administrative Law in California.
Congress has authorized $2.3 million for ACUS through 1982, much
of this for implementation of the Government in the Sunshine Act,
and in a report accompanying the authorization noted, "the Conference merits and needs . . . a significantly increased authorization
. . . to keep pace with economic developments over the next few
years."[29] The Senate Committee on Governmental Affairs has
recommended restructuring ACUS and charging it to:

> actively monitor the way agencies plan and manage
> their regulatory responsibilities and propose pro-
> cedures to improve the effectiveness of agency opera-
> tions . . . with respect to . . . the development of
> regulations . . . licensing, ratemaking, handling in-
> formation, adjudication, program enforcement, dis-
> pensing grants and benefits, handling complaints,
> paperwork reduction, interaction with state regulatory
> programs, caseload management, court litigation, and
> some aspects of personnel management. . . . ACUS
> should significantly expand the services presently pro-
> vided to Congress. [30]

The committee report cited reasons why ACUS would perform the
functions assigned more satisfactorily than would OMB. In addition, the committee recommended that Congress authorize sunset
review for all regulatory agencies and "concurrent submission of
budget and legislative proposals by regulatory agencies to the Congress and OMB."[31] These recommendations appear highly compatible with proposals for institution of legal and procedureal review or a regulatory budget.

   As distinct alternatives, and in combination with other approaches, the procedural reform options described thus far have
been implemented in varying degrees in state or federal government, yet this experience has not been evaluated extensively. We
now move to consider other procedural reform options, several of
which can be evaluated on the basis of experience.

ECONOMIC IMPACT ANALYSIS

   Economic analysis of the consequences of regulatory measures
is intended to identify the balance and distribution of costs and bene-

fits resulting from government action. Economic impact analysis is difficult to perform, even where the rules for analysis are clear: Costs and benefits are not easily defined; the relationships between direct and indirect costs often are not easily discernible; the estimation of costs is highly sensitive to assumptions; and the price of good staff work is high, and high-quality analysis typically requires a long time to perform. Economic analysis seldom produces wholly unambiguous results upon which decisions can be made. In order for economic analysis to be used it must be performed well and understood by decision makers, yet few decision makers possess the skills necessary for full comprehension. As such, its use has presented serious problems in the past to federal decision makers.

An evaluation of the value of economic analysis as a procedural reform measure involves a review of its use over the past eight years in three presidential administrations. Ex ante economic impact analysis has been performed by executive branch regulatory agencies since 1974.[32] Through 1976, it was undertaken in the Inflation Impact Statement (IIS) Program, changed under Carter to Economic Impact Statement (EIS) Program. Responsibility for program administration was vested primarily in the President's Council on Wage and Price Stability (CWPS). This approach was justified initially as a weapon in the fight against inflation under President Ford. Initially, the officials responsible for the program interpreted its objectives in a somewhat different light. As they saw it, the proper goal of the program was an improvement in the decision making of regulatory agencies. They interpreted this to mean that regulatory decisions should reflect sound microeconomic analysis—getting agencies to take account of the costs and benefits of proposed regulations and legislative recommendations.

According to James C. Miller III, one of the officials responsible for the economic impact program, prior to 1977 he and the others were under no illusion that such analysis would dominate regulatory decision making, but hoped that by mandating that it be carried out, some of the more deplorable propensities of the regulators could be countered. He explained:

> What program officials wished to avoid was the tendency for agencies to serve special constituent interests, often at great cost to the general public; to view the objects of their regulations as natural enemies, to be dealt with punitively; to forge ahead with regulatory and legislative proposals without knowing enough about the problem being addressed or the effects of the proposed solution; and to resist suggestions for alternative, more efficient ways of dealing with economic problems.[33]

The departure from the anti-inflation objective that occurred in the implementation of the IIS program was rationalized by the following formula: If the proposal would generate tangible and intangible benefits in excess of costs, it was anti-inflationary; if it generated costs in excess of benefits, it was inflationary. There is little evidence that regulation, per se, has much direct, consistent impact on inflation. Nor for that matter is the relationship between welfare and inflation unambiguous. Consequently, the applied welfare analysis required by the IIS and later the EIS program in some instances pointed in directions that would have increased price indexes. This created inconsistencies that were never wholly resolved within CWPS.[34]

How was the IIS/EIS program supposed to have worked? Initially, executive departments were required merely to certify that they had carried out an economic analysis of their proposals. In the case of recommendations for legislation, certification was to be filed with the Office of Management and Budget and, in the case of proposed regulations, with CWPS. Later, following the discovery that certifications were false in many cases, departments were required to file impact statements for review by OMB/CWPS on all major proposals meeting a specific set of criteria and to certify in the Federal Register that consideration had been given to the economic consequences of each proposed regulation. In addition, regulatory agencies could be required to justify their classification of a proposal as one not requiring review by CWPS.[35]

Agencies were directed by CWPS to include the following information in economic impact statements: an analysis of the principal costs and, where practical, secondary costs and benefits; a comparison of anticipated costs and benefits; and a review of alternatives to the proposed action.[36] The Council on Wage and Price Stability then reviewed both the proposed regulation and the professional quality of the accompanying impact statements.

As noted earlier, the officials responsible for this program hoped that if economic analysis were performed, it would influence agency decision making. It seems that this hope was not realized. Few if any decisions seemed to have been influenced by this program in its first few years of operation. This ought not to be greatly regretted: Decision making is unlikely to be improved by incompetent analysis. Most of the early IIS/EISs were of poor quality: Cost estimates were frequently dubious, benefit estimates incomplete, and consideration of alternatives nearly nonexistent.[37] Perhaps one reason for the quality of these analyses was that they were typically prepared after proposals had been approved by the decision-making authorities within the regulatory agency and were intended only to justify decisions based upon other considerations.[38]

The program's initial lack of success was generally attributed to two factors: lack of clout and poor timing.[39] CWPS had little influence, and regulatory agencies quickly learned that they could afford to ignore its criticism of their IIS/EISs and provide perfunctory justification for treating a proposal as "not major."[40] Two agencies dropped out of the program—the Federal Energy Agency (FEA) and the Department of Agriculture (USDA). The OMB had clout, but was not particularly interested in the success of the IIS/EIS program. In addition, as the IIS/EIS did not have to be drawn up until after the regulatory proposal was fully prepared and published in the Federal Register, it frequently was not.[41]

As a consequence of experienced frustration with the EIS program, Executive Order 12044 was issued by President Carter in March 1978 to improve regulatory review. The order required executive agencies, excluding independent regulatory agencies not under the direct control of the president,[42] to do the following:

Involve agency heads at the earliest stages in developing regulations for which they will be held accountable.

Prepare a regulatory analysis for each major rule, assessing its economic effects and the alternate means of achieving its objectives.

Select the least burdensome acceptable alternative.

Develop an evaluation plan to review the effectiveness of all new regulations.

Use simple, understandable language in writing rules.

Publish a semiannual agenda of regulations under development in each agency.

Involve the public in regulatory decisions.

Systematically review existing regulations to evaluate whether they are achieving their objectives and whether costs are being minimized.

Independent regulatory agencies were encouraged to adopt the executive order requirements as their own.[43]

E.O. 12044 was intended to correct the quality and timing problems and to strengthen the role of CWPS in the regulatory review process. In addition, by involving the White House Economic Policy Review Group in regulatory matters, it was intended to promote executive branch coordination in the development of regulation.[44] Regulatory agencies within the executive branch were required to secure approval of the quality of their regulatory analysis from the Regulatory Analysis Review Group (RARG).[45] The analysis was to be made public, and RARG approval was required before the proposal could be published in the Federal Register. Responsibility for resolving disputes between RARG and the initiating agency rested with the Economic Policy Review Group, composed of the chairman of the Council of Economic Advisors, the secretary of the treasury, the director of OMB, the secretary of labor, the secretary of commerce, and the secretary of state.

Despite these changes and others made subsequently, many of the problems with EIS were not addressed, and because of this it is doubtful that the full potential of the economic impact analysis programs implemented under Carter would have been realized. These problems included lack of OMB support, inconsistency on the part of reviewers, overemphasis in review of new and proposed regulations relative to existing rules, and perhaps most importantly, an absence of coordination of economic analysis and the review process itself.

The OMB required initiating agencies to comply with the EIS program within existing budgets and with existing personnel. It was argued that agencies already possessed sufficient capacity for economic analysis and that the EIS program would merely redirect that effort. Perhaps this was true, perhaps not. In any event, under Carter, the EIS program was given the means to compel analysis. If the resources had been appropriated, it is likely they would have been redirected to comply with the requirements. However, without the analytical resources, the requirement for economic analysis presented an almost impossible hurdle, nipping new regulatory initiatives in the bud. Some may have applauded such an outcome, but this was not the same thing as improved regulatory decision making, unless the social costs of all proposed regulations were greater than their benefits.

We think it is possible that this decision reflected a propensity on the part of the OMB to limit the amount of analytical talent available to agencies. In turn, this propensity was very likely based upon a realistic appraisal of the consequences of funding analysis, especially economic analysis. Improved economic analysis may have permitted agencies to make a better case for a larger budget and may have made it harder for the OMB to oppose expenditure increases. As we noted earlier, budget analysts are typically far more concerned with controlling government spending than they are with the cost-effectiveness of government decisions. [46] Cost-benefit analysis ought to be directed as much against this bias as it is against biases of decision makers within regulatory agencies.

The Council on Wage and Price Stability's reaction to the EISs prepared by the initiating agencies was frequently inconsistent. This inconsistency reflected both the limited resources devited to the EIS review and conflicting objectives within CWPS. In the first place, response of CWPS to the content of most proposals was in no way proportional to their net consequences. For example, CWPS strongly objected to every single proposal made by the Environmental Protection Agency and the Department of Transportation, despite the fact that the EISs filed by these agencies often indicated substantial net benefits.

In addition, CWPS "jumped through the hoops" in the early days to avoid endorsing proposals that were contrary to the objective of holding down the consumer price index, despite the fact that these proposals often met the net-benefit criterion established by the EIS program. This conflict of objectives and CWPS's consequent unpredictability led the Federal Energy Administration to drop out of the program. [47]

Despite problems with economic impact analysis, after issuance of E.O. 12044 and subsequent promulgation of E.O. 12174 (November 30, 1979), the pace of regulatory review, reform, and the application of economic analysis under the Carter administration quickened. Creation of the Regulatory Council and its publication of five semiannual issues of the <u>Calendar of Federal Regulations</u> improved communication on regulation within government and the provision of information on regulatory proposals and actions to the public. Publication of the <u>Calendar</u>, <u>Regulatory Reform Highlights</u>, and other documents gave the appearance of greater coordination in the use of economic and other types of analyses and in the review process itself, even if this coordination was more a goal than an achievement. The staff of the Regulatory Council worked with agencies to gather and disseminate information and to increase consideration of various innovations in regulatory enforcement policy. [48] As noted in Table 6.4, a number of procedural and substantive regulatory policy reforms were instituted in the latter stages of the Carter administration, indicating that the long-standing drive toward regulatory reform enunciated in the early 1970s in President Nixon's "quality of life" review and continued under Ford and Carter finally was beginning to show concrete results.

The final major procedural reforms affecting the conduct of economic impact analysis instituted under Carter were enacted in the Paperwork Reduction Act and the Regulatory Flexibility Act, the latter signed by Carter in late 1980 after his loss to Ronald Reagan. In addition, Carter proposed additional procedural review initiatives to Congress in his last year in office that were not enacted. The Paperwork Executive Order (E.O. 12174) and the act required agencies and departments under the direct authority of the president to prepare budgets indicating the time utilized in the private sector to comply and respond to federal regulations. An initial submission of the paperwork budget indicated that approximately 786 million hours were spent annually responding to 5,000 federal reporting requirements. About three-quarters of this time was consumed in

completing tax forms. In addition, the order and act authorized a
sunset procedure for review of existing regulation with a five-year
sunset deadline for the life of federal reporting requirements; establishment of a computerized management information system (information locator) in OMB; and the use of innovative "market-oriented"
approaches to regulation. These measures also strengthened OMB's
role in the review process by assigning it responsibility for approval
of agency reporting requirements. OMB's role in the review process
was increased through these authorizations, but the review procedures
envisioned by Carter and his staff were not implemented fully before
Carter left office, although during the latter phases of his administration, the Office of Regulatory and Information Policy (RIP) in OMB
increased the application of economic analysis to proposed regulations.

In response to E.O. 12174 and the act, during 1979 and 1980 the
Regulatory Council devoted considerable staff time to the development
and bureaucratic marketing of management improvement techniques,
including methods for increasing public participation, increasing the
use of plain English in writing rules, reducing document processing
time, simplifying compliance monitoring and reporting rules, encouraging the use of voluntary rather than mandatory standard setting,
and employing innovative regulatory techniques. Among these were
so-called market-oriented regulatory approaches, including, in addition to general efforts to remove constraints to competition, the following:

Marketability of rights to use scarce resources
Use of performance standards in place of design and engineering standards in compliance measurement (including the EPA's
"bubble policy" to allow air-polluting firms to make internal trade-
offs in abatement technologies as long as they maintained or reduced
their existing emission levels)
Tiering rules to the size of regulated firms
Use of economic incentives, such as differential fine and fee
schedules to reduce and compensate for creation of negative externalities, and the differential industry subsidies

The specific provisions of E.O. 12174 were subsequently suspended
by President Reagan's Executive Order 12291, but implementation of
a number of the approaches noted above was continued within a number of agencies, although restricted severely by budget reductions
and concomitant cuts in regulatory analysis staff.

The Regulatory Flexibility Act required agencies to solicit
cost and benefit information from private sector firms and, as noted
above, to design regulations and reporting requirements appropriate
to the size and resources of regulated firms, that is, tiering regula-

tions to mitigate the adverse impact on smaller businesses. The act did not require cost-benefit to be the criterion by which regulations would be judged, but did authorize collection of data so that economic analysis could be performed. The provisions of the Regulatory Flexibility Act were continued under Reagan, some of them reiterated and their definitions made more specific in E.O. 12291 (February 1981).

Finally, Carter proposed to Congress the enactment of an even broader Regulation Reform Act to embody a number of the reforms noted above under Executive Orders 12044 and 12174 and others suggested by the staffs of the Regulatory Council, CEA, OMB, CWPS, the Department of Commerce, and his own White House Staff. The Regulation Reform Act was to be a capstone accomplishment of procedural reform to accompany a quite laudable record of substantive reform. In his last years in office Carter had proposed substantive reforms in economic regulation of the trucking industry, railroads, telecommunications, the banking and finance industry, trade and anti-trust practices, and a number of changes in environmental, safety, and health regulation, many of which were enacted, typically with substantial modification by Congress (see Table 6.4).

Many of the procedural changes intended to improve economic analysis and the regulatory review process approved at the end of the Carter administration were suspended with the election of Ronald Reagan. However, the zeal to review regulation and to improve the review process was certainly not diminished in the transition to a new administration. Some of the more important procedural changes recommended by the Carter administration were implemented quickly under Reagan. The key change in the review process instituted under the Reagan administration was to shift the responsibility for coordination and conduct of economic analysis and general regulatory review to OMB and its Office of Information and Regulatory Affairs (OIRA), headed by James C. Miller III under the direction of the Task Force on Regulatory Relief (TFRR). The TFRR was appointed by President Reagan on January 22, 1981, chaired by Vice-President George Bush, with the membership including the OMB director, the chairman of the President's Council of Economic Advisors, the secretary of the treasury, the attorney general, the secretary of commerce, the secretary of labor, and the president's adviser for policy planning, with Miller serving as executive director to the task force in his capacity as director of OIRA. Miller was appointed subsequently as director of the Federal Trade Commission.

The objectives of TFRR were to evaluate major agency regulatory proposals, especially those having an impact of $100 million or more on the economy; review existing regulatory policies having significant economic effect; coordinate the development of regulatory legislation for the administration; and enunciate the administration's position on the purpose and operational objectives of regulatory agencies. [49] In addition to creation of TFRR, the administration sought to reduce regulation by the appointment of cabinet-level departmental secretaries and agency directors who shared the new administration's critical view of the regulatory burden.

Under the provisions of Executive Order 12291 issued by President Reagan in February 1981, economic impact analysis was embraced more fully than it had been under the Carter administration. As noted, Carter administration regulatory review had been conducted decentrally by CWPS staff, the Council of Economic Advisors (CEA), the interagency Regulatory Analysis Review Group (RARG), OMB's Office of Regulatory and Information Policy (RIP), to some extent the Office of Statistical Policy in the Department of Commerce (OSP), and other Executive Office of the President and White House staff members. This review attempted to involve regulatory agencies to a considerable extent in the review process, but did not always succeed in this effort. And OMB's reluctance to fund regulatory analysis in agencies has been noted.

Almost immediately after taking office, Reagan terminated RARG and the Regulatory Council, and after a period of some confusion, merged approximately 90 staff analysis positions from CWPS, OSP, RIP, and elsewhere into OIRA. Regulatory Calendar submissions by agencies and calendar process were continued despite the termination of the Regulatory Council, which had prepared and published four editions of the Calendar of Federal Regulations (CFR). [50] Continuation of the Calendar attested to the effectiveness of this instrument for coordinating information on rules and adopting actions and for making this information known to the public.

As noted, under the authority of Executive Orders (12044 (Improving Government Regulation) and 12174 (Paperwork Budget), the Carter administration had required information on the costs and benefits of proposed rules to be prepared by agencies, but net costs or benefits were not required and, more importantly, were not employed as primary decision criteria in any formal way. [51] However, Reagan's E.O. 12291 required that cost-benefit analysis be conducted by agencies, that net benefits be stated, and that net benefits be shown in order for a rule to be approved. Among the criteria established by E.O. 12291 were maximization of social benefits and minimization of social costs, minimization of costs given a specific regulatory objective, the impact of regulation on the economy, and impact on future regulatory actions of other federal agencies. The other criteria notwithstanding, this last requirement has proven difficult to fulfill. The executive order required agencies to prepare regulatory impact analyses (RIA) specifying alternatives to regulations proposed and net results of cost-benefit analysis. The order also requested agency

plans for review of regulations postponed by a Reagan Presidential
Memorandum issued in January 1981 almost immediately after the
inauguration.

Reagan delayed implementation of regulations at the end of
Carter's term for 60 days to permit his staff to review these proposals according to the criteria specified in E.O. 12291. The postponement applied to agencies in 12 departments, including Commerce, Interior, Agriculture, Labor, Transportation, and the Environmental Protection Agency. Rules established in conformance
with Administrative Procedures Act (APA) requirements and those
pertaining to the military, foreign affairs, government procurement,
and the Internal Revenue Service were exempt from the postponement review. [52]

At the end of the review period, the administration announced
that of 172 regulations postponed, 100 had been approved, 35 rejected and returned to agencies or withdrawn by agencies, and 37
postponed for further review. During the postponement period 96
additional proposed rules were approved; most of these were emergency regulations or rules mandated by statutory law or court rul-
ings. [53]

After straightening out some of the typical transition confusion
over staff assignments, changes in review procedures, relationships
between OIRA and OMB budget staff, and those between departmental
and agency executive offices and staffs, the Reagan administration
proceeded to apply the net-benefit criterion very strictly to rules
proposed by agencies. However, the administration's efforts to apply benefit-cost analysis to worker health and safety was dealt a
sharp blow by the Supreme Court's decision in the cotton dust case
(June 17, 1981). The Court ruled that OSHA work-place health standards could be applied where the agency could demonstrate that actual benefits would accrue, even where industry compliance costs
were substantial. This ruling appeared to reject strict benefit-cost
analysis as the basis of health decisions. A year earlier, a Supreme
Court ruling on OSHA benzene standards upheld a 1978 appeals court
decision that the benefits of regulation in improved worker health
would have to be demonstrated in order for a rule to stand. In making the ruling, the Court implied that OSHA might employ some form
of risk analysis in rule setting and that the cost-effectiveness and
feasibility of rules still should be considered. In addition, it noted
that better information on compliance costs would have to be provided
by industry to improve OSHA decisions. [54] We address the information issue in discussion of the regulatory budget and worker health
and safety standard setting in Chapter 7.

In June 1981, the Reagan administration issued a status report
on regulatory review indicating that of 847 regulations reviewed by

May 27, 1981, 56 had been rejected and returned to agencies at an estimated savings of $15.5 billion to $18 billion to the economy. James C. Miller III announced plans to review approximately 100 major regulations by December 31, 1981, including transportation, motor vehicle, occupational and consumer health and safety, affirmative action, and environmental regulations, and to propose revisions to existing regulatory acts scheduled for reauthorization by Congress, for example, the Clean Air Act Amendments. [55]

While the Reagan administration moved quickly to streamline executive regulatory review procedures and to increase the application of economic analysis in its own review, similar efforts were not made to improve regulatory analysis in agencies. Instead, due to budget cuts, agencies found themselves hard-pressed to vie success-fully with the administration in defense of existing rules and in institution of new regulations. The Reagan administration added to the length of time and number of steps required for review. Perhaps taking a lesson from the tactics of environmentalists and other interest groups that have resisted the construction of dams, nuclear power plants, and other public works projects through procedural delay, the Reagan administration lengthened the review route for agencies seeking approval of new regulations.

The first step in lengthening the review process was to continue to require preparation of two regulatory impact analyses (RIA) as done previously under Carter, but to subject these analyses to more critical review. A preliminary RIA was required t. accompany the Notice of Proposed Rule Making (NPRM), and a second RIA had to accompany the final rule submitted for review to OIRA 30 days prior to publication in the Federal Register. Each of the RIA was reviewed by OIRA, and in some cases other presidential staff, for compliance with the rigorous analytical requirements required by E.O. 12291. [56] The second step was to require that preliminary RIA for all major proposed rules be submitted to OIRA 60 days prior to publication in the Federal Register. In addition, the public comment period following publication of the NPRM in the Federal Register was maintained at 30 to 90 days, as under Carter. The combination of the several procedural changes instituted under Reagan added at least 90 days to the regulatory review process, with an approximate of the total number of days required for approval extended to a range between 210 and 300 days.

A comparison of the phases of proposal and review for new regulations utilized by the Carter and Reagan administrations is shown in Table 6.3. As is apparent in the table, the Reagan administration's review schedule is perhaps procedurally more straightforward than that used under Carter. However, the key difference between the two procedures is not revealed in the procedural steps.

TABLE 6.3

Comparison of Regulatory Review Schedules

Carter: E.O. 12044	Reagan: E.O. 12291
Step 1: Advanced Notice of Proposed Rule Making (ANPRM was not used universally by agencies)	Step 1: ANPRM
Step 2: General public comment period (variable length of time provided by agencies)	Step 2: Preparation of preliminary RIA to be provided to OIRA 60 days prior to publication of NPRM
Step 3: Notice of Proposed Rule Making (NPRM) published in Federal Register	Step 3: NPRM published in Federal Register
Step 4: Second public comment period (30 to 90 days)	Step 4: Public comment period (30 to 90 days)
Step 5: Preliminary RIA prepared	Step 5: Preparation of final RIA (FIRA) to be submitted to OIRA with proposed rule 30 days prior to publication in the Federal Register
Step 6: Preparation of final draft of proposed regulation	Step 6: Review of proposed regulation by OIRA (30 days)
Step 7: Review of final rule by CWPS, OMB, and RARG (30-day review period)	Step 7: Receive OIRA approval of final RIA
Step 8: Receive RARG approval of final RIA	Step 8: Publication of new regulation in the Federal Register
Step 9: Publication of new regulation in the Federal Register	Step 9: Regulation becomes effective 30 days after publication in the Federal Register unless specified otherwise
Step 10: Regulation becomes effective 30 days after publication in the Federal Register unless specified otherwise	
Step 11: Final regulatory impact analysis published	
Total time: Approximately 120 to 210 days for major rules	Total time: Approximately 210 to 300 days for major rules

Rather, it is in the enforcement of requirements that agencies submit proposed rules to a strict cost-benefit test, show how costs are minimized and benefits are maximized relative to other policy options, and, in addition, indicate the effects on the economy and on the regulatory programs of other agencies. The additional preparation effort and time required for agencies is only one element of the change. The more dramatic difference is in the potential for OIRA to reject agency RIA, requiring additional analysis in compliance with review criteria. As noted by George Eads, this may be contrasted with the procedure employed under Carter where agencies were, in the end, required to "identify costs and benefits, to quantify them insofar as possible, and either to choose cost-effective solutions or to explain why they had not. Moreover, the burden of proving that proposed rules were not cost-effective lay not with the agencies but with senior White House aides."[57]

Despite the lack of coordination in the process under Carter, the review of agency analyses involved consultation among the staffs of RARG, CEA, RIP, and other regulatory analysis units. Under Reagan, the review process has been highly centralized in OIRA and in OMB, and more adversarial to agency staff, but understandably not to Reagan-appointed agency heads and cabinet-level department secretaries who themselves have added to the procedural delay. Within agencies, not only has there been a shouldering of responsibility for economic analysis in compliance with E.O. 12291 but a greater scrutiny of analysis by executive offices, evidencing a generalized resistance to the proposal of new rules.

OIRA has pressed agencies for better economic analysis, good of and by itself, but in many cases exceeding agency analytical capacity. Thus, through the development and use of economic impact criteria and the elevation of OIRA to the role of central judge of the adequacy of analysis, the Reagan administration intentionally placed agencies at a distinct disadvantage in what has become a protracted adversarial game of executive branch regulatory politics.

The application of economic impact analysis under the Reagan administration has been the strongest effort to enforce this approach to regulatory reform implemented under any president. However, this effort has been criticized along a number of lines. It has been alleged to have strongly reduced agency participation and effectiveness in the rule-making process and to have impaired public participation effectiveness through reduced opportunity and altered timing for public comment.[58] It has also been criticized for the absence of restrictions on contacts between OIRA/OMB and agency staffs, both at the preproposal phase, where Carter required that OMB contacts with agencies be recorded but Reagan requires no documentation, and after rule publication in the Federal Register. Carter administration officials were to minimize contacts with agencies and others to prevent conflict of interest in the regulatory process, whereas the Reagan administration has not maintained such controls. This has caused one observer to note that the new regulatory political game belongs to the swift, enterprising, and influential. [59]

Conflict of interest issues notwithstanding, perhaps the most serious criticism of the Reagan administration's approach is that while OIRA has required more and better economic analysis, it has not funded agencies so as to cause this analysis to be produced. The pitfalls of economic and cost-benefit analysis are legendary: in quantification of indirect costs and benefits, valuing externalities, comparing individual utilities, and so on. This is not to say that it can't be done, only that for it to be done well requires training time and, in some cases, new staff. As we have described, agency skills in economic analysis were not fortified significantly under Carter, mostly due to OMB resistance. Instead, RARG, CWPS, CEA, and other staff provided this skill when utilized. However, under Reagan no such interagency or even limited high-level analytical skills became available to regulators. Agency budgets were seriously reduced in the administration's efforts to balance the budget and reduce inflation. The result of all this was to require better analysis but not to receive it; to overpower agency staffs in the rule proposal process but not to teach or lead them. In its first year, the Reagan administration sought to reduce regulation primarily by attempting to eliminate proposals for new rules. This may be contrasted sharply with a policy that might attempt to increase the net social benefit of government interaction with the private sector through refinement of the regulatory process.

These results have been most frustrating to economists and others who believed they had made some headway with agencies in the last year of the Carter administration in terms of inculcating a desire to deregulate and to experiment with new reporting, monitoring, and compliance techniques, for example, marketability of rights, performance standards, and voluntary standard setting. Still, the Reagan administration's efforts to require identification of net costs or benefits, to pay attention to private sector compliance costs that are for the most part passed on to the consumer, and the strong emphasis on comprehensive and orderly sunset review of existing regulation represent movement in the right direction to improve regulatory decision making and perhaps to increase the likelihood that high-quality economic impact analysis will be accomplished. Fulfillment of this promise depends, of course, on how these measures are implemented, particularly in terms of the manner in which agency incentives in policy development, enforcement strategy, and so on are affected by OIRA and OMB actions and the extent to which agencies are funded to produce high quality economic impact analysis.

A chronology of selected regulatory reform events from 1974 through 1981 is provided in Table 6.4 to clarify the sequence of major procedural and substantive reform actions implemented under Ford and Carter and in the initial phases of the Reagan administration.

TABLE 6.4

Selected Regulatory Reform Events, 1974 through 1981

August 24, 1974: Legislation enacted creating Council on Wage and Price Stability. Authorizing legislation permitted CWPS to intervene in regulatory approval process

September 8, 1974: Summit Conference on Inflation convened; economists endorse deregulation

November 27, 1974: Executive Order 11821 issued by President Ford, establishing the Inflation Impact Statement (IIS) program; authorizing CWPS reviews of major regulatory proposals issued by executive agencies

January 1975: The director of the Domestic Council Review Group on Regulatory Reform appointed as chairman of the Securities and Exchange Commission

January 13, 1975: The Securities and Exchange Commission adopted Rule 19b-3 outlawing price fixing in brokerage industry

February 1975: Senator Edward Kennedy's Governmental Operations Subcommittee began hearings on Civil Aeronautics Board regulation of airlines

May 1975: Senate Judiciary Committee Hearings held on regulation of cable television

May to June 1975: Senate Banking Committee Hearings held on Financial Institutions Act

June 5, 1975: Securities Act Amendments of 1975 uphold Rule 19b-3

July 1975: Senate Resolution 71 approved to fund joint study of regulation by Government Operations and Commerce Committees

December 12, 1975: Federal statutes approved allowing states to repeal fair-trade laws

February 5, 1976: The Railroad Revitalization and Regulatory Reform Act of 1976 enacted, giving the Interstate Commerce Commission considerable latitude to move in the direction of deregulation and authorizing greater flexibility in setting rates and permitting exit and entry

May 13, 1976: Presidential Task Force to Streamline Regulations announced by President Ford. The first targets were the Occupational Safety and Health Administration, the Federal Energy Authority, and the Export Control Administration of the Department of Commerce

September 3, 1976: The Sunshine Act enacted, requiring agencies to conduct meetings in the open and to keep transcripts of meetings for public review

September 1976: House of Representatives Hearings held on Motor Carriers Reform Act of 1975

October 1976: House Commerce Committee held hearings on regulatory reform

December 7, 1976: CWPS review of Inflation Impact Statement program published

December 17, 1976: House Subcommittee on Economic Stabilization held hearings on inflationary impacts of government regulation

December 31, 1976: Executive Order 11949 issued extending IIS program through December 31, 1977, and renaming it the Economic Impact Statement program

March 1977: Alfred Kahn appointed chairman of the Civil Aeronautics Board with agenda of airline industry deregulation

November 1977: House Rule 6010 enacted making entry into the air cargo industry virtually free and giving operators wide discretion in setting rates

March 23, 1978: Executive Order 12044, Improving Government Regulation, issued by President Carter expanding the EIS program, calling for zero-base review of existing regulation, and establishing authority for regulatory control and coordination with the Regulatory Council and the White House Economic Policy Review Groups; CWPS EIS Unit assigned as Regulatory Analysis Review Group staff and increased in size from 6 to 12 economists; order requested agencies to improve public participation in the regulatory process

June 1978: The interagency Regulatory Analysis Review Group (RARG) authorized by Executive Order 12044, was established including representatives of all cabinet-level departments except Defense, State, Treasury and including OMB, CEA, EPA, and the Office of Science and Technology Policy

(continued)

Table 6.4, continued

September 5, 1978: The Civil Aeronautics Board deregulated air fares and route restrictions de facto

October 1978: Congress passed the Natural Gas Policy Act (portion of 1978 Energy Act) permitting gradual deregulation of wellhead price of natural gas, relaxing rules on interstate gas transportation and other rules

October 5, 1978: U.S. Court of Appeals ruled that OSHA must perform benefit-cost analysis before issuing substantial health regulations

October 17, 1978: The Department of Commerce hosted a seminar on regulatory reform exploring the feasibility of the regulatory budget, costs and benefits of regulation, and alternatives to regulation

October 1978: OSHA eliminated 928 unnecessary or duplicative safety and health regulations

October 24, 1978: Congress passed the airline deregulation bill (14 CFR Part 200-209)

October 31, 1978: President Carter issued Presidential Memorandum, "Strengthening Regulatory Management," establishing the Regulatory Council

November 1978: House Subcommittee on Communications held hearings on the Communications Act of 1978, changing the focus of the law by supporting regulation of communications only to the extent "market forces are deficient," and treating regulation as a supplement to, rather than a replacement for, competition

November 1978: Congress passed and President Carter signed the Depository Institutions Deregulation and Monetary Control Act

February 1979: The Joint Economic Committee of Congress unanimously endorsed the regulatory budget concept

February 28, 1979: The Regulatory Council issued its first semiannual Regulatory Calendar

March 27, 1979: ICC exempted railroads from rate, route, and service frequency controls for fresh produce shipment

April 1979: President Carter announced the phased decontrol of prices on domestically produced oil

June 1, 1979: Implementation of decontrol of the price of new, domestically produced oil (discovered after January 1, 1979) and "marginal" oil produced from small wells (less than 35 barrels per day)

August 1, 1979: The Joint Economic Committee of Congress held hearings on regulatory budgeting and the need for cost-effectiveness in the regulatory process

August 1979: Price controls over domestically produced heavy crude oil removed

September 1979: OMB report issued on agency performance under E.O. 12044

November 16, 1979: President Carter directed the Regulatory Council, OMB, and the Small Business Administration to develop a national policy to reduce the effect of federal regulation on small business

November 30, 1979: President Carter issued E.O. 12174 requiring departments to prepare paperwork budgets to be submitted to OMB estimating the amount of time spent in the private sector responding to federal regulations; establishing a five-year sunset provision for reporting requirements; authorizing a computerized paperwork management information system (information locator) in OMB; giving OMB authority to approve reporting requirements for most agencies; encouraging agencies to employ innovative and market-oriented approaches to regulation

December 1979: EPA implemented the "bubble" policy to encourage state governments to employ performance standards for polluting firms to permit tradeoff among the mixes of emission control measures

December 1979: Federal Deposit Insurance Corporation reduced regulatory burden for small banks, including deposit requirements

December 26, 1979: Department of Treasury revised banking regulations, removing and modifying 200 pages of CFR rules on banking and securities underwriting

January 1980: The FCC reduced entry controls over the cable television industry and rules restricting international data transmission competition and consumer telephone purchase

January 11, 1980: Rules to implement the provisions of E.O. 12174, the paperwork budget, were published in the Federal Register

January 1980: President Carter shortened the schedule for decontrol of prices of domestic oil, to be completed by October 1, 1981

January 1980: ICC removed and modified accounting and reporting requirements for small trucking firms

(continued)

169

Table 6.4, continued

May 1980: ICC removed trucking route restrictions and interlining requirements for approximately 1,400 of 16,000 regulated trucking firms; eliminated rules prohibiting affiliated companies from carrying each others' freight to reduce empty operating miles; removed restrictions on intermodal shipping agreements with railroads

June 1980: Motor Carrier Act passed and signed, partially deregulating the interstate trucking industry

July 2, 1980: The U.S. Supreme Court rejected as too stringent OSHA work-place benzene standards; the Court upheld the ruling established by the U.S. Court of Appeals in October 1978 that OSHA must provide substantial evidence of benefit in order to sustain its rules; the Court endorsed the concept of risk-benefit analysis and rejected the notion that exposure levels to toxic substances should be maintained at lowest technologically achievable levels regardless of cost

September 1980: Congress passed and President Carter signed the Regulatory Flexibility Act, that became effective January 1, 1981, requiring agencies to solicit cost and benefit information from business and industry and to design regulations relative to the size and resources of regulated firms

November 1980: OMB issued second report on agency performance under E.O. 12044

November 1980: Securities and Exchange Commission removed and revised reporting requirements for financial institutions and publicly traded companies

December 1980: President Carter signed the Paperwork Reduction Act implementing provisions of E.O. 12174

January 22, 1981: Task Force on Regulatory Relief announced by newly elected President Reagan; Vice-President Bush appointed chairman

January 28, 1981: President Reagan announced decision permitting complete decontrol of oil prices

January 29, 1981: Reagan administration issued Presidential Memorandum, "Postponement of Pending Regulations," ordering regulatory agencies to delay the implementation of new regulations for 60 days to permit review by TFRR and, subsequently, the Office of Information and Regulatory Affairs in OMB

February 17, 1981: President Reagan issued E.O. 12291 establishing criteria for evaluating existing and proposed regulations, including net benefit or cost identification; required RIA to be submitted to OIRA; continued the Regulatory Calendar in OMB (October and April); revoked Carter's E.O. 12044 and 12174

March 25, 1981: Reagan administration terminated the Regulatory Council; Vice-President Bush requested the independent regulatory agencies to comply voluntarily with Sections 2 and 3 of E.O. 12291

March 30, 1981: Vice-President Bush for TFRR reported that during the 60-day postponement review period 172 rules were reviewed, 100 approved, 35 rejected or withdrawn, 37 held for review, and 96 other rules were allowed to become effective

June 12, 1981: Vice-President Bush for TFRR announced that of 847 significant regulations reviewed by May 27, 1981, 56 had been returned to agencies at a savings of $15.5 billion to $18 billion to the economy; announced plans to review 100 major existing regulations by December 31, 1981

June 13, 1981: Vice-President Bush issued report "Materials on President Reagan's Program of Regulatory Relief"

June 17, 1981: The U.S. Supreme Court upheld OSHA cotton dust standards, rejecting the proposition that strict benefit-cost analysis may be applied to worker health standards; accepted the position that OSHA rules could be imposed where benefit is demonstrated even where compliance costs are substantial

June 25, 1981: The Depository Institutions Deregulation Committee authorized the phased decontrol of interest rate ceilings, to begin August 1, 1981, and proceed annually through 1984

August 1981: OSHA Director Auchter announced plans for comprehensive reform of agency standards, safety inspection procedures, complaint response practices, and inspection exemptions

---

On the basis of our analysis of the changes in regulatory review procedures that have taken place since 1974, we would propose that if any economic impact-oriented regulatory analysis program is to be successful, not only must the analyses prepared by initiating agencies and OMB be improved but also the central review unit must adopt a uniform set of rules for evaluation of proposals and abide by them. These rules would include standard measures for intangibles and common procedures for handling risk and uncertainty. The review unit also must have sufficient and skilled staff resources to carry out its mission. In addition, the criteria for selection of proposals for review should not be overly concerned with price effects. Instead, the reviewers should give greater attention to the reversibility of the consequences of proposed regulation than has been the case in the past. For example, regulations that primarily increase operating costs and have uncertain consequences should not be required to meet the same standard as those that primarily increase capital expenditures for plant and equipment. In the first case, we can complement ex ante cost benefit analysis with ex post performance evaluation once the program is in place; in the second, we must depend on ex ante analysis to make the right decision.

Finally, it must be noted that a good economic impact analysis program cannot spend all of its resources evaluating new regulation. It is unlikely that the resources devoted to careful review of all proposed new regulations would not be better spent on a comprehensive, but selective review of the stock of existing regulations. There is no reason to believe that incrementalism will produce satisfactory results overall if the proposed increments are not judged against an existing base. We note that this lesson apparently has been learned to some extent, judged by the priority the Reagan administration assigned to the review of existing regulation. A shift in emphasis to give greater attention to existing regulation also has been reflected in the congressional agenda, largely as a result of Reagan administration actions proposing the removal of a number of existing rules and rescinding regulatory policy changes initiated but not implemented under the Carter administration. In addition, the congressional regulatory review agenda has been set to a great extent by the necessity for amendment and repassage of a number of major regulatory acts scheduled for reconsideration in the early 1980s.

Our summary assessment of economic impact analysis is, in essence, that it ought to be done; ex ante economic analysis ought to form the basis for decision making on regulatory policy, especially where costs and benefits can be measured with some accuracy; and good economic analysis is expensive and difficult, but not impossible to perform. We believe that the substantive reform of regulatory policy to be undertaken in the 1980s ought to center around the development of the capacity for more and better economic analysis. An indication of how this may be achieved is provided in Chapter 7; the remainder of this chapter continues the consideration of procedural reform, which we believe is ultimately necessary in order to permit the results of improved economic analysis to be considered and used profitably in the federal regulatory policymaking process.

ZERO-BASE REVIEW

Zero-base review of existing regulation would require that all statutes and administrative rules be analyzed relative to their cost-effectiveness, economic impact, fit with legislative intent, and so on, as if they were newly proposed measures. Under the Ford and Carter administrations, existing regulations were excluded initially from the IIS/EIS programs out of fear of "analysis paralysis." As William Lilley observed, when questioned about extending the program to existing regulation:

> I don't know how you would get at that. If I were head
> of a line agency, I could make an awfully compelling
> case . . . that this would be a license to bring me to
> a stop. If some agency had power to require me to
> justify all my extant regulation, I would never get any-
> thing done. If you granted such a power, it would have
> to be used justly and carefully. [60]

Executive Order 12044 required executive branch regulatory agencies to review all existing regulations and to remove the obsolete, the contradictory, and the ineffective. This approach was characterized as "zero-based regulation"[61] and has been continued under E.O. 12291. E.O. 12044 produced almost immediate results. The Occupational Safety and Health Administration recalled approximately 1,100 regulations. HEW dropped 25 percent of all back-logged regulations and extensively reviewed existing regulations, reducing the total number of pages by nearly one-third.[62] Other agencies instituted similar review. While the change in administrations makes it difficult to draw certain conclusions as to the consequences of this particular effort, it appears that predictions of disaster were unfounded—review itself did not immobilize. It appears that executive pressure, firmly applied, will direct an agency review away from those areas where it is least likely to be effective. But executive pressure alone is probably not sufficient to promote effective performance, even where what is desired is fairly well understood.

This last conclusion is based upon the response of OSHA to Carter administration efforts to retarget its regulatory activities away from worker safety and toward worker health. These efforts were only half successful. OSHA modified its approach to safety hazards, dropping hundreds of superfluous regulations and modifying its enforcement strategy, but was reluctant to come down hard on health hazards. In a few cases, OSHA adopted severe and costly standards, but few work-place health standards were set. Executive

pressure on OSHA may have resulted in paralysis, but not necessarily for the reasons anticipated. It appears that OSHA was para-
lyzed by fear of criticism for making mistakes, a likely consequence
of a strategy oriented toward health hazards. [63]

We conclude that it is not enough merely to understand a regulatory problem, and pressure from above may not be sufficient to
enforce a proper regulatory response to problems. Regulators must
be given the incentives and resources to attack problems over which
they are likely to have the greatest influence. It appears that the
failure of the Carter administration to provide OSHA with an appropriate set of incentives is not explained by the difficulty of the task,
but that the issue was overlooked. Unfortunately, this seems to have
continued under Reagan.

Zero-base regulation, at least so far as it has been practiced
to date, may be contrasted with the two remaining proposals, both
of which are oriented primarily toward modification of the incentives
faced by regulators.

FEDERAL ASSUMPTION OF COMPLIANCE COSTS

James Bennett and Manuel Johnson have proposed that the private sector should be compensated for costs mandated by government regulations, in which case compliance costs would be a cost
to government. [64] The perverse consequences resulting from the
exemption of these costs from the budget process would then be
avoided. Bennett and Johnson are concerned only with the paperwork burden, but the logic of their proposal should apply equally
well to other government-mandated costs. How would it work? To
answer this question, we must first identify which costs are relevant. The general answer to this question is: the same costs that
are reflected in the federal budget. The more specific answer is:
the direct cost of those actions taken by firms to comply with regulation that would not have been taken in the absence of regulation,
as reported in firms' accounting, engineering, and other records.
There are a number of ways of estimating costs and a large number
of cost concepts from which to choose. The answer we posit to the
question assumes that consistency with existing government accounting is desirable.

Current national accounting practices identify two balancing
items in the federal budget, expenditures and revenues. On the expenditure side is exhaustive expenditure, such as goods and services
bought from other producers, wages and salaries of government employees, and transfer payments. On the revenue side are tax revenues and receipts from sales of goods and services. These items

are balanced either by a residual item, called a surplus, on the expenditure side or by a deficit on the revenue side. It is standard practice in government to treat only the components of the expenditure item as costs—such direct inputs into programs as resources, labor, and time. If it were desirable for the federal government to assume the costs of complying with the regulatory requirements of federal government agencies and programs, consistency would require that compliance costs be treated as a purchase of goods and services and that they reflect only the direct inputs to compliance with regulatory programs.

This does not mean that only costs that can be readily estimated or evaluated are relevant to regulatory decision making or that only these costs should be considered by regulatory decision makers. What is done customarily in public sector program analysis is to transfer "hard-to-measure" costs to the benefit side of the equation, treating them as negative benefits. By definition, costs are more tangible and easier to measure than benefits. Assumption of compliance costs implies that comparisons between regulatory and nonregulatory actions would be easier if all "easy-to-measure" costs were treated alike and all "hard-to-measure" costs were shifted to the benefit side, as is the case in the analysis of other public programs. This logic rests upon the prior assumption that the direct, incremental costs of regulation are fairly easy to identify. We cannot say with certainty that this is so, but the Arthur Andersen & Company study done for the Business Roundtable makes a plausible case that it is possible to establish credible methodologies for measuring the directly attributable incremental costs of individual regulations.[65]

There are a number of problems associated with this proposal. Perhaps the most serious is that it may provide firms with an incentive to engage in a regulated activity in order to be paid for not doing it.[66] In addition, there is the possibility of strategic behavior on the part of firms.[67] Theoretical treatments of these issues make it seem that these problems can be avoided, but only with great difficulty.[68] In this case, we are inclined to believe that the theorists have overestimated these difficulties. This conclusion is based, to an extent, upon the experience of similar state-level programs. California and other states have implemented procedures by which states reimburse local governments for state-mandated costs.[69] At first, in California, this program encountered many of the problems noted (perverse incentives, strategic behavior), but local governments and the State Department of Finance learned how to deal with them. It appears that a key to the success of state-mandated cost programs has been that supporters of a proposed program have a prior incentive to underestimate costs, while state budgeteers are prone to overestimate them. Consequently, it is mutually advantageous for both parties to specify fully the characteristics and consequences of a program before its enactment. [70]

As a response to paperwork burden, then, compensation may be a satisfactory solution. This conclusion may apply to most aspects of regulatory enforcement, though as a general complement to regulation federal cost compensation is of dubious value. One does not have to believe that regulation is intended to prevent the "bad acts of evil businessmen" to believe that polluters should bear the burden of reducing emissions. [71] Furthermore, so far as the objectives of regulation (as opposed to its enforcement) are concerned, if it were possible to design an efficient scheme to compensate firms for the cost of compliance, it should be possible to substitute an alternative instrument of public policy for regulation, such as pollution or safety taxes.

THE REGULATORY BUDGET

The regulatory budget is intended to make the federal government treat compliance costs as if they were a cost to government without actually assuming them. What is proposed is an annual summation of all costs generated by an agency. The budget of a regulatory agency would reflect two kinds of costs: administrative and enforcement costs of government regulatory activity, costs that are now reflected in the federal budget; and mandated compliance costs, private sector compliance costs that are not included presently in the federal budget—the same kinds of costs that would be reported if the federal government were to assume directly compliance costs as discussed in the proposal above. [72] From an accounting standpoint, that main difference between this proposal and federal assumption of compliance cost is that under this proposal, the revenue item would be automatically modified to balance compliance costs. This action would be more or less consistent with the procedure followed in accounting for tax expenditures. Tax expenditures are special provisions in the tax laws that provide for preferential treatment and, consequently, result in revenue losses. In government accounts, the revenue item reflects the tax that would have been paid in the absence of the proposed deduction, and the expenditure item reflects the deduction as a transfer. According to Robert Crandall, under a regulatory budget:

> Agencies would be instructed not to exceed the budget
> total in any year, but would be free to determine how
> much to spend in each program in their domain. EPA

could be given, for example, $40 billion per year to
grow by a fixed percentage annually. It would then
have to decide whether to spend $1 billion by requiring
scrubbers for all electrical utilities, or by seeking reductions in, say, water pollution. This proposal would
have the additional advantage of provoking an annual debate in Congress on the size of EPA's or OSHA's budget. Such a debate would force the proponents to measure the benefits of the various regulatory programs,
something now totally lacking in the political process. [73]

Implementing the regulatory budget would require considerable reorganization of the process by which Congress and the president authorize and control government regulatory actions and expenditures. Note that the budgetary process comprehends both expenditure planning and control of outlays. Consequently the budget
cycle may be decomposed into two phases, budget preparation and
budget execution. As is the case with the expenditure budget, the
phases of the regulatory budget process would be further subdivided
into formulation of estimates and proposals, negotiation of proposals,
enactment of proposals into law (budget preparation), spending,
monitoring and control, and postaudit and evaluation (budget execution).

In the federal budget process, budget preparation begins approximately 18 months prior to the start of the budget year with a
call for spending estimates and concludes in formal enactment of
the congressional appropriations bill under the president's signature.
Execution of the budget begins on the first day of a federal fiscal
year, October 1, when agencies commence spending under authority
of the appropriations law, and terminates when spending accounts
have been closed, following postexpenditure audit.

The regulatory budget process would operate parallel to and as
a component of the existing federal expenditure budget process. The
collection and utilization of information on the costs of regulation
would be organized to match the structure and timing of the existing
budget cycle. Regulatory budget estimates and proposals would be
prepared according to guidelines issued by the Office of Management
and Budget. Regulatory agencies would prepare proposals to continue existing regulatory activities and requests for authorization
of expenditures for new proposals. New proposals would include
activities authorized under prior separate legislation but not yet
funded and new initiatives advocated by regulatory agencies not specifically authorized through prior legislative action.

Agency budget submissions would include descriptions of current and proposed regulatory activities, justification statements

for new proposals noting prior legislative authorization, economic rationale, technical feasibility and advisability, and so on and current and proposed expenditures for government administrative costs. The final component of agency regulatory budget submissions to be considered by OMB and the president would be statements of current private sector compliance activities and their costs, estimates of budget year costs (outlay authority) under existing regulatory budget obligational authority, and estimates of proposed increments. Eventually, current cost statements would be drawn from notational cost compliance accounts that would be established once the annual regulatory budget was enacted by Congress and signed by the president.

Once enacted, the budget is a spending plan that details the timing and purpose of outlays or expenditures. Budgets are divided into separate accounts. In order to comprehend both government administrative enforcement costs and compliance costs borne by regulated firms, a dual accounts structure would be required for the regulatory budget. Each regulation or regulatory program would be treated as a separate account, or accounts might be based upon regulatory objectives, with each rule identified as a cost center. The accounting system would record private sector compliance costs in notational regulatory program accounts. These notational accounts would be indexed to administrative accounts in which actual government enforcement and administrative expenditures incurred by regulatory agencies would be recorded. This would permit monitoring, control, and reporting on the execution of the budget both in terms of government and private sector compliance costs.

Traditionally, in the expenditure budget process, accounts may be observed to have two basic components—the base and the increment. It is assumed that the regulatory budget would operate according to the traditional incremental base budgeting model rather than, for example, as a zero-base budget, although a ZBB option might be explored once the fundamental regulatory budget process has been established. The base would be composed of those regulatory costs of government and the private sector that result from existing statutory and administrative requirements. The increment would be composed of proposals to add new programs and expenditures to current activities. As is the case with traditional incremental base budgeting, it may be expected that increments proposed to the regulatory budget would be scrutinized more carefully by the OMB and Congress than the base. However, this scrutiny may be expected to stimulate constant review of priorities and activity levels within regulatory agencies. And, if the traditional incremental approach fails in this respect, the regulatory budget accounts structure may be utilized in a zero-base (or modified ZBB) review of regulatory program expenditures.

The previous description serves to outline the general manner in which the regulatory budget would operate. However, there are many critical aspects of implementation that deserve further attention. These include methods for budget preparation, estimation of private sector compliance costs, government incentives to reduce private sector costs in negotiation and enacting the budget, and, whether in the end, the process of negotiation of costs between the representatives of government and business would produce reliable data.

PREPARATION OF ESTIMATES— COST COMPLIANCE INFORMATION

Considerable sophistication in the initial preparation of estimates for the regulatory budget would be required. Under the procedures envisioned here, agencies might not be held responsible for preparing initial estimates of private sector costs. Rather, these cost estimates could be provided by OMB. The costs to the private sector of proposed new regulation could also be estimated by OMB. It seems advisable that OMB not be permitted to use its "acknowledged" technical expertise as an excuse to exclude the agency from a role in defining its base. The bargaining that goes on between agency and OMB during the negotiation phase of the budget cycle is critical to the effectiveness of the traditional budget process. At the same time, the technical problems associated with compliance cost estimation are not trivial. While it may be fairly straightforward to record and verify current expenditures for compliance, the determination of future costs and indirect costs, such as efficiency loss costs, would be a more difficult task. Let us explore these issues in turn: current expenditures, future costs, efficiency loss costs.

Once regulatory legislation were passed and expenditures were authorized in the regulatory budget, private firms would be notified that regulatory compliance expenditures for a specific period, for example, a regulatory fiscal year, should be recorded, audited, and submitted to the government. Guidelines for this activity would be provided to business firms by OMB. These guidelines would establish the basis for private firm participation in budget preparation, describing the types of firm expenditures to be included, that is, the direct costs of equipment, labor, and so on, and indirect administrative costs associated with compliance; and procedures for verifying these expenditure statements through postaudit and reporting them to OMB.

The U.S. federal budget at present does not formally distinguish between noncontinuing operating expenditures and capital outlay expenditures that occur for a fixed period of time during project construction. The regulatory budget would operate compatibly with this procedure. In the regulatory budget, nonrecurring compliance expenditures would be treated as separate items and would not be included in the budget base. [74]

Once private sector compliance expenditures were reported, these expenditures would be recorded in notational accounts linked by accounting code to government regulatory program expenditure accounts. The data recorded in notational accounts would thus comprise aggregate current private sector compliance expenditures. Normally we expect firms to be somewhat reluctant to comply with additional government requests for information; in this case, however, compliance should be perceived as in the interests of business. This observation is based upon the assumption that firms want government decision makers to know how much regulation costs, and will want this knowledge to influence future decisions on whether to regulate.

In estimating future costs of proposed regulations, we would expect private sector representatives and firms to play a larger role in budget preparation than is normally the case with client or target groups. Firms would be notified of an intended rule change in the Federal Register following agency responses to the call for budget estimates. Agency proposals would provide information for Register listings. Estimates of future private sector compliance costs would be made by OMB, based upon the audited accounting reports of current costs provided by businesses, OMB, and agency cost analyses. It can be expected that firms would prepare their own estimates of compliance costs if they perceived it to be in their interest to participate in cost estimation.

With regard to estimation of efficiency loss costs, we would hope that existing federal EIS procedures that consider these costs would continue in effect under a regulatory budget. However, there appears to be no justification for including such costs in the budget. The regulatory budget, like the expenditure budget, would identify direct expenditures incurred in regulating, that is, specific expenditures for regulatory compliance rather than all of the economic costs associated with compliance. The costs included in the regulatory budget are not the costs that would be used in conducting a cost-benefit analysis. Efficiency loss costs would not be included, even though they occur, because these costs are not comparable with the types of government costs identified in budgets.

NEGOTIATION AND ENACTMENT INCENTIVES

Regulatory budget hearings would be held by OMB to review agency program maintenance and change proposals. In some cases it can be expected that agency and business representatives would provide alternative projections of compliance costs. Although actual participation by business representatives in budget hearings is not anticipated in this proposal, representatives of the private sector would have ample opportunity to present data and arguments in regulatory budget hearings before Congress.

The result of OMB budget hearing would be the regulatory budget base and three sets of change proposals to be reviewed and further negotiated before Congress. These sets would be proposals supported by OMB and also supported by agencies; proposals supported by agencies but not by OMB; and proposals supported by the OMB but not supported by agencies. The president would present the regulatory budget to Congress accompanying the proposed expenditure budget, and Congress would review the budget in the same manner in which the expenditure budget is analyzed and enacted. The results of congressional action would be forwarded to the president for approval as a component of the congressionally approved budget bill. Once enacted in the first regulatory budget, the expenditures authorized would compose the base budget upon which estimates for the succeeding budget year would be made.

Execution of the regulatory budget would parallel the procedures employed in the expenditure budgetary process. However, a key problem to be resolved in regulatory budget execution is decision authority and the extent of control over the transfer of funds from notational to administrative accounts. The exercise of this authority and control is critical to the operation of the regulatory budget. As noted, notational accounts would be employed to maintain a record of the compliance expenditures of private firms. But these accounts would not necessarily be treated like the "real money" in the administrative accounts of regulatory agencies.[75] A major part of the rationale for the regulatory budget is that it will create incentives for regulatory agencies to reduce the total cost of achieving specified regulation objectives. To be effective, these incentives rely to a considerable extent on the ability to transfer funds from notational to administrative accounts.

It is assumed that this incentive would operate in the following manner. In assuming a greater proportion of regulatory costs, for example, for an existing regulation, a government agency would cause an increase in its own administrative revenue account through transfer of funds from a notational account. The agency thus would gain "real," spendable resources by reducing private sector compliance costs. Congressional appropriation of monies to the revenue side of administrative accounts to enable these transfers, up to a specified amount, would have to be provided in the regulatory budget prior to their occurrence in order to create the reward system for agencies. In the same manner, when an agency operated to increase private sector costs of compliance, the revenue account of the regulatory agency would be reduced. Funds would be transferred between notational and administrative accounts on a one-to-one basis. In most cases such transfers would only be justified if they permitted regulatory objectives to be met at lower total costs or if increased regulatory performance were achieved at the same cost.

Revenues and expenditures in notational accounts would balance nominally. The expenditure side of notational accounts would show total private sector compliance expenditures, after these were reported and audited. The revenue side of notational accounts would contain an amount equal to reported private sector expenditures. In actual practice, the revenue side of notational accounts would not contain "real money" in a sum equal to the expenditure side. Large savings, if earned by the agency, would only be available for expenditure by the agency after they were appropriated by Congress and approved by the president in the annual regulatory budget review process. However, some funds would be routinely appropriated by Congress into notational revenue accounts, up to a specific limit relative to the size of the budget of the regulatory agency and its corresponding private sector compliance expenditure level. These routine appropriations would enable the immediate transfer of funds into the budgetary revenues accounts of regulatory agencies. Thus, the revenue side of notational accounts would be subdivided into two categories: a total amount technically available to agencies, which would balance to private sector compliance expenditures, and a lesser amount, which would be immediately accessible to agencies.

The location and range of decision authority and control over fund transfers would influence strongly the extent to which the regulatory budget process operated efficiently. On one hand, fund transfer control would have to be sufficiently flexible to encourage agencies to reduce total regulatory costs. On the other, control would need to be maintained so that agencies would not aggrandize themselves at the expense of the regulatory mission.

Experience in control of fund transfers in the federal expenditure budget indicates that there is no optimal level of flexibility; the amount of scrutiny given by OMB to fund transfer request varies with the perceived trustworthiness of the agencies. Agencies that use their flexibility to increase the efficiency and effectiveness of their program are rewarded with greater delegations, and vice versa.

As is the case with expenditure budgetary control, in the regulatory budget a minimum fund transfer authority would be delegated to OMB for approval, for example, up to $10 million. Above this amount, transfers would be formally reviewed before Congress. Fund transfer authority up to some smaller amount would be delegated to agencies, based upon their performance. In addition, similar control would be exercised over the timing of fund transfers and intertemporal fund transfers.

The formal purpose of fund controls would be to ensure the accuracy and appropriateness of transfers relative to regulatory objectives. At a more fundamental level, authority to delegate authority to transfer funds would provide the control agency with powerful means of rewarding efficiency and of punishing inefficient decision making. It can be expected that postaudit and evaluation of regulatory budget accounts would provide information upon which to judge the effectiveness of controls. As is the case with the expenditure budget, postaudit and evaluation would enable adjustment of both OMB and agency budgetary monitoring and control procedures. And, in order to verify the accuracy of reported compliance costs, government postaudit would require firms to submit externally verified audit reports to OMB for review at the end of the regulatory fiscal year.

A final check would operate to provide incentives for regulatory agencies to minimize private sector compliance costs. This would result from the simple fact that as regulatory agency budgets grew when agencies assumed larger portions of total compliance costs, these budgets could be trimmed by Congress, the president, and the CBO and OMB. These cuts would, however, not destroy agency incentives to maximize revenues but rather would intensify them. As regulatory policy is clarified and some programs are eliminated or reduced, the agency will continue to attempt to increase its budget for regulatory programs still in operation. In a period of tightfistedness in regulatory budgeting, such increases will likely be most easily achieved through reduction of private sector compliance costs. This is the way the new budgetary games should be played. Agencies will be forced to trade off weak and compliance-costly regulatory programs for programs that would clearly show net economic benefits, holding regulatory outcomes constant.

It should be noted at this point that we would not expect regulatory policy or politics to be constant. Indeed, policy changes in this area may be expected to be frequent, given the impact of technology, political philosophy, fluctuations in interest group power and public opinion, and so on. The point here is that changes resulting from these factors will occur, but that the regulatory budget would permit a better organized and more stable review of existing and proposed regulations, and that its incentives would tend to work toward reducing government regulatory and private sector compliance expenditures as opposed to the existing system, which provides incentives to increase regulatory programs and expenditures.

We should also note that, in many cases, net economic benefit may be an unacceptable criterion to a particular interest group or point of view. Disputes over the valuing of social benefits are likely to create disagreements over the "true" net benefits of alternative policies. A regulatory budget would not automatically reduce or resolve these disputes. Rather, it would provide a better framework within which disputes could be negotiated, partially because it would encourage more explicit quantification of both economic and social costs and benefits. While proponents and critics of the regulatory budget might agree that the process would lend itself best to the resolution of disputes and dilemmas in the area of economic regulation—regulation of prices, market entry, and so forth—the process would also be employed to evaluate social regulation and regulatory programs. We can only reiterate that even in this area we believe the regulatory budget would help clarify difficult dilemmas, but it would be no panacea.

Implementing the regulatory budget would be difficult, but the types of problems identified here are those constantly encountered in budgeting: estimating costs, organizing accounting structures, keeping reports up to date. There is little reason to believe a priori that they are any less solvable here than elsewhere.

WOULD IT WORK?

The objective of the regulatory budget would be to increase consideration of priorities and trade-offs by regulatory authorities. It might also promote increased use of economic analysis in regulatory decision making. However, it probably would not prevent the executive and Congress from giving greater attention to some costs than to others, such as administrative costs versus compliance costs or compliance costs versus user costs.

Despite the newness of the concept and some absence of operational specificity, a number of objections to the notion of a regulatory budget have been raised. The first is that it would lead to an overemphasis on costs and an underemphasis on benefits.[76] Second, it might result in hard-to-measure costs being ignored.[77] Third, because compliance costs are not actually a part of the public accounts, they could be rigged by regulators, regulatees, or budgeters. There appears to be some logic to each of these objections. We would argue, however, that these criticisms reflect misconceptions about what a regulatory budget is supposed to do and how it would operate.

First, it is not evident to us that treating compliance costs in a manner similar to other public expenditures would necessarily lead to an overemphasis on costs. Public spending behavior does not appear to be overly cost-conscious at present, although this may be changing. Acknowledgment that budgets are simply expenditures plans, and that the benefits generated by most public-funded activities are hard to measure, should not cause us to infer automatically that better understanding and more consistent handling of costs would lead to less appreciation of benefits. In fact, the reverse might be true; the regulatory budgetary process could provide a powerful incentive for program advocates to identify and measure alternative benefits.

Second, we believe it unlikely that a regulatory budget would exacerbate the tendency to ignore hard-to-measure costs, especially those costs that are spread across a large number of individuals. Again, the adversary relationships built into the regulatory budget process would seem likely to provide incentive for program opponents to identify and estimate hard-to-measure costs, to assess their ultimate incidences, and to point out distributional consequences.

Third, we acknowledge that objections with regard to rigging of estimates may be valid. Still federal decision makers have shown that they are able to take similar notational costs very seriously, as in their treatment of tax expenditures. A priori, there is little reason for us to believe that the nonadministrative portion of the regulatory budget would be considered "funny money." However, it would be important to test this hypothesis, as well as others presented here, in a pilot implementation of the concept. There are real problems yet to be resolved in research and testing of the regulatory budget proposal, for example, in reporting and accounting for compliance expenditures. It is possible that compliance expenditures could be rigged, but there is also reason to believe that these costs could be identified accurately from business firm records. Furthermore, each of the participants in the process would have an incentive to rig these costs in different directions. In the end, the checks and balances and negotiation inherent in the budget process would be relied upon to help ensure that estimate would be made fairly.

Given the attention directed to reform of the traditional federal budgetary process over the past several years, our confidence in its effectiveness may be surprising to some readers. Nevertheless, there are indications that traditional budgetary processes work fairly well to aid government officials in decision making. Experimentation with budget reform has not only demonstrated the tenacity of the traditional budget process but has also provided evidence that the process does work to promote efficiency and effectiveness in government.[78] Considerable attention has been devoted to understanding budgeting as a decision-making process. A fair amount is known about how the participants in this process interact, the roles played by the participants and their motivations and the standard operating procedures they use to interpret imperfect information, persuade, and bargain.

We know, for example, that bureaucrats, regulators included, may be expected to seek to increase the size, scope, or influence of their organizations, to increase the satisfactions of their sponsors, and to increase their prestige, prerogatives, and incomes. In most cases, pursuit of these objectives is served by budget maximization.[79] On the other hand, budget analysts working in central administration budget agencies (for example, OMB as opposed to program agency budget analysts who are, in the end, spending advocates) seek to cut or control government expenditures; that is, they are budget minimizers. Under most circumstances, both "spenders" and "cutters" contribute to efficiency and effectiveness in government. Indeed, Aaron Wildavsky has characterized the budgetary process as an institutionalized conflict between these two roles.[80] The scrutiny given the spenders' budget by the cutters forces continuous programming and planning and constant review of priorities and activity levels. This is so because it is simply not in the interest of budget-maximizing bureaucrats, subject to effective central control, to allow an obsolete activity or ineffective program to continue to drain resources from other activities and programs thought to be more attractive to agency executives and sponsors. To grow, bureaucrats must show that increases in their budgets will finance new activities that are as or more important than those presently carried out by their department and more important than those carried out by others. Otherwise, they will be criticized for not allocating funds for the highest priority activity.[81] In passing we might wonder whether the same dynamic applies where budgets are reduced. We suspect it does. Decreases threatened must be shown to be as or more harmful than other activities undertaken by the department and more harmful than cuts that might be made in other departments.

However, with respect to external consequences of regulation such as compliance costs, no central control presently operates through the budgetary process. As a result, there is no incentive for the regulator to prune from his repertoire obsolete or low-priority items, let alone to find the least costly means of accomplishing the purposes of regulation. Furthermore, shifting costs to the private sector appears to have satisfied the interests of both regulator and government budget analysts. Through cost shifting

the regulatory agency can increase its influence without spending
more "government" money, and the budget analyst can curb public
spending without sacrificing benefits to program supporters. [82]
Given these understandings, the regulatory budget seems particularly attractive to address critical gaps in the existing system of
regulatory review. However, several important additional criticisms of the regulatory budget concept must be addressed. [83]

The first is that a regulatory budget would be ineffective without some form of voucher control, and the second is that in some instances the incentives for government decision makers proposed
would operate to produce undesirable consequences. In response to
the first criticism, as noted earlier, we believe the accounting problems are solvable and that, despite its cost, the benefits of the procedure would prevail. However, without having observed a test of
the regulatory budget we concede that our assessment is merely an
hypothesis.

The second criticism is more serious. It notes that the regulatory budget would cause government regulatory agencies and OMB
to concentrate on direct costs and to ignore indirect costs. Following this line of criticism, this behavior might result in a government strategy with perverse private sector economic consequences.
For example, in implementing EPA goals for air quality, the "bureaucratic" strategy might be to simply discourage new industry or
industrial expansion. By doing so, goals are met (to preserve "ambient" air quality) at little or no increased direct cost to government and industry. The agency has done its job in creating no new
regulation, and OMB is pleased at no new expenditures for regulation. However, the efficiency loss and other economic costs to the
nation under this strategy could be considerable. We should observe
that this result would be preferable to some. For example, among
others, Oregon has pursued such a policy with regard to the location
of new industry in the state. This causes some to argue that the
economic cost to the state resulting from this approach is too great,
that, for example, the state suffers the economic weakness and instability characteristic of a single-industry economy owing to absence of diversification in its forest-products-based private sector.
However, others would argue that the benefits derived from this
policy in preserving the quality and livability of the environment in
Oregon are worth the cost of economic instability, unemployment,
and so forth.

We acknowledge that incentives exist for regulatory decision
makers to concentrate on direct costs, but not that these incentives
are likely to produce automatically a regulatory strategy that would
discourage private sector economic development. White suggests
that the solution to both agency cost estimation bias and compliance

avoidance is establishment of incentives through noncompliance fees set at the marginal compliance cost level. This would eliminate "cheap cost avoidance." His outline indicates that the process would operate through industry self-assessment, balancing the tendency for regulatory agencies to underestimate costs. [84] In our scenario for the regulatory budget, decisions on regulatory strategy would not lie exclusively with agencies or OMB, nor do they presently. We would expect Congress, the president, and representatives of industry, environmentalists, and the other interest groups to continue to play roles in negotiating regulatory strategies. Indeed, one of the strengths of the regulatory budget in our view is that no agency would have unilateral control over regulatory strategy setting. Still, as noted earlier, we cannot deny the influence of OMB and regulatory agencies in current regulatory decision making, nor the absence of effective congressional participation. [85]

As a consequence of these and other criticisms presented earlier, we are inclined to believe that a pilot implementation of the regulatory budget concept would provide a valuable opportunity to evaluate it more carefully. We are aware that some consideration was given to this idea in OMB during the Carter administration. OMB analysts studied the feasibility of the regulatory budget and there was some evidence that this review was favorable. [86] OMB developed a model regulatory cost accounting procedure and drafted legislation that would implement it. A pilot implementation of the regulatory budget to be carefully evaluated over a reasonable period of time, perhaps four years, would seem to the authors to be a reasonable investment at this point.

In testimony before the Congressional Joint Economic Committee hearings on Regulatory Budgeting and Cost-Effectiveness in the Regulatory Process, James C. Miller III observed:

> Despite best-faith efforts by two Presidents—Ford and Carter—and several laudable programs (Inflation Impact Statement, Economic Impact Statement, and Regulatory Analysis), the experience to date leaves much to be desired. For a number of reasons, agencies drag their collective feet when it comes to a benefit-cost requirement.
>
> In my opinion, a Regulatory Budget would turn this around because each agency would have to establish clear priorities so as to maximize benefits within its (regulatory) budget constraint . . . the opponents of the Regulatory Budget are probably correct in that more concern over costs will reduce the pace of regulatory activity. However, such proponents of regula-

tion should not lose sight of the fact that adoption of
the Regulatory Budget might well cause agencies to become more effective in achieving their goals. The reason is that the Regulatory Budget could be an extremely
useful management tool. But we should also ask the
question: if a regulatory initiative cannot be defended
on the basis of a proposed budget, does this not reveal
that the goal itself is not worth the opportunities for-
gone in achieving it?

Now, if a Regulatory Budget is such a good idea,
should not Congress move forward with it expeditious-
ly? Frankly, I recommend caution. The reason is
that with any program of such magnitude, unanticipated
problems, as well as unanticipated opportunities, are
bound to arise. Thus, it would seem advisable to initiate the program slowly and deliberately in order to
learn from experience. [87]

It is not certain whether this experiment would best be performed
within one agency or in a phased implementation across a number
of agencies. We tend to prefer the latter option as a better test of
the usefulness, comprehensibility, and possible comparative advantage of its application in different regulatory policy areas.

CONCLUSION

It is likely that federal regulatory decisions are worse, perhaps much worse, than other kinds of government decisions. This
is because the cost of regulation is a cost of government, but it is
not treated as a cost to government. Consequently, the internal
checks that work to promote efficiency and effectiveness in government are not fully operative where regulation is concerned; in some
cases, they may exacerbate the problem. To improve government
decision making in this area, a number of institutional changes have
been proposed; each appears to have some merit.

An ex ante review of major regulatory proposals is necessary
to improve both agency decision making and executive branch coordination. If review is to be more than an uncritical check on regulatory initiatives, regulatory agencies must have the analytical resources required to do quality analysis. Reviewing organizations
must be consistent and objective in evaluating proposals. [88]

A comprehensive ex post review of a body of regulations is
possible. Executive pressure through procedural and administrative review of the type described in this chapter can compel a regu-

latory agency to go through its regulations and trim away at least some of the obsolete, the foolish, and the ineffective. However, pressure cannot compel "wise behavior" on the part of the regulatory authority.

Both economic impact analysis and the zero-base regulation effort, but particularly economic review, have promoted the development of the kind of information required to improve regulatory decision making. These review mechanisms serve the decision facilitation function, but they do not, and perhaps cannot on their own, promote the decision-influencing function. They do not materially increase the likelihood that the information generated will be used to make better regulatory decisions.

Both federal assumption of compliance costs and a regulatory budget could serve the decision-influencing function. Both confront regulatory decision makers—regulators, budget analysts, even members of Congress—with a set of incentives that should lead them to make better decisions. By requiring explicit public identification of regulatory costs and by forcing trade-offs between regulatory and other activities, both should promote increased scrutiny of regulatory costs and benefits. [89] That is, they could provide an institutional context for both ex ante review of proposed regulations and ex post evaluation of existing rules, and thereby promote better regulatory decisions.

Federal assumption of all compliance costs is not appealing on distributional grounds, although the idea may have some merit so far as enforcement and monitoring costs are concerned. We believe this notion ought to be subordinate to the more general concept of a regulatory budget. Of course, a number of complex design problems, some of which have been identified here, would have to be solved in order to implement a regulatory budget. These problems seem soluble, given that a commitment is made to implementation. We believe that a regulatory budget could be administered with reasonable precision and that most of the hypothetical benefits cited to result from its use would be realized. Viewing government-mandated regulatory expenditures, tax expenditures, and other expenditures as almost interchangeable ways of effecting public purposes and allocating resources is so sensible that it must eventually prevail.

NOTES

1. For examples of some of the government reports, publications, and other documents that have noted the problems to be resolved through reform and have carried recommendations for reform

in the past, see President's Committee on Administrative Management (Brownlow Committee), Report of the Committee with Studies of Administrative Management in the Federal Government, 1937; Louis J. Hector, "Problems of the CAB and the Independent Regulatory Commissions," Yale Law Journal 69/6 (May 1960):931-46 (originally prepared as a memorandum to President Eisenhower, September 10, 1959); Emmette S. Redford, "The President's Committee on Government Organization," November 17, 1960; James M. Landis, Report on Regulatory Agencies to the President-Elect, Committee Print, Subcommittee on Administrative Practice and Procedure, Committee on the Judiciary, U.S. Senate, 1960, pp. 81-87; President's Advisory Council on Executive Organization (Ash Council), A New Regulatory Framework: Report on Selected Independent Regulatory Agencies, 1971; Subcommittee on Oversight and Investigations, Committee on Interstate and Foreign Commerce, U.S. House of Representatives (Moss Committee), Federal Regulation and Regulatory Reform, October 1976, pp. 487-501, 547-49; Committee on Government Affairs, U.S. Senate (Ribicoff Committee), Study on Federal Regulation, Vol. 1, The Regulatory Appointments Process, January 1977, pp. ix-x, and Vol. 5, Regulatory Organization, December 1977; Subcommittee on Administrative Practice and Procedure, Committee on Judiciary, U.S. Senate, Public Participation in Federal Agency Proceedings Hearings, 94th Congress, 2nd session, January-February 1976; James M. Graham and Victor H. Cramer, Appointments to the Regulatory Agencies: The Federal Communications Commission and the Federal Trade Commission (1949-1974), printed at the direction of the Committee on Commerce, U.S. Senate, 94th Congress, 2nd session, April 1976; Special Sub-Committee on Legislative Oversight, Committee on Interstate and Foreign Commerce, U.S. House of Representatives, Independent Regulatory Commissions, H.R. Report 2711, 85th Congress, 2nd session, 1959; Simon Lazarus, "Half-way Up from Liberalism: Regulation and Corporate Power," in Corporate Power in America, ed. Ralph Nader and Mark Green (New York: Grossman, 1975); Simon Lazarus, The Genteel Populist (New York: Holt, Rinehart and Winston, 1974); and Simon Lazarus and Joseph Onek, "The Regulators and the People," Virginia Law Review 57 (1971):1069-108; Marver Bernstein, Regulation: Government by Independent Regulatory Commission (Princeton, N.J.: Princeton University Press, 1955); Mark V. Nadel, The Politics of Consumer Protection (Indianapolis, Ind.: Bobbs-Merrill, 1971); Paul Sabatier, "Social Movements and Regulatory Agencies: Toward a More Adequate— and Less Pessimistic—Theory of 'Clientele Capture,'" Policy Sciences (1975):301-42; James Q. Wilson, "The Politics of Regulation," in Social Responsibility and the Business Predicament, ed.

James W. McKie (Washington, D.C.: Brookings Institution, 1974), pp. 135-68; Mancur Olson, Jr., The Logic of Collective Action (Cambridge, Mass.: Harvard University Press, 1965); Alan Stone, Economic Regulation and the Public Interest (Ithaca, N.Y.: Cornell University Press, 1977); and Mark Green, ed., The Monopoly Makers: Ralph Nader's Study Group Report on Regulation and Competition (New York: Grossman, 1973); Henry J. Friendly, A Look at the Federal Administrative Agencies: The Need for Better Definition of Standards (Cambridge, Mass.: Harvard University Press, 1962); Kenneth C. Davis, Administrative Law of the Seventies (San Francisco: Bancroft-Whitney, 1975); Theodore Lowi, The End of Liberalism (New York: Norton, 1969); Attorney General's Committee on Administrative Procedure, Administrative Procedure in Government Agencies, Senate Document No. 8, 77th Congress, 1st session, 1941, Committee on Administrative Procedure, U.S. Senate; the U.S. Commission on Organization of the Executive Branch of Government (First House Commission), The Independent Regulatory Agencies: A Report with Recommendations (Washington, D.C.: U.S. Government Printing Office, 1949); the U.S. Commission on Organization of the Executive Branch of Government (second Hoover Commission), Legal Services and Procedures (Washington, D.C.: U.S. Government Printing Office, 1955); Commission on Federal Paperwork, Final Summary Report (Washington, D.C.: U.S. Government Printing Office, 1977); Subcommittee on Administrative Law and Government Relations, Committee on the Judiciary, U.S. House of Representatives, Congressional Review of Rulemaking Hearings, 94th Congress, 1st session, October-November 1975; Subcommittee on Administrative Practice and Procedure, Committee on Judiciary, U.S. Senate, Administrative Procedure Act Amendments of 1976, Hearings, 94th Congress, 2nd session, April-May 1976; Herbert Kaufman, Red Tape: Its Origins, Uses and Abuses (Washington, D.C.: Brookings Institution, 1976).

2. See The Challenge of Regulatory Reform, a Report to the President from the Domestic Council Review Group on Regulatory Reform, January 1977, p. 20. See also Economists' Conference on Inflation Report, Vol. 1 (September 5, 1974), pp. 11-13.

3. The support for this judgment is rendered in Chapter 4 of this book. Essentially, much of this neglect stems from the small component of the total federal budget devoted directly to funding regulatory agencies and as a result of misguided attentions to the solution of the wrong or less important problems in regulation.

4. Based upon an interview with Richard Simpson, former director of Consumer Product Safety Committee, August 6, 1978. Also see Nina Cornell, Roger Noll, and Barry Weingast, "Safety Regulation," in Setting National Priorities: The Next Ten Years,

ed. Henry Owen and Charles Schultze (Washington, D.C.: Brookings Institution, 1976).

5. Cornell, Noll, and Weingast, op. cit. For example, in worker health and safety regulation, in addition to establishing tolerable hazard levels or standards, the regulators must decide where to focus the regulatory effort, determine the kind of standards to employ, select a detection strategy, and make a trade-off between detection effort and penalties for violators. Frequently it appears that decisions made with respect to these issues are more consistent with the objective of minimizing administrative costs and, thereby, public spending, than with any other objective. Regulation is typically targeted where enforcement costs are lowest, not necessarily where the total cost of reducing the hazard is lowest. Design standards are generally preferred to performance standards, perhaps because compliance with a design standard may be ascertained by means of a single inspection, whereas performance standards require continuous monitoring. Reactive detection strategies, combined with punitive penalties, are more frequently employed than are comprehensive, ex ante detection strategies and low penalties. All of this is evidence of a commendable concern with public expenditure. Nevertheless, exclusive concern with public expenditures can lead to substantial inefficiency and ineffectiveness.

6. Ibid., pp. 479-500; and James Bennett and Manuel Johnson, "The Political Economy of Government Paperwork," Policy Review (Winter 1979):27-43.

7. Cornell, Noll, and Weingast, op. cit., p. 502.

8. Ibid., p. 477.

9. Ibid., pp. 477-500. This statement and the following discussion of evaluative criteria is based upon Joel Demski and Gerald Feltham, Cost Determination: A Conceptual Approach (Ames: Iowa State University Press, 1976), pp. 3-13.

10. Robert P. Biller, "On Tolerating Policy and Organizational Termination: Some Design Consideration," Policy Sciences 7, no. 2 (June 1976):146-47. See also Robert D. Behn and Martha A. Clark, "The Termination of Beach Erosion Control at Cape Hatteras," Public Policy 27, no. 1 (Winter 1979):99; and Robert D. Behn, "How to Terminate a Public Policy: A Dozen Hints for the Would-Be Terminator," Policy Analysis 4, no. 3 (Summer 1978): 393.

11. Eugene Bardach, "Policy Termination as a Political Process," Policy Sciences 7, no. 2 (June 1976):123-26.

12. Behn, op. cit., pp. 394-402.

13. L. R. Jones, "Termination Gamesmanship: The Strategic Use of Evaluation and Feasibility Analysis," paper presented at the Western Social Science Association Conference, Public Administration Section, San Diego, Calif., April 23, 1981, pp. 8-12.

14. For an explanation of the policy cycle concept, see Judith V. May and Aaron B. Wildavsky, eds., The Policy Cycle (Beverly Hills, Calif.: Sage, 1978).

15. Robert D. Behn, "The False Dawn of Sunset Laws," The Public Interest, no. 49 (Fall 1977):103; Allen Schick, "Zero-Based Budgeting and Sunset: Redundancy or Symbiosis?" The Bureaucrat, Spring 1977, pp. 12-30. See also Herbert Kaufman, Are Government Organizations Immortal? (Washington, D.C.: Brookings Institution, 1976).

16. Government Code Section 11340, (a), (b), (c), State of California. See also "More Government Innovation from the Golden State," Regulation 4 (January/February 1981):8.

17. Office of Administrative Law, "Instructions for the AB1111 Review of Existing Regulations," Sacramento, Calif., pp. 2-3.

18. It should be noted that although cost statements were requested from agencies, cost was not one of the five criteria prescribed by AB1111, nor has it been employed as a formal review criterion by OAL.

19. Government Code Section 11347.3, State of California.

20. Government Code Section 11349.6 (b), State of California.

21. Chapter 1, Statutes of 1981, State of California; Monroe E. Price, "The New Office of Administrative Law: Dragon-Slaying in California," School of Law, University of California, Los Angeles (December 1980), p. 34.

22. All data presented in the analysis of OAL actions and performance were provided by OAL. Some of the calculations from these data are our own, for example, comparative rates of disapproval of proposed regulations between 1980 and 1981 and the three-year period 1977-78 to 1979-80.

23. Price, op. cit., p. 42.

24. George Eads, "Harnessing Regulation: The Evolving Role of White House Oversight," Regulation 5 (May/June 1981):19-26; Robert S. Gilmore, "Congressional Oversight and Administrative Leadership," The Bureaucrat 10 (Fall 1981):32-38.

25. See, for example, Study on Federal Regulation, U.S. Senate Committee on Government Operations/Governmental Affairs, 6 volumes (Washington, D.C.: U.S. Government Printing Office, January 1977 to December 1978); and Joint Economic Committee, "Regulatory Budgeting and the Need for Cost-Effectiveness in the Regulatory Process," 96th Congress, 1st session, August 1, 1979 (Washington, D.C.: U.S. Government Printing Office, 1979).

26. Antonin Scalia, "Viewpoint: Regulatory Reform—The Game Has Changed," Regulation 5 (January/February 1981):14.

27. Eads, op. cit.; Christopher C. DeMuth, "The Regulatory Budget," Regulation 3 (March/April 1980):29-44; Susan Tolchin,

"Presidential Power and the Politics of RARG, " Regulation 2 (July/
August 1979):44-49.

28. President Kennedy issued the executive order creating
the second temporary Administrative Conference of the United States
on April 13, 1961. The origins and functions of ACUS were exam-
ined by the Committee on Governmental Affairs (6-volume study),
U.S. Senate, Vol. 6, Framework for Regulation (Washington, D.C.:
U.S. Government Printing Office, December 1978), pp. 244-55.
The budget for ACUS for 1978 was $914,000. Ibid., p. 254. ACUS
was assigned responsibility for implementation of the Government
in Sunshine Act and has conducted regulatory studies, such as on
the procedural aspects of the Consumer Product Safety Act.

29. Ibid., p. 255.

30. Ibid., pp. 255-56.

31. Ibid., Vol. 2 (February 1977), pp. 128, 135.

32. See Executive Order 11821, Inflation Impact Statement
(White House, November 27, 1974); this was extended through De-
cember 31, 1977, by Executive Order 11949, Economic Impact
Statement Program (White House, December 31, 1976) and expanded
by Executive Order 12044, Improving Government Regulations (White
House, March 23, 1978); see also Federal Register, May 31, 1978,
Part II, "Improving Government Regulations: Proposals for Implementing Executive Order 12044"; Commerce Department 23170,
HEW 23119, Renegotiation Board 23197, Water Resources Council
23199; and "Use of Cost Benefit and Other Similar Analytical Methods of Regulation, " Federal Register, March 6, 1979, p. 12198.
In the IIS program, the attention given to allocative efficiency seems
to have been a by-product of the concern with inflation. The link between these two issues is not, however, readily apparent to an outside observer. Inefficient regulation is by definition a drag on the
economy, but its effect is not necessarily cumulative or increasing.
Even if it is accepted that stagflation is somehow exacerbated by
supply constraints, to demonstrate that regulation leads to inflation
(a continuous, general increase in prices) it must first be demonstrated that the drag on the economy resulting from regulation is
both increasing and increasing at an increasing rate.

33. James C. Miller III, "Lessons of the Economic Impact
Statement Program, " Regulation, July/August 1977, p. 15. This
analysis is largely based upon Thomas D. Hopkins, An Evaluation
of the Economic Impact Statement Program (Washington, D.C.:
Council on Wage and Price Stability, December 7, 1976). See also
Bruce K. Mulock, "Economic and Inflation Impact Statements, " U.S.
Library of Congress, Multilith 78-157E, 1978; and Kathryne L. Ber-
nick, "The Inflation Impact Statement Program and Executive Branch
Coordination, " draft for the ABA Commission on Law and the Economy Study of Federal Regulation, Washington, D.C., May 18, 1977.

34. Bernick, op. cit., pp. 13-17; also Miller, op. cit., p. 17.

35. Hopkins, op. cit., pp. 17-18.

36. Executive Order 11821; see also ibid., p. 17.

37. Hopkins, op. cit., pp. 38, iii, iv; The 1977 Joint Economic Report, Report of the Joint Economic Committee, Congress of the United States, on the January 1977 Economic Report of the President, March 10, 1977, p. 95; and "Testimony of William Lilley, Acting Director of CWPS," Inflationary Impact of Government Regulations, Hearings Before the Subcommittee on Economic Stabilization of the Committee on Banking, Currency and Housing, House of Representatives, 94th Congress, 2nd session, December 17, 1976, p. 8, as cited in Bernick, op. cit., p. 11.

38. Miller, op. cit., p. 18.

39. Information has value only to the extent that it increases the probability that a better decision will be made. Because apparently no decisions were directly affected by the information generated by the IIS/EIS program, this information had no value. The program did have a cost, albeit small; consequently, by its definition, the IIS/EIS program was "inflationary." However, the initial efforts associated with the program may be justified in terms of the agencies' learning how to prepare cost-benefit analysis. This is the kind of intangible benefit typically ignored in the impact statements.

40. Bernick, op. cit., pp. 8-18. The IIS/EIS program must be distinguished from CWPS self-initiated intervention under its legislative authority. Lilley cites several examples of success under the latter on pp. 9-10, 24 of Bernick, op. cit. Section 3(a) of the Council on Wage and Price Stability Act of 1974 (Public Law 93-487, as amended by P.L. 94-78, 1 U.S.C. 1904 note) directs the council to review and appraise the various programs, policies, and activities of the departments and agencies of the United States for the purposes of determining the extent to which those programs and activities are contributing to inflation; and intervene and otherwise participate on its own behalf in rule making, rate making, licensing, and other proceedings before any of the departments and agencies of the United States, in order to present its views as to the inflationary impact that might result from the possible outcome of such proceedings. Notably, "such intervention is not limited to proceedings in which an IIS is involved." The majority of CWPS interventions have been where the proposal is not "major" (where the agency did not identify a proposal as major but CWPS disagreed, or where the proposing agency is not even participating in the IIS program). Hopkins, op. cit., p. 18.

41. Hopkins, op. cit., pp. iii-v; Bernick, op. cit., pp. 9-19.

42. Thirty-six regulatory agencies were not independent of the Executive Office of the President at this time.

43. This description was provided by the U.S. Regulatory
Council, Regulatory Reform Highlights (Washington, D.C., April
1980) p. 5.

44. Miller, op. cit., p. 18.

45. Ibid. The RARG's analytical efforts were carried out by
the same group of analysts at CWPS who reviewed IIS/EIS. Apparently this practice was in part intended to reduce some of the internal conflicts of objectives within CWPS (interview with CWPS staff,
August 1978). For an analysis of RARG and its milieu, see Christopher C. DeMuth, "Constraining Regulatory Costs—Part I: The
White House Review Programs," Regulation, January/February
1980, pp. 13-26; and Tolchin, op. cit. With regard to RARG's impact it appears that only in a few cases was it directly influential,
for example, in lowering DOE's Fuel Use Act cost index regulations
in March and October 1979, and EPA's selection of a "weight of evidence" rather than "fixed rule" approach on the regulation of carcinogens adopted in 1980. The principal influence of RARG (CWPS
staff) was exerted through criticism of agency regulatory proposals
and provision of assistance in economic and other types of analysis.

46. Cornell, Noll, and Weingast, op. cit. On the OMB's propensities, see Allen Schick, "The Budget Bureau That Was: Thoughts
on the Rise, Decline, and Future of a Presidential Agency," Law and
Contemporary Problems 35 (Summer 1970):519-39; and Gary Bombardier, "The Managerial Function of OMB: Intergovernmental Relations as a Test Case," Public Policy 23 (Summer 1975):317-54. Also
see Aaron Wildavsky, "A Budget for All Seasons? Why the Traditional Budget Lasts," Public Administration Review (November-
December 1978); Fred Thompson and William Zumeta, "Control and
Controls: A Reexamination of Control Patterns in Budget Execution,"
Policy Sciences 13 (1981):25-50.

47. Miller, op. cit.; and from interview with CWPS staff and
ex-staff members in August 1978. In a number of instances, CWPS
documents equate maximization of net benefit with maximization of
consumers' surplus. This slip is indicative of the conflict within
CWPS. It must be understood that applied welfare economics is not
a common skill in the U.S. federal bureaucracy. The CEA and
Treasury have traditionally been dominated by macroeconomists.
And, while it might seem that the OMB would be a hotbed of cost-
benefit analysis, it is not. Indeed, one senior official in OMB said
"What we look for are MBA types and some economists. Agricultural economists and labor economists are OK, but none of these
applied welfare types; they can't seem to understand what budgeting
is about." This is one of the problems FEA had in meeting CWPS's
expectations; they had great difficulty going from the input-output
models, which they used to formulate policies, to an elaboration of
costs and benefits.

48. U.S. Regulatory Council, op. cit., pp. 9-12. See also USRC, Regulating with Common Sense: A Progress Report on Innovative Regulatory Techniques (Washington, D.C., October 1980); and USRC, Innovative Techniques in Theory and Practice: Proceedings of a Regulatory Council Conference (Washington, D.C., July 22, 1980). See Kahn, op. cit. pp. 1-9.

49. "Statement of the Vice-President George Bush Regarding the Membership and the Charter of the Presidential Task Force on Regulatory Relief," January 30, 1981, p. 2.

50. U.S. Regulatory Council, Report from the Director (Washington, D.C., July 1980), p. 2. Under Carter the first Calendar of Federal Regulations was published February 28, 1979 (44 FR 11388 et seq., 9/28/79), the second on November 28, 1979 (44 FR 68202 et seq., 11/28/79), the third on May 30, 1980 (45 FR 36844 et seq., 5/30/80), and the fourth November 24, 1980 (45 FR 228, 11/24/80).

51. Eads, op. cit., p. 20.

52. A good description and analysis of these events is provided in Patrick J. Hennigan, "Politics of Regulatory Analysis," Department of Political Science, Columbia University, September 1981, delivered at the Annual Meeting of the American Political Science Association, New York, September 4, 1981.

53. The White House, "Press Briefing on the President's Task Force on Regulatory Relief," James C. Miller III, Executive Director, March 30, 1981.

54. The U.S. Supreme Court's decision in the cotton dust case was made in reference to the American Textile Manufacturers Institute versus Donovan. The benzene ruling was made in response to a suit brought by the American Industrial Health Council representing a number of manufacturing industries. "For Deregulation, a Detour—Not a Roadblock," Business Week, July 6, 1981, p. 26; "The Court Leaves OSHA Hanging," Business Week, July 21, 1980, pp. 67-68.

55. The White House, "Press Briefing on the President's Task Force on Regulatory Relief," James C. Miller III, Executive Director, June 12, 1981; Office of the Vice-President, "Materials on President Reagan's Program of Regulatory Relief," June 13, 1981.

56. "Deregulation HQ: An Interview on the New Executive Order with Murray L. Weidenbaum and James C. Miller III," Regulation, March/April 1981, pp. 14-23.

57. Eads, op. cit., p. 20. (Authors' emphasis added.)

58. Ibid., pp. 25-26.

59. William W. Ross, as quoted in ibid., p. 26.

60. Quoted in Bernick, op. cit., p. 26.

61. Ibid.

62. See Operation Common Sense (Washington, D.C.: Department of Health, Education and Welfare, April 5, 1978); and Getting Our Priorities Straight (Washington, D.C.: Department of Labor, April 30, 1979).

63. Cornell, Noll, and Weingast, op. cit. For a more comprehensive discussion of this point, see Chapter 7.

64. Bennett and Johnson, op. cit.

65. Arthur Andersen & Company, Cost of Government Regulation Study for Business Roundtable (New York: The Business Roundtable, 1979).

66. R. T. Page, Economics of Involuntary Transfers: A Unified Approach to Pollution and Congestion Externalities (New York: Springer-Verlag, 1973), p. 29; E. S. Mills and D. E. Bramhall, "A Note on the Asymmetry Between Fees and Payments," Water Resources Research 2, no. 3 (1966):619-716; W. J. Baumol and W. E. Oates, The Theory of Environmental Policy (Englewood Cliffs, N.J.: Prentice-Hall, 1975), pp. 183, 189-90; and A. V. Kneese and K. G. Maier, "Bribes and Charges for Pollution Control," Natural Resources Journal 13, no. 14 (October 1973):716. The problem here is that assumption of compliance cost may have unwanted incentive effects as far as the affected firms are concerned. In effect, under this proposal, firms would be selling compliance efforts to the government. Consequently, they may be tempted to do something destructive in order to be paid (bribed) for not doing so.

67. M. I. Kamien, N. L. Schwartz, and F. T. Dolbear, "Asymmetry Between Bribes and Charges," Water Resources Research 2, no. 1 (1st Quarter 1966):153; Kneese and Maier, op. cit., pp. 682-86.

68. Baumol and Oates, op. cit., p. 189.

69. See Edmund G. Brown, Jr., The Buck Stops Here: A Proposal for a Federal Fiscal Impact Act (Sacramento, Calif.: Department of Finance, February 22, 1978).

70. Interview with Richard Ray, program budget manager for the State-Mandated Costs Program, State Department of Finance, Sacramento, Calif., July 22, 1978.

71. In theory a bribe is identical in consequence to a charge (such as an accident tax or an effluent charge) plus a lump sum transfer. In terms of allocative efficiency, bribes may be made to produce the same outcome as a tax. However, prices and bribes produce different distributional outcomes. A bribe system implicitly says that the firm has a property right (the right to pollute or to cause accidents) which is being expropriated by the state for which a just compensation is paid. The tax approach implies that no such right exists; rather the firm has simply been exploiting the ignorance or folly of its employees, customers, or the public. Most people

seem to prefer the latter interpretation; at least, their preferences regarding the incidence of regulatory burdens reflect such a perspective. Federal assumption of compliance costs as outlined above would make a smaller claim on the public fisc than one might think. The fact is that compliance costs as they are identified here are costs of doing business and are deductible from corporate income taxes. The federal government now may be said to pay half of the cost of compliance. These tax expenditures aren't tracked. Of course, we would expect the magnitude of regulation-induced costs to be reduced.

72. We should note that some compliance costs result from errors of those who are regulated (auto safety recalls stimulated by government action), where the social cost of noncompliance may be very high. In such cases, government regulatory actions are taken, at least initially, somewhat regardless of the consequent compliance costs and impact on industry. The regulatory budget might not affect regulatory decisions markedly in such circumstances, but the costs of compliance, nonetheless, would be reflected in it. The effectiveness of the strategy employed in such a crisis would, as a consequence, be evaluated.

73. Robert Crandall, "Is Government Regulation Crippling Business?" Saturday Review, January 20, 1979, p. 34; for an analysis that draws many of the same conclusions on the regulatory budget, see DeMuth, op. cit.; see also Lawrence J. White, "Truth in Regulatory Budgeting," Regulation, March/April 1980, pp. 44-46; R. Litan and W. D. Nordhaus, The Regulatory Budget (Washington, D.C.: Brookings Institution, forthcoming); C. C. DeMuth, R. H. Shockson, E. O. Stock, and A. W. Wright, "The Regulatory Budget as a Management Tool," Joint Economic Committee, 96th Congress, 2nd session, May 29, 1979.

74. The procedure for recording capital expenditures by businesses incurred in compliance with regulation could also list these costs as items separate from the base in notational accounts.

75. In principle, of course, administrative accounts established for agencies in the enacted budget do not actually contain money either. Budgetary accounts are also accounting entities that show periodically allotted and updated expenditure balances relative to the purposes for which monies have been appropriated. In essence, "real money" is held in Treasury-administrated accounts, transferred in and out as treasury and controller functions interact to make money available when needed to cover government payrolls, to pay agency bills, and so on.

76. "Statement of Harry S. Havins, Director, Program Analysis Division, U.S. General Accounting Office," in Cost of Regulation to the Consumer, Hearings Before the Committee on Commerce,

Science and Transportation, U.S. Senate, 95th Congress, 2nd session, November 21 and 22, 1978, pp. 75-76.

77. Ibid.; see also "Statement of Mark Green, Director, Public Citizen's Congress Watch," ibid., p. 245.

78. Wildavsky, "A Budget for All Seasons?" op. cit.

79. Aaron Wildavsky, Budgeting: A Comparative Theory of Budgetary Processes (Boston: Little, Brown, 1975), Chap. 2; William Niskanen, Bureaucracy and Representative Government (Chicago: Aldine-Atherton, 1971); William Niskanen, "Bureaucrats and Politicians," Journal of Law and Economics 18, no. 3 (December 1975):617-43.

80. Ibid.

81. Aaron Wildavsky and Arthur Hammann, "Comprehensive Versus Incremental Budgeting in the Department of Agriculture," Administrative Science Quarterly 10, no. 3 (December 1965):321-46.

82. Thompson and Jones, op. cit., p. 7; Cornell et al., op. cit.

83. These criticisms of the regulatory budget were suggested to us by William Niskanen, member of President Reagan's Council of Economic Advisors, upon review of a previous draft of this manuscript.

84. White, op. cit., p. 46.

85. For another view on the need for effective congressional oversight, see Gilmore, op. cit.

86. Office of Management and Budget, "Improving Government Regulation" (Washington, D.C.: U.S. Government Printing Office, November 1980).

87. "Statement of James C. Miller III, Hearings Before the Joint Economic Committee, Congress of the United States, on "Regulatory Budgeting and the Need for Cost-Effectiveness in the Regulatory Process," 96th Congress, 1st session, August 1, 1979 (Washington, D.C.: U.S. Government Printing Office, 1979), p. 26. See also "Statement of Arthur W. Wright," ibid., p. 20.

88. In part, this is also a problem of resources. The Council on Wage and Price Stability team doing analysis for the Regulatory Analysis Review Group had 24 economists, four times the number available during the earlier IIS/EIS period. Nevertheless, as Crandall observed: "RARG has a very small staff; undertakes only a limited number of reviews a year. . . . Clearly, this organization cannot hope to have a major impact on the score of agencies in the executive branch which issue thousands of major regulations a year." "Statement of Robert W. Crandall, Senior Fellow, Brookings Institution," in Cost of Regulation to the Consumer, op. cit., p. 181. We may note that the Office of Information and Regulatory Affairs instituted under President Reagan has a relatively large staff of approximately 90 employees; Eads, loc. cit.

89. Ibid., pp. 180-81.

7

SUBSTANTIVE REFORM
AND ECONOMIC ANALYSIS

The previous chapters developed the perspective that although substantive reform of regulation is likely to be achieved through improved economic analysis, understanding that this is the case does not prescribe for us how economic analysis ought to be performed and used. In this chapter we attempt to address the issue of how economic analysis can help us to determine why and how regulatory policy should be altered.

The example chosen to illustrate the issues and problems encountered in attempting to improve the use of economic analysis is health and safety regulation. Health and safety regulation suits our purpose for several reasons: Health and safety benefits are nearly universally sought; regulation in this area is politically and socially sensitive and, in many cases, very costly; the costs, especially indirect costs, of policy failure are difficult to measure; and the valuing of benefits presents some very serious problems to analysis. In addition, it may be argued that the improvement of health and safety regulation ought to be our highest priority for substantive regulatory reform given the possible long-term and widespread consequences of misdirected regulatory policy in this area.

The call for more and better economic analysis is usually taken to mean more and better benefit-cost analysis. Unfortunately, past attempts to incorporate benefit-cost analysis into the decision-making processes of government have not been very successful. One reason for the failure of these attempts is that, in many cases, it is difficult to identify the objectives of policy and, consequently, to distinguish between benefits and costs. By focusing the discussion that follows on regulatory policies that are intended to promote health and safety, this problem may be largely avoided. As noted, very few people would question that greater safety or better health is a benefit. Other problems remain, however. In particular, this chapter explores some of the conceptual and data problems that are encountered in performing analyses of regulatory proposals, assesses their significance, and tries to show how they might be overcome or avoided.

THE SCOPE AND PURPOSE OF HEALTH AND SAFETY REGULATION

Coincident with a huge increase in expenditures for medical treatment and health care that has occurred since 1960 has come a substantial increase in government activity aimed at reducing health and safety hazards in the environment. This has been accompanied by considerable effort by individuals to increase personal health— increased interest in weight control and diet, exercise to manage stress, reduction in cigarette consumption, a dramatic shift to low-tar and nicotine brand cigarettes, and so on. Much of the expansion of government activity has taken the form of regulation of business. New statutes were passed and a number of new regulatory agencies created, examples of which are shown in Table 7.1. In addition, existing agencies such as the Food and Drug Administration (FDA) were given new responsibilities for protecting people from health and safety hazards.

There should be no doubt that the hazards addressed by these agencies are real. For example, experts believe that between 60 and 90 percent of all cancers are caused by chemical carcinogens in the environment and, hence, that they are ultimately preventable."[1] Auto accidents are the third most important cause of death in the United States. A substantial proportion of these deaths are preventable.[2] Finally, prior to the establishment of the U.S. Mine Safety and Enforcement Agency in 1969 there were 100 deaths attributable to mine-related accidents and illness for each 10,000 man-years worked, a rate nearly eight times higher than in the next most dangerous major industry, railroading.[3] The rate is now half what it was and falling rapidly.[4] There also should be little doubt that the control of health and safety hazards in the environment is a legitimate function of government in a market economy. Their presence tends to reflect market failures of a type that can only be corrected by public intervention. And there is no doubt that, in the absence of public action, too little attention would be paid to the reduction of environmental and worker and consumer health and safety hazards.[5]

TABLE 7.1

New Regulatory Agencies, 1969-75

1969	Mine Enforcement and Safety Administration (MESA): responsible for reducing health and safety risks faced by coal miners
1970	National Highway Traffic Safety Administration (NHTSA): responsible for reducing highway hazards, accident rates, and mitigating the consequences of highway accidents (also certifies compliance with auto emission standards)
1971	Environmental Protection Agency (EPA): responsible for reducing health risks in the environment, including the control of air and water pollution and solid waste disposal
1972	Consumer Product Safety Administration (CPSA): responsible for reducing health and safety risks in the work place
1975	Nuclear Regulatory Commission (NRC): responsible for reducing health and safety hazards (in the general environment and the work place) associated with the nuclear fuel cycle

However, to say merely that some form of public action is justified leaves a number of questions unanswered:

What is meant by "too little attention to the reduction of health and safety hazards"? Is it possible to pay "too much attention" to hazard reduction?

On what basis should society choose between hazard reduction (ex ante) and post hoc remedies?

What forms of public action would best accomplish a reduction in health and safety hazards?

Answers to these questions are not easy. Nevertheless, one may conclude that health and safety policy as presently implemented is frequently inconsistent and, perhaps, that public intervention has gone too far in seeking to reduce some hazards and not far enough in seeking to reduce others. Second, that public policy frequently fails to choose wisely between prevention and post hoc remedies. And, third, that the instruments chosen to effect a reduction in hazards are frequently inappropriate. These are significant problems. Their persistence reflects the complexity and obscurity of the issues involved and the difficulty of choice among complicated, often untried solutions.

It is increasingly understood that government cannot legislate all hazards out of existence and that, if it could, it would be too costly to do so. What government should do is less clear. To show that this is the case, we shall explain what might be called the regulatory optimum or ideal, why it is so hard to put it into practice, and what would have to be done to make it easier.

THE REGULATORY "OPTIMUM"

In theory, a "risk neutral, rational society"[6] would seek to minimize the sum of the damage resulting from environmental hazards to health and safety and the cost of reducing hazards. This means that steps should be taken to ensure that preventive measures are taken whenever prevention is less costly than the damages that would occur without it. This is the efficiency goal of public intervention to reduce health and safety hazards. Furthermore, a "just" society would probably try to prevent sudden, drastic losses that fall on relatively few people. This is one facet of the equity goal of public intervention in this area.[7] In theory, there is no conflict between these two goals. An efficient, just society would take steps to ensure that those persons who suffered injury as a result of hazards too costly to prevent would be fairly compensated for their pains. Indeed, such a compensation scheme would automatically provide the information needed to determine how much effort to spend on reducing various hazards—they would be reduced up to the point where marginal prevention costs equaled marginal compensation costs but not all social costs are compensable.[8] This ideal is shown in Figure 7.1.

In Figure 7.1, control or prevention costs are shown as a linear function of effort; this is so by definition. The damage schedule is drawn to show decreasing returns to additional hazard reduction efforts—that is, the schedule is concave or quasi-concave to the origin. Total costs will be minimized where an additional dollar spent to reduce hazards reduces expected damage by the same amount. It should be noted, however, that for each damage schedule, there may be several cost-control schedules, each representing a different hazard prevention technology. Selecting the best prevention technology means selecting the control cost schedule with the least slope. Also, in many cases, there may be a fairly substantial range of hazard reduction effects (in Figure 7.1, Pmin, Pmax) over which the sum of prevention and damage costs will be roughly equivalent to the minimum (Po). Generally speaking, the more linear the damage schedule, the broader this range.

FIGURE 7.1

The Regulatory "Optimum"

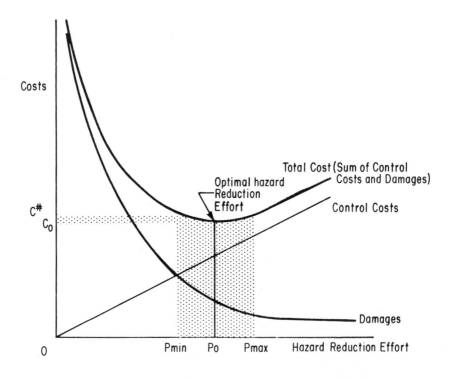

Finally, a just society would try to ensure that the costs of preventing hazard damages and compensating victims are "fairly" apportioned. This is the other facet of the equity goal of public intervention in this area. Once again, in theory, there is no conflict between this goal and the goal of efficiency; those responsible for making the decision causing the hazard should bear its cost. If the net result of such charges were deemed "unfair," this problem could be dealt with through direct income transfers.

Theory Versus Practice

Unfortunately, the theoretical optimum is, or likely to be, unattainable in practice. Certainly the information needed to employ these theoretical insights is lacking. In particular, the relationships between hazards and preventive activities are frequently poorly understood. Indeed, many hazards have not been identified. Furthermore, in many cases it is impossible to say with any degree of certainty what is "fair compensation" for an injury. For many, the loss of life or limb may be incommensurable with money—the form that "compensation" almost always takes. And with regard to the consequences of many environmental hazards, it is practically impossible to assign responsibility for their cause to a given individual or firms. Moreover, even if this information were obtainable, it is likely that the cost of obtaining it, prior to formulating policy, would often greatly exceed the marginal costs of an imperfect policy solution. Finally, it might be noted that, although it can be argued that collective (particularly societal) decision making ought to be risk neutral,[9] it seldom is neutral.

Does this mean, therefore, that an understanding of the theoretical optimum is irrelevant? Not at all. At best, it can guide us in our choice of alternative policy instruments. At worst, it can help us determine what we don't know that is important to the design of effective policies and, thereby, permit us to design policies that may compensate for our ignorance. And it can help us identify areas where further analysis can have a substantial payoff in terms of improved policy making.

Information Needed to Obtain the Health and Safety Optimum

What must we know in order to minimize the sum of damages resulting from environmental hazards to health and safety and the cost of reducing hazards? Referring to Figure 7.1, one must identify the total damage schedule, and, for a given damage schedule, identify the hazard reduction schedule with the least slope. Identification of the total damage schedule may be broken down into three separate steps: determination of the change in hazard level brought about by a change in government policy (for example, the reduction in sulfate emissions resulting from the requirement that all coal-fired generators have smokestack scrubbers); determination of the change in the incidence of adverse incidents (for example, deaths or workdays lost due to illness) resulting from a change in the level of hazard—this is called the dose-response relationship where health hazards are concerned; and determination of the change in damage costs resulting from a change in the incidence of adverse events.

It will be noted that the first two relationships are clearly questions of fact, while the third is a question of values. This qualitative difference is frequently cited as evidence of the irrelevance of the formulation of the health and safety optimum depicted above.[10] It is not. Of course, with respect to the first two relationships, perfect certainty (at least so far as means and properties of distribution are concerned) is theoretically obtainable—at a cost—through either the evaluation of ex post experience or ex ante analysis. On the other hand, we cannot, in theory, hope to be so certain about questions of value.

In practice, however, we frequently have a better understanding of this relationship than of either of the other two. For example, we can be fairly certain that dying is "bad," but we are perfectly ignorant of any number of hazards in our environment (some hazards have not been brought to our attention). Moreover, owing to the indirect consequences of public action, we cannot always know how much a hazard can be influenced by public action once it has been identified. Indeed, it seems likely that analytical efforts designed to reduce our ignorance about the value of life and limb might have a greater payoff in terms of improved decision making than would similar investments in understanding either of the other two relationships. This information would be relevant to policymaking about every kind of health and safety hazard, while information about the first two relationships, particularly the second, is hazard-specific.

What do we know about these relationships? What can we know? What are the limits of our understanding? What implications have the answers to these questions for policymaking?

Determination of the Change in Hazard Levels Resulting from a Change in Government Policy

As we have insisted throughout this volume, the first decision to be made has to do with the selection of the appropriate policy instrument or institutional arrangement. Furthermore, an array of policy instruments is employed to reduce hazard levels, although this purpose is not always consciously recognized. These include not only direct regulation but also mandatory compensation schemes, the assignment of property rights, and information provision as well. We have also argued that there exists an appropriate criterion for choice among these institutional arrangements and that we possess a fair amount of knowledge upon which to base a choice. With effort, we may know a great deal more. However, our knowledge or evidence base is not at this time sufficient to overcome the biases that predispose political leaders and bureaucrats to choose regulation. Consequently, we have repeatedly stressed the importance of designing and evaluating alternatives to regulation.

Nevertheless, in this chapter, we assume that this decision has been made and that regulation was the right choice. Hence, the decisions that we are concerned with here have to do with the choice of regulatory mechanisms and their configurations. Paradoxically, despite the extensive use of regulation as a means of hazard reduction, we know very little about the relative advantages of alternative regulatory mechanisms.

What do we know? We know that hazards can be reduced by directly prohibiting them or by requiring some corrective action to reduce them. We also know that the effectiveness of these prohibitions will be influenced by the effort made to enforce them and that, in theory and with considerable effort, regulatory arrangements may be so configured as to produce the identical hazard reduction outcomes that would obtain under alternative institutional arrangements.

How much a given hazard will be reduced will not, however, depend simply on the target hazard level specified in the regulation. Where corrective action is mandated, the connection between the action mandated and the hazard level and the enforcement strategy adopted by the regulatory agency will both have a bearing on the amount of hazard reduction actually obtained.

Enforcement has two aspects: detection of violators and their punishment. Once responsibility for compliance with regulation has been assigned and the kind of standard selected (either design or performance), detection may be either proactive, based upon inspection or monitoring to determine compliance, or reactive, with detection following the occurrence of damages. If detection is proactive, inspections may be comprehensive and continuous or random and sporadic. Penalties may be either tied to the cost of compliance or be punitive. [11] The probability that a sanction will actually be imposed is also a function of the algorithm used by the regulatory agency's legal staff in deciding which cases to prosecute, evidentiary rules, and, of course, the legal resources of the non-complying firm.

It should be noted that there is evidence that firms will frequently comply with regulations whether or not they are enforced. Random inspection can obtain compliance levels of 80 to 90 percent. Comprehensive inspection, combined with an appropriate system of penalties, can increase compliance levels to nearly 100 percent. An example of this is the Connecticut Department of Environmental Protection's (DEP) enforcement program. In this instance, the DEP determined the cost of bringing each firm in the state up to "standard." A monthly levy was then imposed on each firm until it complied with the law. This assessment was based upon the rate that would amortize the cost of bringing the firm into compliance with DEP standards and had the effect of removing the incentive to delay or to avoid compliance by guaranteeing, in effect, return on investment in pollution control devices equal to the return on an equivalent commercial investment. This does not mean that all that might be known about the trade-offs between detection and penalty is known. The DEP enforcement program may be seen as a limiting case—minimal penalties combined with comprehensive inspection. Other solutions are more common. It seems unlikely, however, that this situation reflects a rational assessment of alternative enforcement strategies. [12]

Furthermore, each element of the enforcement strategy adopted by a regulatory agency interacts with all of the others to determine the degree to which hazards are reduced. Moreover, the effectiveness of a given regulatory approach may be influenced by other regulations and other existing means of promoting hazard reduction. In some cases, elements of the regulatory mix will work at cross-purposes to each other. On the other hand, apparently flawed elements of the regulatory mix may interact in such a way as to compensate for each other's weaknesses. For example, generally speaking, the severity of the penalty should be made inversely proportional to the probability of detection. However, under certain circumstances, one might imagine that a combination of high design standards, reactive monitoring, and punitive sanctions might be nearly optimal, at least insofar as the behavior of the firms subject to regulation reflected an economic rather than a moral calculus.

In this instance, where the cost of compliance represented the least costly means of reducing a given hazard or where the efficacy of alternative means was highly uncertain, we would expect the firm to comply with the standard. If, however, the hazard could be reduced with certainty by some less costly means known to the firm, it would be free to choose that option. Only where the cost of abating the hazard substantially exceeds the expected cost of failing to do so would the firm take no action.

Indeed, one may not conclude that, simply because a regulatory agency sets some standards at too high a level or rejects less costly but equally effective abatement technologies, overall resources are misallocated. As we will explain, identification of the appropriate hazard abatement level and technology can be very costly. It might, therefore, make sense for a regulatory agency to behave in an outrageous manner when forced to specify standards, in a limited number of instances, to induce trade associations to generate reasonable consensus standards. It might even make sense for an agency to target its enforcement activities, not where problems are most serious, but where they will get the most publicity. Our point is that, although regulation may seem a straightforward, even simple, approach to the reduction of hazards to anyone concerned with trying to understand its effects, there are few, if any, firm conclusions one can draw with regard to the potential effectiveness or efficiency of regulation in general.

Instead, one must first specify a hazard, its properties (or, more correctly, our understanding of its properties), a target level of hazard reduction, an enforcement strategy, and a situation.

Regulatory practice is another matter. The elements of a regulatory strategy are seldom combined in an appropriate, consistent, organized fashion. More than anything else, the failure of the regulators to employ consistent, appropriate strategies is reflected in their failure to pay heed to a single basic principle of management: The best way to get something done is to figure out who is best located to deal with a situation and give that person the authority and the responsibility to deal with it properly.

This is of course both a diagnosis and a prescription. For example, we tend to prefer performance to engineering standards, in large part because we assume that firm personnel are generally better situated and motivated to figure out how best to meet regulatory targets than are engineers located in Washington laboratories. This same logic underlies our tacit endorsement of many of the recent innovations in the environmental regulatory area—bubbles, offsets, and so on—as well as our earlier favorable discussion of smog and accident taxes, marketable emissions rights, and the like.

Several factors explain the regulators' failure to combine targets, standards, and enforcement into a coherent, efficient regulatory strategy: flawed enabling legislation, interest group pressures, ignorance. However, these factors may be subsumed into a single factor: The absence of external pressure to improve performance and very likely real negative incentives to undertakings that may improve the efficiency with which regulatory objectives are obtained, but that also involve some risk. For example, a MESA administrator who adopts a standard enforcement strategy may not be criticized for failing to maximize overall efficiency. On the other hand, if the administrator does undertake nonstandard procedures to increase overall efficiency and something goes wrong, he or she may be out of a job. The inability to appropriate gains from increased efficiency, combined with the high risks associated with error, simply does not provide bureaucratic officials with incentives to try to improve public sector performance.

The interesting question here is, Why is this the case with respect to regulation? We would contend that the explanation usually given for the lack of incentives to efficiency in the public sector is not very satisfactory, that is, an inability to measure the consequences of an organization's activities. The fact is, as far as health and safety regulation is concerned, performance can be measured—environmental quality, imperfectly; emissions, more satisfactorily; work-place exposures to chemical hazards, accidents, and so on can all be measured. Furthermore, regulatory performance often is measured, and when it is, these measures frequently appear to influence regulators' decisions, especially with respect to the design and execution of regulatory programs. But if we cannot explain absence of incentives to overall efficiency or the misincentives that had led to risk avoidance by an inability to measure regulatory performance, how, then, does one account for the behavior of the regulators?

At the risk of sounding overly repetitious, our answer is fairly simple. Students of public management tend to overlook the fact that efficient choice requires both cost and performance measures. This is the case because the absence of cost measures is seldom at issue. Nevertheless, proper incentives are just as likely to be absent where performance can be measured, but costs cannot be or are ignored; as where costs are measured, but performance cannot be or is ignored. So long as regulatory decision makers are more attentive to their own costs, the probability that any given hazard reduction strategy will represent the most efficient solution to the problem of reducing hazards is low. This generalization may safely be applied to the decision to employ regulation, as opposed to alternative policy instruments, and to the selection of an enforcement strategy.

However, even if the incentives were right, ignorance would remain a significant barrier to the identification of optimal regulatory strategies. Much more can be learned. Because the lessons that can be learned with respect to the use of these mechanisms can be profitably applied to a wide range of hazards, such research should be given a fairly high priority. At the same time it should be understood that, in some cases, reducing one hazard will create new hazards or lead to unintended behavioral changes exacerbating others. In the evaluation of hazard reduction programs, these indirect consequences ought not to be ignored. However, it is not clear whether this is a problem of instrument selection or of hazard identification.

Determination of the Change in Incidence of Adverse Effects Resulting from a Change in the Level of Hazard

With respect to the relationships between hazard levels and adverse incidents, we frequently know far too little and learning more will be costly. As noted above, information about such relationships may be gleaned either ex post, by working backward from the etiology of accidents, sickness, and premature death, or ex ante, by testing products, chemicals, and so on to determine their hazard potential.

Where ex post analysis is concerned, considerable damage must be done before a hazard can be identified. And even after a great deal of damage has been done, it may not be possible to trace damages back to a single hazard. This is particularly likely to be the case insofar as health hazards are concerned. The causes of illness are seldom simple or immediate. Consequently, ex post analysis can frequently do no more than suggest possible health hazards, and then only after considerable damage has been done.

On the other hand, ex ante analysis is expensive,[13] testing on humans may be dangerous, and testing on animals is often inconclusive. Even if testing weren't expensive, dangerous, or inconclusive, the mind boggles at the task of testing all products, chemicals, and so forth for their hazard potential. There are over 10,000 consumer products on the market and 50,000 to 70,000 chemicals in routine use. At this time, fewer than 1 percent of the chemicals in routine use have been partially tested. Moreover, there is increasing evidence that chemicals interact synergistically to cause some illnesses, including cancer. Obviously, there is no way to test the hazard potential of all the possible combinations and permutations of chemicals in the environment (50,000 x 49,999 x 49,998 . . .). Indeed it is not possible to test the 17 or so new drugs introduced each year in the United States for synergistic effects (the number of theoretically possible effects is about 300 trillion).[14]

It is possible that the best strategy would start with ex post epidemiological analysis to identify possible hazards and would then proceed to more rigorous testing of these candidates. Where safety hazards are concerned, present techniques of ex post analysis and ex ante testing in combination may prove reasonable guides to policy. Work-place and product safety hazards can be satisfactorily identified through the analysis of clinical records and case histories.[15] Laboratory testing can frequently isolate product or work-place attributes responsible for the injury and determine whether or not they can be corrected. However, actual practice is distinctly inferior to what is currently possible.[16] Where health hazards are concerned, the prognosis must be more pessimistic. What is needed here are intellectual breakthroughs in data collection, analytical design, and testing procedures.

Finally, even where hazard potential can be identified, it may not be possible to specify the exact relationship between hazard level and the incidence of adverse effects. For example, it is known that there is a statistically significant relationship between air pollution and human health.[17] However, the size of the effect and the relative importance of various pollutants are not known precisely.[18] This means that even if the value question were settled, a precise damage function could not be established. However, good estimates of the upper bound on the size of this effect are available, and these, combined with qualitative information on the shape of damage schedules, may be a sufficient basis for action. This is so because where the slope of the damage schedule is understood to be roughly linear, basing hazard reduction efforts on a good guess will not produce substantially inefficient outcomes (see Figure 7.1). On the other hand, where the damage schedule is dramatically curved to the origin, small variations in the level of hazard reduction effort may be critical. Consequently, qualitative understanding of damage schedules is one of the keys to sound policymaking in this area.

Of course, there are some relationships between hazard levels and adverse effects that are fairly well understood. To cite some examples, the effects of radiation on health are fairly clear,[19] and some of the consequences of changing vehicle safety standards are highly predictable.[20] In each of these instances, adverse outcomes are probabilistic. However, where hazard levels are specified, both the mean and the variance of expected damages can be estimated with a high degree of accuracy. Nevertheless, it does not follow that where this knowledge exists, health and safety policy is necessarily more consistent or more closely conforms to the regulatory optimum than in other areas. That this is the case appears, in part, to be due to an unwillingness to place a value on adverse health effects.

Determination of the Change in Damage Costs Resulting from a Change in the Incidence of Adverse Effects

Analysts generally reject the notion that the value of human life and well-being are infinite, but there is no consensus as to the proper values to use in the assessment of damages done to human health. Indeed, it is impossible to hope that we might resolve all the puzzling issues that are involved in valuing injury and death prevention. However, it is not necessary to do so to improve public policymaking.

For example, according to R. Wilson, some of the safety standards on nuclear reactors imply a marginal cost of $750 million for each death prevented,[21] whereas the corresponding figure for highway maintenance activities appears to be on the order of $20,000. Spending resources on the former at the expense of the latter seems ridiculous. Most would agree a life is worth more than $20,000 and less than $750 million. The question is how much more or how much less. If we could be reasonably certain that a life is worth more than $200,000 and less than $2 million and, if the estimates cited above are accurate, it is possible that the variance in the cost-effectiveness of public programs in the United States could be reduced to one-tenth of 1 percent of what it is now.

In fact, analysis of these issues has progressed to the point where we can say that it is probable that the average value of a life falls between these two figures. Furthermore, it is likely that additional analysis can significantly increase our confidence in such estimates. Because this kind of analysis is inexpensive and is applicable to a wide range of public policies, not only to questions of health and safety regulation, it seems reasonable that this is a particularly attractive field for further research. The questions to be answered are: Roughly speaking, what is a life worth? Can injuries be compared with fatalities? And when is one life worth more than another?

The greatest amount of analytical attention has been given to the first of these questions.

What Is a Life Worth? Traditionally, the most commonly used figure for the value of a human life has been the discounted or present value of lifetime earnings (estimated to be about $275,000).[22] However, this figure has been criticized as omitting from consideration the value to the individual of his life over and above his earnings. To get at this problem, analysts have attempted to infer the value people place on their lives from the choices they make. This is usually done by evaluating the risk premium associated with danger-ous jobs. This analysis typically produces figures on the order of $300,000 to $1,000,000 per life.[23] However, this analysis is not wholly satisfactory for several reasons: First, people who choose to work in risky industries or jobs may be less risk averse than are most of us. There is some evidence to support this notion. People who work in such industries tend to be younger, are less likely to be married, and are more likely to smoke.[24] Second, people who work in risky industries or jobs may tend to underesti-mate the risk. People are not good natural statisticians. They tend, in fact, to base their expectations of the future on their past experiences.[25]

Consequently, other estimates of the implicit value placed on human life as revealed by the choices people make are:

$450,000—based on the decision not to use seat belts[26]
$500,000—based on the decision to drive 65 mph (where permitted by law) rather than 55 mph[27]
$800,000—based on the decision to stop smoking, and the price elasticity of demand for cigarettes[28]
$1,000,000—based on the decision to jog three hours a week[29]

This range may seem substantial; however, it is far less than a single order of magnitude.[30] Given the quality of information avail-able to people on the risks they are assuming, the difficulty of evaluating it, and quality of the data available, these estimates are more consistent than they may first appear. Accepting these variations in the value of life cannot possibly account for the value of life implied by certain regulatory decisions.

Can Injuries Be Compared with Fatalities? The second question has received less attention. Consequently, less is known about trade-offs between injuries and fatalities. The Consumer Product Safety Commission (CPSC) has developed a much criticized index that weights the severity of a large number of adverse health consequences, including death. These weights range from 10 for a sprained ankle to 2,516 for a death.[31] Steven Kelmon[32] points out that the relative weight assigned to death by the CPSC was reduced from 34,721, because that figure was felt to be too high. Other similar indices have been developed,[33] but we cannot be confident that they are any better or worse than the CPSC's. Most of this analysis is based upon survey data. While it is interesting to know that some people say that certain injuries (for example, genetic damage to an unborn child)[34] are more awful than death itself and that others (for example, sprained ankles) are fairly trivial, it would be desirable to see if sample survey results could be validated by revealed preference.

When Is One Life Worth More than Another? The third question has been subjected to considerable speculation but almost no empirical analysis. Nevertheless, it is clear that four of five factors enter into the evaluation:[35] the variance of the damage function; the degree to which the hazard is voluntarily assumed; the degree to which the hazard is assumed as a result of participation in socially approved activity; the degree to which the propensity to assume a hazard is related to differences in self-evaluation of life's worth; and the degree of the familiarity of the hazard (in terms of revealed preference, people prefer to die in familiar ways, such as .automobile accidents versus nuclear power meltdowns).

The variance of the damage function is, perhaps, the most problematic of these issues. It is known that people are not risk neutral. That is, they will not necessarily be indifferent between a situation in which ten persons will die with certainty and one in which there is a 1 percent probability that 1,000 people will die. Because the benefits of hazard reduction are necessarily probabilistic, this suggests that it might be proper to weight expected deaths based upon the variance of the estimate. However, it is not clear how this should be done. One study, for example, suggests that about 50 percent of the population is made up of risk takers (that is, they would prefer a 1 percent probability of 1,000 deaths to a certainty that ten persons will die); 25 percent are risk averse; and 25 percent are risk neutral.[36] Interestingly, it has been suggested that better educated, more articulate individuals have a substantially greater propensity to social risk aversion. Furthermore, risk averse individuals are more intense about their preferences. [37] Finally, there is some evidence that formal training in Bayesian statistics increases the tendency toward risk neutrality. [38] Perhaps this is because both risk aversion and risk-taking behavior partially reflect an inability to deal with probabilities and consequently erroneous risk assessments—with risk takers erring on the side of optimism and the risk averse on the side of pessimism. [39]

Nor does it appear that anything certain about social risk preferences can be learned from social decisions. In the majority of cases it appears that social decision making is risk taking; for example, considerable sums of money will be spent to rescue a trapped miner, [40] but much less is spent to reduce the probability that fairly large numbers of miners will be trapped. But a number of decisions indicate significant risk aversion, such as nuclear reactor safety standards. [41] Indeed, if one were trying to impose some logic on the observed pattern of U.S. health and safety policy, one might conclude that it is almost as if a conscious decision had been made to assume the most favorable state of nature would obtain in a number of cases, the most likely in others, and the least favorable in still others.

It might be noted that such a pattern of responses cannot be judged wrong or irrational. Of course, if all health and safety policies were submitted to systematic, consistent ex ante evaluation, the public interest would likely best be served by risk-neutral decision making. However, where each problem is addressed independently on an ad hoc basis, where the basis for the decision reflects real uncertainty or fails to reflect a sound assessment of the probabilistic information that is available, the public interest may be served best by a mix of policies that reflects both pessimistic and optimistic as well as neutral expectations. According to Charles Lindblom, such an approach to policymaking may generate wrong-headed individual policies, [42] but the sum of the consequences produced by the full range of policy decisions may not be too far from the optimum—particularly when the cost of obtaining, processing, and using information is considered. It might also be noted that the appropriate response to new information is different under these alternative policy formulation strategies. Under the first, new information should be used to revise prior expectations. Under the second, it must be treated as the sole basis for the policy decision. Both strategies require a readiness to make policy changes as further information becomes available. However, the first assumes an efficient search for new information. The second takes a passive approach to information collection. It is assumed that wrong-headed policies will bring themselves to the attention of decision makers. Consequently, if this approach is flawed, the flaw is that it is biased in favor of attention to the immediate and the determinant and against the more distant and indeterminant.

Unfortunately, regulation's comparative advantage (as an instrument of government action) is greatest where it is directed at the distant and indeterminant. Perhaps, it is this flaw that accounts for the apparent inconsistency with regard to the treatment of risk that characterizes health and safety policy, in that it simply reflects mistaken risk assessments. Perhaps it reflects the sometimes strange concentration of interest group demands and alliances. Perhaps it represents real preferences. The point is that we do not know. Until we find out, the last possibility ought not to be ignored. This means that ex ante analysis of health and safety regulation should comprehend properties of the distribution of outcomes other than the mean. This can be accomplished through the skillful use of sensitivity and a fortiori analysis.

Most of the health and safety regulatory agencies have a potential for protecting people from themselves by making it impossible for them to make the choices they would make if they were fully informed. Again, this is a question of values—who should be protected from their own bad judgment and by how much. Regulatory paternalism is an issue that deserves more attention. This is not to imply that the sole purpose of a regulatory agency ought to be to determine the risks associated with a given job or product and to provide that information to workers and consumers and then let them decide whether or not they wish to bear the risk. In some cases, it is indisputable that a hazard should simply be prohibited, as in CPSC's crib and bicycle standards. [43] The problem arises when a government intervenes to require or prohibit behavior that people would choose for themselves if they were fully informed of the probabilities and the consequences.

The automobile airbag issue illustrates many of the problems encountered when government tries to protect people from themselves. Opponents of passive restraint laws argue that if people wanted airbags or other passive restraints they would demand them as optional accessories on vehicles. Because consumer demand has been underwhelming, opponents claim that regulations requiring passive restraints are an unnecessary infringement on personal choice. They also claim that the same degree of protection could be obtained through the use of manual seatbelts. On the other hand, proponents point out that passive restraints would save 8,000 lives a year. They grant that manual lap and shoulder belts, if used, provide the driver with about as much protection as is provided by passive restraints and that they are much less costly to produce.

However, manual lap and shoulder belts are more inconvenient to use. If the inconvenience of buckling up each time one gets in a car is assumed to be worth 10¢, the total cost in the United States of installing and using manual lap and shoulder belts appears to be nearly double the cost of installing and using a passive restraint system ($2 billion versus $1.2 billion per year). [44] This estimate is supported by polls showing passive restraint standards to be about five times as popular with the public as mandatory seatbelt laws. [45]

If the facts are as stated, why don't people choose to buy passive restraints? To do so would be perfectly consistent with other choices regarding risks in the environment made quite frequently. One answer is that, as an option, passive restraints have been expensive—the list price has ranged from three to ten times what it would be if they were standard equipment. [46] This implies a value per life saved of $360,000 to $4 million, which is on the high end of the scale. Even so, between 1970 and 1977, at least 10,000 airbag systems were purchased as optional equipment at prices up to $1,200 each. [47]

Congress forced the National Highway Traffic Safety Administration to delay its proposed passive restraint standards. In doing so, it was implicitly placing a fairly low value on a human life. Similar decisions have been made with regard to automobile size standards. One can only infer that the voluntary assumption of hazard entered into these decisions. At the same time, it cannot be inferred that Congress has a great deal of respect for freedom of choice, per se. For example, the 55 mph speed limit implies either that Congress assigned a rather high value to a life or that fast driving is not a wholly approved of activity. The latter interpretation seems more plausible.

Again, the question might be asked, Do these decisions represent social preferences? How much weight should be given such preferences, and when do they come into play? And, again, the answer is "We don't know."

An additional related issue has to do with whether or not health and safety policy should be based upon the average value of life, on individual willingness to pay (and, therefore, on differing tastes and perceptions of risk on the part of those it is trying to protect), or on some measure of the social value of the individuals and groups being protected. Our health and safety policies appear to reflect all of these positions in different contexts. Finally, some policies appear to reflect the belief that some hazards are more awesome than others. Inasmuch as the best evidence suggests that these assessments are in error, it is suggested that people care about the cause as well as the probability of death; they would rather drown, die in traffic accidents, or die in a coal mine accident than die of radiation poisoning. Here, too, it can be asked whether this is a valid perception or a post hoc rationalization of previous policy errors. There is reason for believing the latter. The fact is that lifesaving programs that are wholly federally funded tend to place a far lower implicit value on a life than is the case with some regulatory programs.[48]

Even if the largest inconsistencies in health and safety policy reflect real preferences, it is not clear that these preferences ought to be incorporated in public policies. In the case of well-understood spillover hazards, they certainly should be. But in the ca ɘ of worker and product hazards, perhaps they ought not to be. One of the more persuasive justifications for paternalistic policies in this area is that the high costs of learning about and understanding various hazards can be avoided by the delegation of this task to a central authority. If this is the purpose of such policies, shouldn't paternalism be consistent, shouldn't policies reflect the best judgment of the experts and not the uninformed opinion of non-experts? Isn't there a conflict between the objective analysis of a hazard and its possible remedies and the interpretation of social values? If so, which is the proper task for the regulators to perform?

CONCLUSION

The promotion of health and safety is a complex and difficult task. Much of what we would like to know about health and safety hazards is not known. If we had more information about these issues, we could make better decisions. However, information is costly. This means that among the most critical of the decisions that must be made are those that have to do with how much and what kind of information should be obtained.

What do we know? Seven factual propositions are particularly relevant to the formulation of health and safety policy.

First, we can generally make a fairly sound choice as to the best public policy instrument to use to reduce a hazard. The market and the liability system can best cope with easily identifiable and avoidable product and worker hazards. Where hazard levels or consequences are easily measurable, tax compensation schemes or the assignment of rights are more efficient and less equitable than direct regulation. Regulation makes the most sense in uncertain areas with which market mechanisms cannot cope (such as uncertainties about the weather and complex, poorly understood health hazards).

Second, regulatory activities must be properly targeted. This means that regulatory agencies must have sufficient resources to carry out the research and economic analysis required to identify hazards and to determine the best means of dealing with them.

Third, external review of proposed regulatory standards should try to determine whether or not regulations are directed at problems they have the best chance of solving (the choice of instrument) and try to determine whether or not the damage prevention effort proposed is roughly right given the factual information available.

Fourth, confidence in the "rightness" of the level of damage prevention effort is contingent upon an understanding of damage schedules. Ignorance is most serious where the damage schedule is dramatically curved toward the origin. Where this slope is understood to be roughly linear, basing hazard reduction efforts on a good guess will not result in substantially inefficient outcomes, regardless of the slope or intercept of the damage function. On the other hand, in the case of a program concerned with the reduction of harmful emissions, if the emission reduction effort is characterized by increasing costs and the dose-response relationship is nonlinear, small variations in the level of the reduction effect will be very important. This suggests that if analytical dollars are to be allocated so as to obtain the biggest payoff, they should be, first, directed at obtaining a qualitative understanding of damage schedules. Quantitative understanding of damage schedules should be sought only where there is prior reason to believe that they are nonlinear.

Fifth, a cost-benefit analysis can promote the objectives of external review. A key problem of administrative decision making is that the costs relevant to administrators are not necessarily the same as those that "objectively" exist after a choice has been made. The natural propensity to view costs narrowly has frequently resulted in the choice of regulation, where other instruments would be more appropriate. It has also resulted in both under- and overprevention of hazards. The strength of cost-benefit analysis is that it forces consideration of a wider array of costs, thereby reducing the opportunity for public decision makers to let their personal cost and risk preferences influence decisions.

Sixth, it is possible to assign reasonably consistent values to health and safety benefits. This is the case despite the fact that precise values of human life and limb cannot be obtained.

Seventh, as a society we must be prepared to act on the basis of information that is available and to modify policy as new information becomes available.

To accompany the economic analysis of specific hazard reduction proposals, what additional research should be done in this
area? Our understanding of the problems encountered suggests the
following research priorities:

Research to understand better the alternative forms of public
intervention to reduce hazards. This includes the design of alternative mechanisms and systematic experimentation with and evalua-
tions of tax compensation schemes, information provision, and so on
    Research to find shortcuts for the identification of hazards and
dose-response relationships. This means the development of
quicker, cheaper tests, statistical procedures, sampling techniques,
and so on
    Research to get better upper-bound estimates of damages and
damage reduction costs
    Research to obtain a better understanding of damage costs.

The first and fourth priorities are stressed because this information is broadly applicable to a wide range of health and safety
issues. In a sense, this information reflects a fixed cost of better
decision making. The third priority is emphasized because if it is
feasible to obtain comprehensive information of this kind, this would
materially aid decision making in the area of health and safety policy. The second priority is stressed because obtaining comprehensive dose-response information is simply too costly at present to
be justified. However, good dose-response information would
greatly improve health and safety policy decisions. If the cost of
obtaining this information can be significantly reduced, health and
safety policy can be greatly improved.

NOTES

    1. Talbot Page, Robert H. Harris, and Samuel S. Epstein,
"Drinking Water and Cancer Mortality in Louisiana," Science,
July 2, 1976, p. 55.
    2. The National Highway Safety Needs Report (Washington,
D.C.: U.S. Department of Transportation, April 1976), p. 8.
    3. Implications of Environmental Regulations for Energy Pro-
duction and Consumption, Vol. 6, Analytic Studies for the U.S.
Environmental Protection Agency (Washington, D.C.: National
Academy of Sciences, 1977), pp. 115-16.
    4. Ibid.
    5. To say that government action may be justified is not the
same as saying whatever action the government takes is justified.

Just as there are flaws in the market that produce inefficient outcomes, there are flaws in the process of collective choice that tend to produce inefficient outcomes. Even where collective action is justified, the actions taken by government may make us worse off than if nothing had been done. See Richard B. McKenzie and Gordon Tullock, Modern Political Economy (New York: McGraw-Hill, 1978), pp. 340-57; James M. Buchanan, The Basis for Collective Action (Morristown, N.J.: General Learning Corporation, 1971).

     6. It must be stressed that risk-taking aversion refers here to choices between outcomes with higher and lower probabilities, not to the normal human propensity to avoid threats to themselves. This distinction may be illustrated by the U.S. Food and Drug Administration's drug control policies. By keeping all drugs off the market until they are proven both safe and effective, one can be certain that some injuries are avoided. However, this means that some drugs might not be developed, drugs that might do considerable good. There is sufficient evidence to show that the expected reduction in damages resulting from more rapid pharmaceutical innovation would more than offset the damages caused thereby. However, the benefits of increased pharmaceutical research are highly uncertain. Therefore, technically speaking, the FDA's policy is risk taking. However, because the FDA is held to be responsible for damages caused by drugs it certifies as safe, but is not given credit for the benefits of drug use, FDA bureaucrats naturally tend to be cautious in granting approval to new drugs. In the everyday usage of the term, they are risk-averse. See Sam Peltzman, Regulation of Pharmaceutical Innovation: The 1962 Amendments (Washington, D.C.: American Enterprise Institute, 1974); David Schwartzman, The Expected Return from Pharmaceutical Research (Washington, D.C.: American Enterprise Institute, 1975); W. M. Wardell and Louis Lasagna, Regulation and Drug Development (Washington, D.C.: American Enterprise Institute, 1975); and Robert B. Helms, ed., Drug Development and Marketing (Washington, D.C.: American Enterprise Institute, 1975). This does not mean that drugs do no harm. As Melman et al. point out: "between 150,000 and 450,000 patients per year enter hospital . . . either with or solely because of a drug reaction . . . those being treated for a drug reaction have a 30 per cent chance of developing another while being treated for the first." However, "80 per cent of the adverse drug reactions . . . [are] due to . . . known pharmacological effects of drugs given in the wrong doses." In addition, some drugs are prescribed incorrectly. If 90 percent or more of the damage done by prescription drugs is the result of physician error, and much of the remainder is the result of idiosyncratic reactions, it is doubtful that FDA regulations do very

much to correct the situation. Melman et al., "Medical Benefits and Risks Associated with Prescription Drugs: Facts and Fancy," in Helms, op. cit., pp. 5-8. See also P. C. Fishburn, The Theory of Social Choice (Princeton, N.J.: Princeton University Press, 1973); B. Fischhoff, P. Slovic, and S. Lichtenstein, "How Safe Is Safe Enough? A Psychometric Study of Attitudes Towards Technological Risks and Benefits," Decision Research Report no. 76-1 (Eugene: Decision Research, a Branch of Perceptronics, University of Oregon); and P. Slovic, B. Fischhoff, and S. Lichtenstein, "Cognitive Process and Societal Risk Taking," in J. S. Carroll and J. W. Payne, eds., Cognition and Social Behavior (Potomac, Md.: Lawrence Erlbaum, 1976).

7. Nina Cornell, Roger Noll, and Barry Weingast, "Safety Regulation," in Setting National Priorities. The Next Ten Years, ed. Henry M. Owen and Charles L. Schultze (Washington, D.C.: Brookings Institution, 1976), p. 463.

8. See Anthony Fisher and Frederick M. Peterson, "The Environment in Economics: A Survey," Journal of Economic Literature 14, no. 1 (March 1976);20, Figure 1.

9. K. J. Arrow and R. C. Lind, "Uncertainty and the Evaluation of Public Investment Decisions," American Economic Review 60, no. 3 (June 1970):364-78. See also A. C. Fisher, "Environmental Externalities and the Arrow-Lind Public Investment Theorem," American Economic Review 63, no. 4 (September 1973): 722-25.

10. See David Burnham, "Marshall Splits with Carter Aides on Estimating Costs of Regulations," New York Times, May 9, 1977, p. 51.

11. On the logic of "punitive sanctions," see Alfred Blumstein et al., eds., Deterrence and Incapacitation: Estimating the Effects of Criminal Sanctions on Crime Rates (Washington, D.C.: National Academy of Sciences, 1978). See also Colin S. Diver, "A Theory of Regulatory Enforcement," Public Policy 28, no. 3 (Summer 1980):257-99.

12. See Connecticut Enforcement Project, Economic Law Enforcement, Vol. 1, Overview (Washington, D.C.: U.S. Environmental Protection Agency, September 1975), p. 7. See also William Drayton, "Economic Law Enforcement," Harvard Environmental Law Review 4, no. 1 (Spring 1980):1-40.

13. Alexander, op. cit.; Alexander, "The Hidden Cost of Drug Safety," Business Week, February 21, 1977, pp. 80, 82, 84; Alexander, "Drugs Beat Bugs, but Bureaucrats?" and "But Are They Safe?" The Economist, November 25, 1978, p. 102.

14. Schwartzman, op. cit.

15. Steven Kelman, "Regulation by the Numbers—A Report on the Consumer Product Safety Commission," Public Interest 36 (Summer 1974):82-102.

16. Ibid. See also N. A. Ashford, Crisis in the Workplace: Occupational Disease and Injury (Cambridge, Mass.: MIT Press, 1976); G. H. Collings, Jr., et al., "Multiphasic Health Screening in Industry," Journal of Occupational Medicine 14 (1972):434-95; R. B. Desjardins, "Occupational Health Information Systems," paper presented at the Joint TIMS/ORSA Meeting, Los Angeles, November 13-15, 1978; David P. Discher, G. D. Kleinman, and F. J. Foster, Pilot Study for Development of an Occupational Disease Surveillance Method (Rockville, M.D.: U.S. Department of Health, Education, and Welfare, May 1975); HEW Publication no. (NIOSH) 75-162; J. D. Forbes et al., "Utilization of Medical Information Systems in American Occupational Medicine—A Committee Report," Journal of Occupational Medicine 19 (1978):819-30; R. Gillette, "Plutonium (II): Watching and Waiting for Adverse Effects," Science 185 (1968):1140-43; F. W. Holcomb, Jr., "IBM's Health Screening Program and Medical Data System," Journal of Occupational Medicine 15 (1973):863-68; Pamela S. Kerr, "Recording Occupational Health Data for Future Analysis," Journal of Occupational Medicine 20 (1978):197-203; T. A. Maugh II, "Chemical Carcinogens: The Scientific Basis for Regulation," Science 201 (1976): 1200-05; R. W. McBurney, D. W. Hillman, and H. Doutchyard, Jr., Diamond Shamrock Corporation Occupational Health Surveillance System (Cleveland, 1977); Sidney Pell, "Epidemiological Requirements for Medical-Environmental Data Management," Journal of Occupational Medicine 20 (1979):554-56; and E. J. Schneider, "Information Systems for Industrial Hygiene," paper presented at the Joint TIMS/ORSA Meeting, New York, May 1, 1978.

17. L. B. Lave and E. P. Seskin, "Air Pollution and Human Health," Science, August 21, 1970, pp. 723-33; L. B. Lave and E. P. Seskin, Air Pollution and Human Health (Baltimore: Johns Hopkins Press, 1977); L. B. Lave and E. P. Seskin, "Health and Air Pollution," Swedish Journal of Economics 73, no. 1 (March 1971):76-95; L. B. Lave and E. P. Seskin "Acute Relationships Among Daily Mortality, Air Pollution and Climate," in Economic Analysis and Environmental Problems, ed. E. S. Mills (New York: Columbia University Press, 1975); National Research Council, Commission on Biological Effects of Atmospheric Pollution, Lead: Airborne Lead in Perspective (Washington, D.C.: National Academy of Sciences, 1972); H. Schimmel and T. J. Murowski, "The Relation of Air Pollution to Mortality, New York City, 1963-1972," paper submitted to the New York State Department of Environmental

Conservation, 1975; V. K. Smith, "Mortality—Air Pollution Relationships: A Comment," Journal of the American Statistical Association 70, no. 350 (June 1975):341-43. U.S. Environmental Protection Agency, Health Consequences of Sulfur Oxides: A Report from CHESS, 1970-1971, Final Report, National Environmental Research Center, EPA-650/1-74-004 (Research Triangle Park, N.C., 1974), NTIS PB-234920/7; and D. Hamilton, Health Effects of Air Pollution (Upton, N.Y.: Brookhaven National Laboratory, 1975).

18. Schimmel and Murowski, op. cit.; B. G. Ferris et al., "Sulfur Oxides and Suspended Particulates," Archives of Environmental Health 27 (September 1973):179-82.

19. National Research Council, The Effects on Population of Exposure to Low Levels of Ionizing Radiation (Washington, D.C.: National Academy of Sciences, 1980); W. K. Sinclair, "Effects of Low-Level Radiation and Comparative Risk," Radiology 138, no. 1 (October 1981):1-9; Arthur C. Upton, "The Biological Effects of Low-Level Ionizing Radiation," Scientific American, February 1982, pp. 41-49; and Eliot Marshall, "New A-Bomb Studies After Radiation Estimates," Science, May 22, 1981, pp. 900-04; and Eliot Marshall, "New A-Bomb Data Shown to Radiation Experts," Science, June 19, 1981, pp. 1164-65. Also see L. A. Sagan, "Human Costs of Nuclear Power," Science 177, no. 4048 (1972):487-93; and U.S. Environmental Protection Agency, Environmental Analysis of the Uranium Fuel Cycle (Washington, D.C., 1972), NTIS PB-235 803. Contrast with U.S. Department of the Interior, Coal Mining Industry Fatalities in 1974 (Arlington, Va.: MESA, 1975). See also National Research Council, Analytical Studies. Vol. 6, Implications of Environmental Regulations for Energy Production and Regulation (Washington, D.C.: National Academy of Sciences, 1977).

20. Secretary of Transportation, The National Highway Safety Needs Report (Washington, D.C.: U.S. Department of Transportation, April 1976).

21. R. Wilson, "The Costs of Safety," New Scientist 68 (1975): 274-75.

22. See, for example, R. G. Ridker, Economic Costs of Air Pollution (New York: Praeger, 1967); or L. B. Barrett and C. Morse, The Cost of Air Pollution Damages (Research Triangle Park, N.C.: U.S. EPA, February 1975).

23. See R. Smith, Compensating Wage Differentials and Hazardous Work, Technical Analysis Paper no. 5 (Washington, D.C.: Office of Policy Evaluation and Research, Department of Labor, August 1973); R. Thaler and S. Rosen, "Estimating the Value of Saving a Life: Evidence from the Labor Market," Conference on Research in Income and Wealth (New York: National Bureau of

Economic Research, 1973. See also M. Jones-Lee, The Value of Life (Chicago: University of Chicago Press, 1976); M. Jones-Lee, "The Value of Changes in the Probability of Death or Injury," Journal of Political Economy 82 (July/August 1974):835-49; J. P. Acton, Evaluating Public Programs to Save Lives: The Case of Heart Attacks, Rand Corporation Report R-950-RC (Santa Monica, Calif., January 1973); and J. Linnerooth, "The Evaluation of Public Programs Affecting Population Mortality," Ph.D. thesis, University of Maryland, 1977. Several of the issues addressed here were first raised in T. C. Schelling, "The Life You Save May Be Your Own," in Problems of Public Expenditure Analysis, ed. S. Chase (Washington, D.C.: Brookings Institution, 1968); and extended in B. C. Conley, "The Value of Human Life in the Demand for Safety," American Economic Review 66, no. 1 (March 1976):45-55; and E. J. Mishan, "Evaluating Life and Limb," Journal of Political Economy 79 (July/August 1971):687-705.

24. F. E. Lundin et al., Radon Daughter Exposure and Respiratory Cancer: Quantitative and Temporal Aspects, Report from the Epidemiological Study of the United States Uranium Miners, NIOSH Joint Monograph no. 1 (Washington, D.C.: U.S. Public Health Service, 1971).

25. Fischhoff et al., op. cit.

26. It is estimated that wearing seat belts would reduce the per person probability of death by 1.5×10^{-4}. Based upon an informal survey, it was determined that 40 percent of those who do not use seat belts would do so if they were paid 10¢ each time they got into the car and buckled up. Assuming the car is used twice a day, 365 days a year, the decision not to use a seat belt implies that the value placed on life is equal to or less than $487,000— $EV = V(P)$ or $\$73 = V(1.5 \times 10^{-4})$; solving for V we find: $V = \$486,667$. See G. Blomquist "The Value of Life Saving: Implications of Consumption Activity," Journal of Political Economy 87 (June 1979):540-58.

27. Charles A. Lave, "The Costs and Benefits of the 55 MPH Speed Law," Working Paper, University of California, Irvine, 1977.

28. Given a price elasticity of demand of .12, the estimated 14 percent reduction in consumption of cigarettes attributed to increased awareness of the risks of lung cancer may be treated as the equivalent of a $1.18 increase in the price of a pack of cigarettes. Consequently, we have a loss of consumers' surplus equal to 59¢ per pack. Assuming consumption of one pack a day, this implies an annual consumers' surplus of $215.35. Since a decision to stop smoking reduces the probability of death by 2.7×10^{-4}, we have $\$215.35 = V(2.7 \times 10^{-4})$; hence, $V = \$797,592$.

29. The absolute maximum reduction in the probability of death that could be associated with this decision is 4×10^{-4}. See W. B. Kannel, P. Sorlie, and P. McNamara, "The Relation of Physical Activity to Risk of Coronary Heart Disease: The Framingham Study," in Coronary Heart Disease and Physical Fitness, ed. R. O. Malmborg and O. A. Larsen (Baltimore: University Park Press, 1971), p. 256; J. N. Morris et al., "Vigorous Exercise in Leisure-Time and the Incidence of Coronary Heart-Disease," Lancet 1 (1973):333-39; L. Epstein et al., "Vigorous Exercise in Leisure-Time, Coronary Risk-Factors and the Resting Electrocardiogram in Middle-Aged Male Civil Servants," British Heart Journal 38 (1976):403-09; S. Shapiro et al., "Incidence of Coronary Heart Disease in a Population Insured for Medical Care (HIP): Myocardial Infarction, Angina Pectoris, and Possible Myocardial Infarction," American Journal of Public Health 59 (1969):1-101; L. Wilhelmsen and G. Tibblin, "Physical Inactivity and Risk of Myocardial Infarction: The Men Born in 1913 Study," in Malmborg and Larsen, op. cit., pp. 251-55.

Assuming the cost of running an hour (net of nonhealth benefits) is equal to the minimum wage of $2.85, the annual cost running three hours a week would be $445. This implies a value of a life of $1,026,000. In this case, the reduction in the probability of death is far higher than the literature warrants and the "reservation wage for jogging" far lower than the average. The average person would have to value his life in excess of $300 million to jog three hours a week—of course the average person doesn't jog three hours a week. It is likely that the marginal jogger overestimates the health benefit of this particular form of torture and assigns a low cost to the activity (some even claim to enjoy it!).

30. Howard proposes a third method based upon the notion of life chance lotteries which he claims is applicable to small-risk situations. By his technique, high risks, for example, 10 percent, would never be accepted at any price and individuals would sacrifice their full income (or more if they can manage it) to avoid such a risk. Based upon reasonable assumptions, Howard's approach produces a value of a life figure of about $1 million for the average person and $2.4 million for a person aged 25 and earning $20,000 a year. Howard also provides a method for estimating the maximum marginal value of eliminating all accidental deaths in the United States, about $110 billion. Interestingly, this figure is three to ten times higher than the values estimated for eliminating all accidental (nonlethal) injuries in the United States. See R. A. Howard, Life and Death Decision Analysis, Technical Report no. ETS DA-78-1 (Stanford: Department of Engineering-Economic Systems, Stanford University, 1979). See also Jan Paul Acton,

Measuring the Monetary Value of Life Saving Programs, RAND
P-5075 (Santa Monica, 1976); Barbara S. Cooper and Dorothy P.
Rice, "The Economic Value of Human Life," American Journal of
Public Health 57 (November 1967):1954-66; Selma Mushkin, "Health
as an Investment," Journal of Political Economy 70 (October 1962):
129-57; Richard Zeckhauser and Donald Shepard, "Where Now for
Saving Lives?" Law and Contemporary Problems 40 (Autumn 1976):
5-45; and articles by Clarke, Dorfman, Fischer, Lipscomb, and
Schutze et al., in Health: What Is It Worth?, ed. Selma Muskin and
David W. Dunlop (Washington, D.C.: Public Services Laboratory,
1979). Also see E. H. Clarke, Demand Revelation and Public
Goods (Washington, D.C.: Woodrow Wilson Center, Smithsonian
Institution, December 1977).

    31. See "Mean Severity," in CPSC, NEISS News 4 (July 1975).

    32. Kelmon, op. cit.

    33. R. L. Berg, ed., Health Status Indexes (Chicago: Health
Research and Educational Trust, 1973); M. M. Chen, J. W. Bush,
and Donald L. Patrick, "Social Indicators for Health Planning and
Policy Analysis," Policy Sciences 6 (March 1975):71-89; S. Fanshel
and J. W. Bush, "A Health Status Index and Its Application to Health
Services Outcomes," Operations Research 18 (November/December
1970):1021-66. See also articles by Chen and Mushkin in Mushkin
and Dunlop, op. cit.; and Martin Bailey, "Earnings, Life Valuation, and Insurance," "Measuring Benefits of Life-Saving," and
"Safety Decisions and Insurance" (Washington, D.C.: Public
Services Laboratory, Georgetown University, 1977).

    34. John W. Lathrop, "Measuring Social Risk and Deter-
mining Its Acceptability," UCRL-81060 (Lawrence Livermore
Laboratory, July 14, 1978).

    35. Ibid. See also Peter Self, Econocrats and the Policy
Process (New York: Free Press, 1975), pp. 74-75.

    36. Lathrop, op. cit.

    37. Ibid. See also Samuel E. Bodily, "Analysis of Risks to
Life and Limb," Darden School Working Paper DSWP-78-22
(Charlottesville: University of Virginia, 1978).

    38. Slovic, op. cit.; S. Lichtenstein and P. Slovic, "Com-
parison of Bayesian and Regression Approaches to the Study of
Information in Judgment," Organizational Behavior and Human
Performance 6 (1971):679-744.

    39. S. E. Bodily, "Evaluating Joint-Life Saving Activities
Under Uncertainty," Lecture Notes in Economics and Mathematical
Sciences 155 (New York: Springer-Verlag, 1978). Bodily also
explains that risk preferences appear to be characterized by increasing marginal disutility, that is, other things equal, the
higher the background risk, the more distasteful is the assumption

of increasing risk. This, along with their greater experience, would tend to explain the caution of older people. Lacking such an explanation, this observation would be inconsistent with deductive approaches to the estimation of the utility of life, which require declining utility with age.

40. Self, op. cit.

41. The public may be particularly cautious about nuclear hazards because government has frequently lied to them about the real risks. For example, the AEC insisted for years that above-ground nuclear testing was "safe." And for many years denied epidemiological evidence showing that it was not.

42. Charles Lindblom, The Intelligence of Democracy (New York: Free Press, 1965), especially pp. 63, 84.

43. Kelmon, op. cit.

44. Background Manual on the Passive Restraint Issue (Washington, D.C.: Communications Department, Insurance Institute for Highway Safety, August 1977); Air Bag and Safety Belt Fact Sheets (Chrysler Corporation, August 1977); and Subcommittee on Consumer Protection and Finance, House of Representatives, Installation of Passive Restraints in Automobiles, 95th Congress, 1st Session, September 9, 12, 1977 (Washington, D.C.: U.S. Government Printing Office, 1977).

45. "Gallup Poll: Public Approves of Airbags," Status Report, August 17, 1977; "Automatic Protection Favored by New Car Buyers," Status Report, August 17, 1977; "MVMA Poll: Air Bags 'Least Objectionable,'" Status Report, October 12, 1976; and Roper Public Opinion Research Center Poll (77-4), conducted March 1977 and reported in Background Manual, op. cit., pp. iv-7.

46. Roper, op. cit., pp. vi, 9-11.

47. A. R. Karr, "Saga of the Air-Bag, or the Slow Deflation of a Car Safety Idea," Wall Street Journal, May 16, 1976, p. 17. On the other hand, fewer than half of 1 percent of all new car buyers chose to buy air bags.

48. Marie-Elisabeth Paté, "Cost per Life Saved in Public Projects and Regulations," paper delivered at ORSA meeting, Los Angeles, November 13, 1978.

8

SUMMARY AND CONCLUSIONS ON REGULATORY REFORM AND A POSTSCRIPT ON THE REAGAN ADMINISTRATION

The purpose of this chapter is twofold. First, it summarizes and organizes the arguments made in previous chapters—both positive and normative. Second, based upon this summary, it seeks to evaluate the regulatory policies and practices of the present administration. Most of the footnote references in the summary portion of this chapter have been eliminated, as they are provided in previous chapters.

RECAPITULATION: REGULATION AND REFORM

We have defined regulation as the imposition of rules by government, backed by the use of penalties, that are intended specifically to modify the economic behavior of firms and individuals in the private sector. An essential characteristic of this definition is its emphasis on rules or commands requiring or prohibiting specified behavior. A second characteristic of this definition is its exclusive concern with economic behavior. Rules based upon moral or ethical precepts are explicitly excluded from this definition of regulation, although we acknowledge that murder, theft, gambling, drug dealing, and so on have an economic dimension and recognize that the imposition of economic regulations implies a moral and ethical obligation to obey.

Using this definition, we have attempted to describe the growth of regulation in terms of its scope, domain, and the effort devoted to its implementation. As we have seen, regulatory activity is pervasive. No industry is exempt from its influence. In many, its influence is overwhelming and, in some, its influence has been growing.

We have assumed that the purpose of any government activity ought to be the promotion of the common good. Generally speaking, this purpose may be accomplished through effective macroeconomic management, income redistribution to achieve a fairer, more equitable distribution of society's resources, or the promotion of a more efficient use of its resources. At best, regulation has only a tangential relation to the design of macroeconomic policies or their performance with respect to such objectives as full employment or price stability. However, we are sufficiently impressed by supply-side arguments to note that the growth of regulatory activity has probably had a significant adverse effect upon the rate at which the economy has expanded. This is so not only because the efforts made by firms to comply with government regulations have raised costs and crowded out other, productive, investments. More importantly, regulation has in practice tended to favor the status quo, thereby slowing the process of creative destruction through which the economy grows, and diverting scarce managerial resources to an unproductive search for advantage in the political marketplace. In far too many industries, regulation has created environments in which the most attractive strategic opportunity available to their participants is the opportunity to establish a market niche protected by the police powers of the state. In such industries, the greatest strategic threat is that a firm's competitors will get to the regulators first. However, to say that regulatory practice influences macroeconomic performance does not imply that it is directly relevant to macroeconomic policies.

As for the redistributive function of government, it is our view that regulation is simply an inappropriate means of achieving a more equitable distribution of resources. Not only is regulation a blunt instrument with which to accomplish this end, its characteristics are such that income redistribution via regulation almost inevitably makes some of the rich richer and most of the poor poorer.

This leaves only one function for regulation to perform: promotion of the more efficient use of society's scarce resources. We have also argued that regulation can serve this end in at least four instances:

When it promotes effective competition

When it permits the public to enjoy economies of scale or scope obtainable only under monopoly of supply

When it compensates for divergences between private and social costs

When it reduces the number of mistakes made by parties to private market transactions by standardizing product or service attributes or working conditions

However, in none of these instances may it be unambiguously concluded that regulation is the best option. In each, the benefits obtainable via regulation might also be secured via alternative institutional arrangements.

Indeed, we have concluded that regulation is seldom the best institutional arrangement for realizing single plant or industry efficiencies. Either some form of franchise and bidding arrangement or public provision will usually dominate regulation. If it is assumed that potential service suppliers understand the demand characteristics of their markets and the production and cost behavior in their industry better than the regulators, and can be prevented from colluding, then a competitive bidding arrangement should ensure the best supply arrangements possible in any particular market. If it is assumed that the regulators are as informed or better informed than are managers in the regulated industry, then private ownership has no significant function or responsibility to discharge.

Under conditions of externality, we conclude that regulation will usually be inferior to the manipulation of market incentives and penalties as a means of reducing externalities. Incentives may take the form of charges (effluent taxes) or marketable rights. It is assumed that where producers can determine better how to reduce externalities than regulators, market incentives will outperform regulation.

In the fourth circumstance, it is asserted that public provision of information—or in the case of information asymmetries, certification, reassignment of liability, or enforced disclosure as in truth in packaging and labeling—will produce more efficient outcomes than will a regulatory program that restricts the range of goods and services made available, enforces standards of quality, or establishes maximum levels of exposure to health and safety hazards. Once again, if it is assumed that participants in private market transactions err only because information is absent, then public provision of information is preferable to regulation. This follows from the observation that public provision of information can meet social and economic objectives without removing alternatives from the market that some consumers and workers would prefer.

At the same time, there are circumstances where we would expect regulation to dominate alternative institutional arrangements. Perhaps the least ambiguous case involves difficult probabilistic judgments and the opportunity for making serious mistakes. In this case, regulation will be lest costly and/or more effective than information provision, for example, simply because the cost of information processing and, thereby, avoiding error can be reduced by delegating the task to an expert. (This strategy is, of course, most likely to produce satisfactory outcomes where individual preferences are known to be fairly similar.) Regulation will usually be the most efficient means of promoting worker health and even safety where the regulators have a better understanding of work-place hazards than have managers at the work site. This same logic also applies to reducing harmful or unsightly emissions. Finally, regulation is probably the least worst alternative institutional arrangement where the supply of a service involves a costly physical connection between service user and service supplier and there are no easily available substitutes for the service. Note that the key characteristic of all of these cases is a high level of uncertainty. To the extent that uncertainty is unavoidable at a reasonable cost or where computational costs are simply very high (and if the mistakes that would be avoided are serious enough to warrant any action at all), regulation can and very likely will be the most appropriate means of coping with the situation. In other words, we are saying that ignorance is an important and a valid justification for regulation. Having made this claim, we would also insist that there is often no justification for ignorance.

With regard to how to evaluate the relative merits of regulation in comparison to other public policy instruments or other forms of market organization, in some cases regulation may be evaluated on the basis of the benefits and costs it produces. Choice of the most appropriate institutional arrangement may be determined based upon the criterion of minimization of information costs; application of benefit–cost and information cost minimization analysis should be complementary rather than conflicting in determining where to regulate.

If regulation has a comparative advantage relative to other government actions in certain instances, why are economists generally so critical of it? One reason is distrust of government decision making in general. In turn, this distrust frequently reflects a distaste for interest group politics and its consequences, an appreciation of the short-term horizon that characterizes political decision making, and cynicism toward many of the claims made about the public interest in political debate.

So far as the choice between regulation and alternative institutional arrangements is concerned, however, we do believe that the economists' bias against regulation reflects a very real tendency of government to rely to far too great an extent on regulation. Regulation is the instrument most familiar to lawmakers, especially those with backgrounds in the law. It is also consistent with the legal approach to problem solving in other areas. Consequently, regulation is often the first solution to a problem that lawmakers choose. Second, the information available to influence government choice between alternatives is often biased in favor of regulation. We would guess that the failure to identify the right institutional arrangements and, where regulation is appropriate, the right regulatory strategy results in annual welfare losses in excess of $50 billion each year.

We have, therefore, referred to movement toward more optimal institutional arrangements as substantive regulatory reform. Substantive reforms involving choices between broad classes of institutional arrangements (that is, regulation and information provision) have been identified as comprehensive reforms; those that have to do with choices among design elements and their configuration within a single institutional arrangement (for example, engineering versus performance standards) have been identified as incremental or marginal reforms. We have also concluded that the greatest payoff to regulatory reform efforts will come as a result of the promotion of comprehensive substantive reforms. In most cases comprehensive reform will require legislative action.

How do we achieve comprehensive substantive reform? First of all, we need better information. Where a major change in institutional arrangements is proposed, at least three kinds of information must be supplied if the proposal is to be taken seriously:

1. Hard evidence that the alternative institutional arrangement will produce more satisfactory outcomes than would more effective or more comprehensive regulation

2. Evidence that the costs of transition to the new institutional arrangement would not eliminate the gains made by the move

3. Evidence that adverse distributional outcomes will not occur.

In most cases, the kind of hard credible information needed to support substantive reform is simply not now available. Consequently, we would conclude that getting this evidence ought to be a high priority. Probably the best way to get the kind of information needed is through an organized program of experimentation with alternative institutional arrangements.

Even if we had this information, however, we could not guarantee the inevitability of reform. We have argued that the regulators behave the way they do because that is often how Congress wants them to behave. Congress wrote the enabling legislation under which the regulators operate, created many of the inconsistencies that force the regulators to work at cross-purposes to each other, and continues to exercise considerable influence on their behavior. Furthermore, we have argued that it is frequently no accident that the means used to obtain apparently worthwhile ends are often unsatisfactory; the existing regulatory apparatus does to a substantial degree reflect the real interests of key elected officials.

To overcome these interests (we would stress that they are not necessarily the interests of Congress as a whole), two additional factors are critical: presidential leadership and the attention of Congress. At a minimum, presidential appointees must, by their actions, direct the attention of Congress to matters of substantive reform.

So far as regulatory policy is concerned, the leadership supplied by both the Ford and the Carter administrations was remarkable, particularly when weighed against previous reform efforts in this area. Their efforts not only changed attitudes toward the use of regulation to achieve public policy objectives but also led to substantive reform and changes in the policymaking process. Perhaps even more important than the substantive achievements of the Ford-Carter years was the thrust of the Ford-Carter efforts. These efforts were distinctive because of their emphasis on improving efficiency and their assumption that economic analysis can identify mistaken regulatory practices and policy, that further mistakes can be avoided, and that past mistakes can be corrected.

To avoid future mistakes and to correct past mistakes, the Ford-Carter administrations relied primarily upon a process of review that subjected proposed new regulations to rigorous, high-level scrutiny and sought to evaluate existing regulations. That is to say, the principal tool with which both administrations sought to fight regulation was regulation. We are, of course, mindful of the wacky incongruity of this response to regulatory failure. Yet if the arguments made in this volume are valid, such a response makes considerable sense. Of course, if regulators do not make mistakes, review is a waste of time. On the other hand, if the reviewers know best how to formulate, design, and execute public policy, regulatory officials have no real function to discharge. But the fact is that neither the reviewers nor the regulators know in every case what to do, let alone how to do it. And, as we have argued, ignorance is, perhaps, the best justification for regulation.

There is no doubt in our minds that well-designed review mechanisms can provide the kind of information that will produce better decisions and lead to substantive regulatory reform. We have described the installation of review mechanisms that promote better decisions as procedural reform.

Certainly, the proper response to ignorance is analysis. However, the elimination of all ignorance is neither possible nor necessarily desirable. As is the case with many good things, analysis is costly. Regrettably, where we are ignorant, the cost of obtaining perfect information usually far exceeds its value. Consequently, the aim of public policy analysis is to be roughly right.

Given this aim, the review mechanisms installed by the Carter-Ford administrations (or the OAL program in California) have, so far, very likely served us rather well. The analysis performed by the reviewers was cheap, the information requirements imposed upon the regulators were minimal, and, where the reviewers were successful, the outcomes of their interventions were generally beneficial. In several instances the reviewers apparently succeeded in blocking regulatory proposals that simply did not make sense. Considering the flow of new regulatory proposals and the rate at which regulatory effort was increasing during the Ford-Carter years, it would have been surprising indeed if the reviewers had not been right far more often than they were wrong.

However, the circumstances that made these early review mechanisms effective no longer obtain. The flow of new regulatory proposals has largely been brought under control. Consequently, it is now time for further procedural reform. The key weakness of the kind of regulatory review Ford and Carter sponsored and that has been carried to its logical extreme by the present administration is that it can keep the regulators from doing the wrong things, but it does not make them want to do the "right" things. Furthermore, placing the full burden of proof on the regulators, while simultaneously denying them the analytical resources required to prove their case, guarantees that they will frequently fail to take action when they should.

In other words, the effect of requiring the regulators to prove conclusively that any action they propose will not only be efficient but more efficient than any other conceivable action is the equivalent of the FDA's requirement that drugs must be proven safe and effective before they can be marketed. As we have seen, under this requirement very few unsafe drugs are marketed, but a significant number of beneficial drugs are kept off the market; perhaps an even greater number are never developed.

Our principal conclusion with respect to procedural reform has to do with the use of benefit-cost analysis. Nearly everyone concerned with improving regulatory policy and practice recognizes the power of this tool to improve decision making. It is powerful not only because it provides decision facilitating information but also because it forces decision makers to consider the full array of the consequences of any proposal, thereby reducing their propensity to let personal cost and risk preferences determine their choices. Benefit-cost analysis is blind to group identities in a way that administrative preferences can never be. However, benefit-cost analysis is useful only when it is, in fact, used to aid decisions.

We argue that review, in general, and benefit-cost analysis, in particular, are likely to be most valuable as a means of facilitating decisions when they are expressly aimed at offsetting biases that would predictably result in mistakes. This argument is, of course, directly analogous to our conclusion that regulation will frequently be the most efficient means of dealing with hazards where cognitive biases eventuate in predictable, costly errors. In making this argument, however, we are not concerned only with cognitive biases (for example, congressional predisposition to legalistic solutions) but also to those that result from organizational processes (for example, everyone's predisposition to treat regulation as a free good).

We would especially stress the value of information that would lead decision makers to choose from a wider array of institutional arrangements. In practice, what this might mean is that the reviewer ought to be primarily concerned with satisfying himself that the regulator had seriously considered and discarded an array of alternatives, before turning to regulation. In any case, there is very little justification for extended debates about the merits of particular estimates of benefits or costs or the details of specific regulatory proposals. On these points the regulatory agency is almost certain to know more than the reviewer.

What we propose here is, in fact, a rather rigorous standard. It would not be easy to demonstrate that alternatives had been seriously considered. However, we would carry this proposal even further and suggest that proposals that call for the use of alternative institutional arrangements ought to be subject to less rigorous scrutiny than proposals which call for more regulation.

Obviously, in making this latter suggestion, we are going beyond decision facilitating to decision influencing. To be quite candid, we are wholly convinced that the most effective counter to biases caused by flaws in organizational process is the redesign of incentives, responsibility structures, and information systems. Information is particularly valuable when it motivates decision makers to make the right decisions. At some point, procedural reform must be concerned with motivating decision makers, with the design and installation of incentives that lead them to make better decisions.

In practice, what this seems to imply is an endorsement of a regulatory budget. Whether or not a regulatory budget would work, we cannot say. We can say, however, that its proponents are thinking about the right issues. The fundamental idea behind the regulatory budget is so sound and so plausible that it must ultimately prevail.

If the preceding conclusions are correct, our prognosis for reform is guardedly optimistic. That it is optimistic at all is the result of our interpretation of the success of the reforms instituted over the past five years and the lessons learned from these successes. Regardless of political preferences and independently of real differences of opinion on the value assigned to such benefits as clean air and water, we ought to acknowledge that in many instances regulation is not the most appropriate public policy instrument to solve the problems at hand.

We have learned over the past few years that some types of economic controls produce perverse consequences and ought to be eliminated: price controls on natural gas and oil, price and market entry controls in the air travel and trucking industries, entry and other supply controls over the communications, financial, and banking industries. We have also learned that benefits accrue through consolidation and relaxation of some accountability-oriented rules in the health and safety area. We have begun to recognize the difference between control applied through specification of technology versus performance standards enforced with sliding fine and fee schedules. Regulatory measures have been "tiered" to fit the size of firms to which they apply. Greater attention has been given to other innovative and market-oriented regulatory measures to influence private sector investment incentives, for example, marketable rights or setting fines to match compliance costs. We are refining our understanding of the manner in which economic and social objectives may be met more satisfactorily through the use of nonregulatory policy instruments such as tax expenditures, contracting, and changes in public and private ownership to solve problems formerly approached exclusively through the imposition of government controls.

And in other areas—including worker health and safety, nuclear and toxic waste exposure and disposal, protection of endangered species and wildlife habitats, and land use—we are developing better evidence to demonstrate that regulation is often appropriate, effective, and productive of long-term, survival-oriented economic efficiencies. This recognition ought to stimulate a rededication to the search for less cumbersome and more effective control strategies and methods and support for those willing to use market-oriented mechanisms of mitigation and control. We firmly believe that a maturation of our philosophy of control can lead to satisfactory resolution of some nasty and pressing socioeconomic dilemmas; ultimately it must be acknowledged that in many instances it is possible to regulate better by regulating less.

POSTSCRIPT

Had this conclusion been written a year ago, our optimism would have been less qualified. During his campaign for the presidency, President Reagan had made regulatory reform a key plank in his economic platform, along with cutting taxes and expenditures

and stabilizing the growth of the money supply. We had very high
expectations as to the incoming administration's commitment to
regulatory reform. Furthermore, our expectations were shared by
many observers of the regulatory scene. Mel Dubnick spoke for
what was then the conventional wisdom when he observed that:

> Negative attitudes took root . . . and are likely to fully
> blossom with the Reagan administration. Indicative of
> this is the high priority Reagan gave to the establish-
> ment of a regulatory relief task force chaired by Vice
> President Bush, and the appointment of a well known
> critic of regulation, Murray Weidenbaum, to head the
> Council of Economic Advisors.[1]

Gradually over the past year, however, there has emerged a widen-
ing gap between our expectations and actual events. As one very
careful student of the regulatory scene recently put it, "The performance of the Reagan administration has . . . been spotty, erratic,
and contradictory."[2]

Much of this administration's energies have gone into the implementation of more intensive, more comprehensive review mechanisms. The most important of the changes made in this area has
been the centralization of ex ante review in the OMB's Office of Information and Regulatory Affairs. Together with the support of
Vice-President Bush, relocation of the regulatory review function
has given the reviewers considerable clout. Furthermore, the administration has placed greater reliance on benefit-cost analysis,
clarified review procedures, and augmented OIRA's analytical resources (while simultaneously reducing the analytical capabilities
of the regulatory agencies). Consequently, it is now much harder
for a regulatory agency to issue new rules and it takes them longer,
too. The impact of these changes is roughly reflected in a substantial reduction in the rate of expansion of the Federal Register.

What we see here, therefore, is more of the same—not necessarily better. There is no indication that the administration is
seriously considering further real procedural reforms, although an
advocate of the regulatory budget concept has been appointed director of OIRA.

On the legislative front, the administration has simply not
made any effort on behalf of substantive reform. So far, this failure cannot be attributed to the lack of opportunities to provide leadership or even to the lack of a reform agenda. The administration
is on record as supporting complete deregulation of natural gas,
freer entry in the broadcasting and telecommunications industries
and banking, extensive revision of the Clean Air Act, and taking the
"S" out of OSHA.

The most favorable interpretation we can put on the Reagan administration's surprising failure to take the lead in changing existing regulatory statutes is that regulatory issues have been crowded off the administration's legislative agenda by more important issues—defending the recent tax cut, controlling domestic expenditures, managing the deficit, and increasing support for national defense. If this is the case, we would certainly not challenge the administration's priorities. In the short run, fighting inflation and unemployment is certainly more important than fighting regulation. Unlike his immediate predecessors, this president seems to think he knows how to do it. Moreover, we understand that the attention of Congress is a scarce commodity—one that no administration can afford to squander.

Nevertheless, the structure of Congress permits it to deal with more than one issue at a time; and in several instances Congress has recently indicated a willingness to act on substantive reform proposals nominally supported by the current administration. In particular, we would note the opportunity to excercise leadership that presented itself when the Clean Air Act came up for renewal. As Walter Guzzardi observed:

> an occasion for reform presented itself last September when the act came up for renewal and was as easy a target as it is ever going to be. But the administration shied away from the issue, with officials from Bush on down insisting that the battle over taxes and the budget had to have priority. . . . Taxes and the budget seem likely to grab all the administration's attentions again this year. [3]

Even now, we believe that the administration could achieve decontrol of natural gas prices if it were willing to do no more than to give a tacit endorsement to a windfall profits tax. [4]

Clearly, from a presidential leadership perspective, the impetus for comprehensive reform of the substance of regulatory policy has weakened considerably in the transition from the Carter to the Reagan administration. Due to the preoccupation of the president and, consequently, the Congress with macroeconomic policy and budgets, confounded by the conflict inherent to fiscal retrenchment and the confusing complexity of the continuing resolution process of expenditure authorization, the pressure for substantive reform has been considerably diffused. [5]

Despite its failure to pursue substantive reform, there have, in fact, been major regulatory changes under this administration. On the whole, however, the direction taken by these changes may best be described as erratic, if not contradictory. On balance, these changes appear to have done as much harm as good. We would guess that this outcome is largely explained by the pattern of appointments made to key regulatory positions by the current administration. Just as the Carter administration's regulatory policies often reflected an ongoing conflict within the administration between pro-efficiency and antibusiness appointees, Reagan's appointees are split between the pro-efficiency and the probusiness. In a substantial number of cases, Reagan has appointed representatives of the regulated industries and trade groups to high positions in the regulatory agencies. Under Carter, common sense had to fight moral posturing; now it has to fight greed.

On the positive side, we would note the Antitrust Division's recent settlement with AT&T. This settlement will accomplish many of the reform objectives sought through legislation under the previous administration. Together with the decision to drop the 15-year-old case against IBM, the initiative taken by the Justice Department promises far more effective competition in the telecommunications industry. However, we would note that unless legislation is passed that would comprehensively dismantle the existing regulatory regime, including a preemption of local and state jurisdiction, one result of this action may be a serious decline in local telephone service and consumer satisfaction.

It should also be acknowledged that the current administration successfully eliminated all remaining price controls on petroleum products and refinery allocations.

On the negative side, we would note a partial reversal of regulatory policy and practice at the ICC, returning us part way to a regime of restricted entry and price controls. The effect of this reversal is reflected in the market value of operating permits. As noted in a recent issue of Regulation magazine:

> If entry into the industry is genuinely free, new entrants should be unwilling to buy the rights to operate in a certain market from existing operators. As one would expect, the value of operating rights dropped to zero under the commission's previous leadership. Now, according to scattered reports, they once again have positive market value. [6]

It appears that airline deregulation has also been partially undone by the administration's persistent failure to deal with the landing-rights issue. In a number of airports serving important and expanding markets, these are, particularly at peak use periods, in very short supply. The supply has been reduced even further since the air controllers' strike of 1981. The problem of rationing these spaces arises not only because of congestion but also as a result of increased protest from citizens residing near airports or under their approach paths. Despite the plausibility of market-oriented solutions to this problem (for example, marketable landing rights or landing fees),[7] The FAA, which has jurisdiction over airport operations, continues to endorse the status quo. This clearly works to the disadvantage of potential entrants and to the advantage of existing carriers on existing routes. Indeed, Guzzardi reports the claim made by many small carriers and potential entrants that the FAA is using its authority "to shield the established carriers from competition, thereby reimposing protection on an industry just barely cut loose of it."[8]

It has been suggested that if there is any consistency to the new administration's policies, it is to be found in its antagonism to the new social regulation. And there is some truth to this claim. But we do not see any hard evidence of an across-the-board administrative repeal of measures intended to promote a cleaner, safer, healthier, or fairer environment; where such a repeal has been observed, old measures have frequently been replaced by plausible and reasonable alternatives. In only two cases, that of the EEOC and the EPA, does it appear that the regulators have retreated from their efforts to obtain previously accepted economic and social objectives. In the case of the EPA it might be suggested that this is as much due to mismanagement as to anything else.[9]

The preferred weapon with which the new administration has sought to control the new social regulation is the budget. But even here, we see no consistency to the pattern of cutbacks. Many of the new social regulatory agencies have suffered substantial budget reductions—up to 40 percent between fiscal 1981 and 1983—including EPA, OSHA, EEOC, NHTSA. But so too have a few of the older regulatory agencies—ICC and FTC. Furthermore, some of the regulatory agencies have been promised augmentations—NRC, FDA, SEC.

We are actually far more upset with the incidence of the cutbacks within agencies than with the size of the cuts or the particular agencies affected. While enforcement activities have been cut back or redirected in a number of areas (not necessarily the worst of all possible outcomes), the budget weapon has been disproportionately aimed at research, development, and analytical activities. We can understand why the OMB might want to monopolize regulatory wisdom, but we are frankly appalled that they have nearly succeeded in doing so. We have argued throughout this volume that ignorance accounts for many of the regulators' mistakes. The OMB seems committed to keeping the regulators ignorant. We would conclude, therefore, that while the OMB's ability to influence and enforce a targeted pattern of impoundments, deferrals, and reductions in spending authority may lead to less regulation, it will almost certainly not result in better or smarter interventions to achieve worthwhile goals.

Our point is that budgetary impoundment, recision, or deferral of previously authorized spending is not regulatory reform, although such tactics may be employed to promote reform or as a result of it. Nor is budget cutting regulatory reform. Deregulation and, particularly, administrative repeal are not necessarily reforms. It certainly is not a reform to retreat from efforts to obtain economic and social objectives through government intervention. Relaxation of toxic waste management measures or even some clean air standards are not necessarily reforms. Regulatory reform is not simply a process whereby government reneges on efforts to protect the environment or the health and safety of its citizens; quite the contrary.

From this perspective, however, the only real consistency we find in the current administration's regulatory policy is its lack of consistency. We remain optimistic about the prospects for substantive regulatory and procedural reform, nevertheless. In the long run, the power of the alternative institutional arrangements discussed in this volume, together with an almost inevitable improvement in our understanding of how to make them work, ought to eventuate in their ultimate triumph. Unfortunately, we no longer believe this triumph will come under the present administration. We would, of course, be pleased to be wrong.

NOTES

1. Melvin J. Dubnick, "Government Regulation: Advice and Analysis," Public Administration Review, March/April 1981, p. 286.

2. Walter Guzzardi, "Reagan's Reluctant Regulators," Fortune, March 8, 1982, pp. 34-37. See also "The Budget Weapon Hits the Regulators," Business Week, February 22, 1982, pp. 34-35.

3. Ibid., p. 36.

4. Walter Guzzardi, "A Back-door Approach to Raising Gas Prices," Business Week, February 15, 1982, p. 50.

5. Christopher DeMuth correctly adds that:

Before Congress will itself act, external changes are required to dislodge the accumulated interests in the status quo and to assure the doubtful of the economy's ability to continue functioning in the absence of federal controls. . . . [T]he history of deregulation is that major administrative reform is a necessary prerequisite of statutory reform. (Regulation, January/February 1982, p. 18)

However, we have also learned that if administrative reform is to stimulate legislative action, the reformers must have a consistent definition of what they want to accomplish. While we would acknowledge that several of the actions taken by this administration have been arresting, they have not reflected a particularly consistent definition of regulatory reform. Furthermore, in the environmental health and safety areas, we simply do not believe that unilateral executive action can do very much to improve the situation, although it may reduce some of the harm done by command and control type regulation in these areas.

6. "Reregulation at the ICC: 'The Congress Made Me Do It,'" Regulation, November/December 1981, p. 7.

7. See, for example, S. C. Littlechild and G. F. Thompson, "Optimal Aircraft Landing Fees: A Game Theory Approach," Bell Journal of Economics, Spring 1977, pp. 186-204.

8. Guzzardi, op. cit., p. 39.

9. See Gil Reshtenthaler, W. T. Stanbury, and Fred Thompson, "What Ever Happened to Deregulation?" Policy Options, May/June 1982, pp. 36-42.

AUTHOR INDEX

ABOUT THE AUTHORS

FRED THOMPSON is associate professor of public policy and management and associate director of the Canadian Studies Program in the School of International and Public Affairs of Columbia University. He has been a visiting professor at UCLA's Graduate School of Management and at the University of British Columbia and has served as a staff consultant to the ECC's Regulation Reference, participating in the preparation of its Interim Report.

Fred Thompson received his B.A. from Pomona College (1964) and his Ph.D. from Claremont Graduate School (1972). He is the author or coauthor of more than 20 publications in such journals as Public Choice, Policy Analysis, Policy Sciences, and The American Political Science Review.

L. R. JONES is assistant professor of public management in the Graduate Program in Planning, Public Policy and Management at the University of Oregon. He teaches and conducts research in the areas of regulatory reform and decision making, public financial management and budgeting, and cutback management. Formerly he taught policy analysis as a member of the Faculty of Business Administration, University of British Columbia. He has extensive consulting experience with government and nonprofit organizations and is director of the Center for Regulatory Evaluation, a nonprofit corporation providing research and consulting services in business-government relations.

L. R. Jones received his B.A. from Stanford University (1967), and his M.A. and Ph.D. from the University of California, Berkeley (1977). He has published articles in Sloan Management Review, California Management Review, Public Administration Review, State and Local Government Review, and The Bureaucrat. He is completing a book on critical mass budgeting and planning.

G4